You Can't Kill the Miracle
I Didn't Know Him, but He Knew Me

Jaime Torres
With
Sandi Huddleston-Edwards

Published by Hear My Heart Publishing

Copyright 2019 by Jaime Torres
Written by Sandi Huddleston-Edwards

ISBN: 978-1-945620-62-1

A product of the United States of America.
This book is a work of non-fiction.

Dedication

With a heart full of gratitude and humility, I dedicate this book to the **Lord Jesus Christ**, Whom I know shed His precious and innocent blood on the cross for me, Who has forgiven me for my sins – past, present, and future – and Who promises me that I will not perish but have everlasting life because of His ultimate sacrifice and my belief in Him.

Jesus' presence in my life has lit an incomparable joy in my soul and has poured a bountiful love into my heart. His goodness and mercy are contagious, and I want to pass it on to you. Through the pages of this book, you will read of my shortcomings, my trials and many tribulations, and my loss of hope. But when I came to know the Lord and accepted Him as my personal Savior, my life was transformed – my life was saved. I now know a joy and peace that transcends all understanding.

My purpose in writing this book is to instill hope and to challenge my readers not to stop dreaming and not to top hoping no matter the circumstances in which they find themselves. It may be a place of desperation, a place of pure darkness you are in where you perceive there is no light, no way out. But let me tell you there is a way out. Because of my Christian journey, I've traveled to seven countries (Panama, Belize, Mexico, Peru, Ecuador, Venezuela, and the Dominican Republic). I have taken my testimony and witness to countless towns and cities in the United States. This is what I want. I want to bring the message of hope so folks can dream again, live again, and fight again. I want the downtrodden not to lay down and surrender. Jesus, the Almighty God, is stronger than anything you are going through. He can pick you up and give you new footing on solid ground. Our God is a forgiving God no matter the sin. Our God is a loving God. He loves you dearly, as a father loves his precious son or precious daughter. All you have to do is put your faith in Him and repent. If you pray the following sinner's prayer, you can be saved and be made whole.

Sinner's Prayer

Dear Father in Heaven,

I want to be forgiven for my sins. I want to dedicate my life to You. I want to live for You. I want You to be my Lord and Savior. All who I am and all that I have are Yours. Because of Your grace and mercy, I believe I have been born again. I am cleansed of my scarlet sins, which have been made as white as snow. I give my life to You freely and completely.

Amen

Acknowledgements

Throughout my life, there have been many people who have touched me deeply and for whom I am grateful for their kindness, patience, and diligence in helping me.

The Bible teaches us that "For everything there is a season, and a time for every matter under heaven" (Ecclesiastes 3:1, NRSV). As a Christian (follower of Jesus Christ), I believe every person we encounter and every relationship we nurture and deepen molds us into the persons we become.

As Christians, we become miracles, whose lives are transformed. We are born again to live in the glory and promise of Jesus' resurrection from death to everlasting life. The Bible, or God's Word, is what heals our broken souls and broken bodies. According to Wayne Jackson in the *Christian Courier,* "A miracle is a divine operation that transcends what is normally perceived as natural law; it cannot be explained upon any natural basis" (qtd in Fisher).

I'd like to mention a few of the miracles who have enhanced my life and kept me moving along the straight and narrow road for which God is calling me to journey.

Grace Torres, my beloved wife
Felton Burke
Chad Burke
Javier Guzman
Sonia Santiago Torres
Gene Lawson
Jorge Valdes
Pastor Stanley Carter

Rep. Mark Meadows
Steve White
Keith Morgan
Curtis Johnson
Rev. Larry and Meredith Cline (Papa and Mama)
Pastor George Logan
Pastor Camp
Chaplain David Turbeville
Rep. Jack Kingston
My Children – Vanessa, Kira, Richard, Michael, Ashley, JonathanDavid, and Isabella Torres.

There are many more people for whom I'd like to mention, but it isn't possible. Just know that you are in my heart and memories. I love you all, and I thank you from the bottom of my heart. *To God be the glory, now and forever.*

Table of Contents

Faithful Servant

What is a true servant of the Lord?
And how can we measure such?
One who is blameless, gentle and humble
Respectable, and faithful in much
One who shepherds the fold with love,
And leads them to fountains of grace
Who feeds them with meat from heaven above
To faithfully finish the race
Who covers the flock with fervent prayer
Lifting each one by name
Standing as guard against the foe
Bearing their burdens and shame
How hard the job must seem at times
And thankless, sometimes, too
Yet in the end, the reward will be
A crown of life for you.

--Caron Cline

Introduction

Pastor Jaime Torres

I want to know Christ and the power of his resurrection and the sharing of his sufferings by becoming like him in his death....
Philippians 3:10 (NRSV)

Pastor Jaime Torres is a man who easily echoes the Apostle Paul's words from 1 Timothy 1:15-16 (NRSV):

> *The saying is sure and worthy of full acceptance, that Christ Jesus came into the world to save sinners – of whom I am the foremost. But for that very reason I received mercy, so that in me, as the foremost, Jesus Christ might display the utmost patience, making me an example to those who would come to believe in him for eternal life.*

Jaime was born in Puerto Rico to an unwed mother of fifteen, who left the island for New York City when Jaime was only nine months of age. Jaime experienced many rejections in his life, but God had scheduled an appointment with Jaime in a federal prison. Since receiving God's mercy and salvation, Jamie often says, "The road has been one of hardship and trials at times, but God has been faithful to me."

Today, Jaime Torres is ministering in local prisons, teaching Bible studies, and preaching the Gospel at every opportunity. Young people hold a special place in Jaime's heart, and their salvation is his priority. He has spoken at various youth rallies in several states, preaching the good news that there is a God, Who loves them enough to send His Son to die for their sins in order that those sins will not be counted against them.

In 2004, United States Representative Gilbert Gutknecht from Minnesota, commissioned Jaime to conduct several youth rallies in his precinct. These became great opportunities from which to reach America's future leaders and citizens.

Jaime was nominated by Georgia's State Representative, Jack Kingston, for the National Hispanic Leadership Summit. This was a two-day conference that included over three hundred Hispanic participants from thirty-six states and the District of Columbia for the purpose of discussing various policy issues with members of the United States Congress and the Bush Administration. Some of the topics discussed were job creation, education, health care, and other opportunities for Hispanic Americans.

Jaime stated, "This conference was a highlight in my life. I had dinner with Senator Kay Bailey Hutchinson of Texas and Senator Bill Fritz of Tennessee. I was so excited I kissed them. That's when they asked me where I was from. When I explained that I'd just come out of prison, they had a funny look on their faces."

Jaime carries a burden for the unity among all people, especially the people of God, regardless of their culture or denomination. The words of Jesus in John 17:20-23 (NRSV) reflect the heart of Jaime Torres.

"I'm a preacher of the Gospel; that's what I love to do," states Jaime with a beguiling smile. "I love to talk about God's goodness. I love people. I love to encourage people. I love His word. I love His presence. I work in Forgiven Ministry's camps all the time. I have a ministry, Jaime Torres Ministries, where I go to ten prisons and do a lot of out-reaching in the streets in the hood. This is what I like to do."

Jaime is a loving father. "I love all of my children and want to be a part of their lives. I enjoy contacting my sons, Richard (Florida) and Michael (Atlanta), and my daughter, Ashley,

(Atlanta). I pray for my two daughters, Kira and Vanessa, (Puerto Rico), for whom I've seen once and have no relationship. I enjoy watching my two youngest children, JonathanDavid and Isabella Grace, discover the world and grow.

Beth and Sandi invite you to read Jaime's memoir, and we pray that you will be blessed and inspired by the sharing of his soul and heart. To God be the Glory!

Prologue

The Turning Point

Insults have broken my heart, so that I am in despair. I looked for pity, but there was none; and for comforters, but I found none. – Psalm 69:20 (NRSV)

I had been in and out of state prisons for much of my adult life. Among these were two of the Fort Leavenworth Military Prison and Riker's Island. But the real turning point in my life came when I was going to spend my whole life in prison.

My female attorney had a grim face as she sat waiting for me to enter the visitation room. After giving me a half-smile, she warned, "Jaime, I have some bad news." Obviously, she wasn't someone who believed in beating around the bush.

I had just sat down when her dire words pierced my ears. My stomach turned over and quickly tied in knots. *What can it be?* I held my breath, not wanting to hear her next words.

"The prosecution is asking for a life sentence." Her words hit me harder than any fist I'd ever encountered.

"Life?" I said stammering. "Why life?"

She only shook her head and moved her eyes to an invisible spot on the table's surface.

Immediately, I knew what this meant. A life sentence in the federal prison is when you don't get out. There is no chance for parole. You die in prison. If you can't afford a funeral, they will bury you in the prison cemetery. You might argue, "Well, federal inmates have televisions and pool tables and nicely colored walls." But to that I'd reply, "Since state prisons don't carry large sentences, they tend to look like dungeons compared to federal prisons, which are cleaner and painted with lively colors."

"Then just shoot me!" I cried. "Please just shoot me." I was scared to be honest. I was scared like a little kid. This was my death sentence, and the prison would become my coffin.

Every night became torture for me as I waited for my court date. I shared a cell with a roommate who slept in the bottom bunk; I slept on the top. I was careful to smother my desperate cries and wet tears in the folds of the spent pillow, so he wouldn't know. Fear gripped my soul. Reality set in. I was never going to see my mother again. I'd never interact with my family members. I felt the walls were closing in.

You know, there are people happily lying on the white sand and basking in the hot sun on thousands of beaches, yet they have no idea that one day soon the doctor will tell them they have cancer. That's when everything in their lives will change. Many of them may not last long afterward. They will receive this as condemnation and lose hope. They may believe there is no way to beat this disease. They may start declining. This is what happened to me.

Even though my attorney had done a wonderful job illustrating my miserable life and how it had impacted my behavior, in my heart, I knew this judge could care less. My attorney had shared key events of my sad life as a plausible explanation for the crimes I had committed and the evilness I had caused against society. But it didn't matter to the court that I had experienced many rejections in my life. What the court would remember is that I had found acceptance from one of the many gangs, which were prevalent in New York City and that I had been a drug dealer.

I stood with hunched shoulders; my body trembled as I heard the words that I'd been found guilty. I'd lost my case. And now I bowed my head as a sign of respect for the judge, sitting on the high bench who would pronounce sentencing on me. My shallow breathing ceased as the judge cleared his throat to speak.

As he recited my guilt and the offenses I'd committed, along with the statutes and laws I'd broken, it became more evident from his monotone voice and the manner in which he avoided any direct eye contact with me that this judge had heard one too many sob stories from countless criminals who had stood where I was now. It was a certainty that he couldn't be moved to a more lenient sentence than life. He thought I was a loser; I was worthless to society; I was a reject who couldn't fit in.

But somehow, he had been moved as he pronounced my fate. "You are sentenced to serve twenty-five years in the federal prison."

I am twenty-eight-years-old, I surmised. *If I serve twenty-five years, I'll be fifty-three-years-old – an old man!* The walls came crashing in. This wasn't a dream. This wasn't a few years; this was a quarter of a century of my life.

Even though I'd somehow dodged a life sentence and should be thankful for that, I was devastated. As they led me away in handcuffs, I stumbled. But other than my attorney who had said, "Jaime, I'm sorry," there was no one in the courtroom who knew me. None of the gang members – my so-called friends – would dare appear in court. There was no one to offer consolation. I felt destitute and alone. I was a lost soul.

But what I didn't comprehend was there was someone who loved me. . . . Someone who could perform miracles . . . . Someone who could forgive me . . . . His name was Jesus. He was in charge. And I'd realize He had a different plan for me.

Chapter One

Lazarus – A Miracle

Now a man named Lazarus was sick. He was from Bethany, the village of Mary and her sister Martha. – John 11:1 (NIV)

I recently received a message from the Lord, and I titled the message, "Even if You Wanted to Kill the Miracle, You Can't Kill the Miracle." Thank you, God. In the following sermon, I will be paraphrasing the Biblical verses based on my understanding.

A certain man was sick, Lazarus of Bethany, the town of Mary and her sister, Margaret. It was Mary who had anointed the Lord's feet with a fragrant and costly oil. Therefore, the sisters sent to Him saying "Lord, behold, he whom thou lovest is sick" (John 11:3, KJV).

For many years I was sick – sin sick, but He loved me.

Unbeknownst to Lazarus, his sisters had a relationship with Jesus. Jesus, the One whom you loved is sick. Isn't it wonderful to know that even in our sickness, He loves us. We see that Jesus replied with something like, Okay, this sickness is not unto death, but then Lazarus died, and Jesus went and raised him from the dead. Why did He do that? There are a lot of reasons. Lazarus was a miracle – the one He loved. "Lazarus, come out" (John 11:43b NIV).

In Chapter 12, it says six days before the Passover, Jesus came to where the miracle was, the one who had been dead.

Lazarus was a miracle. We are all miracles, but we still have issues. But he loved us. Why did Jesus raise Lazarus back up from the dead, whom He had raised from the dead?

"There they made him a supper; and Martha served: but Lazarus was one of them that sat at the table with him" (John 12:2, KJV). Lazarus went from being sick to dying – a castaway – but now here we are told he is sitting at the table with Jesus! The miracle was on his way to hell. The enemy was trying to kill the miracle. The sickness was trying to kill the miracle, but because Jesus loved Lazarus, and because Jesus had a plan for Lazarus, they are sitting at the table together, and Martha is serving them. Lazarus is sitting at the table with Him!

Let's move ahead a bit. Verse 9 says, "Much people of the Jews therefore knew that he was there: and they came not for Jesus' sake only, but that they might see Lazarus also, whom he had raised from the dead" (John 12, KJV). They came to see the miracle.

They heard about this dude who was raised from slinging dope to slinging hope.

You see, they heard Jesus had done this big miracle, and now this miracle is sitting at the table. People wanted to see the miracle!

How is it this guy can go to prison and get his life back?

And a great many Jews knew Jesus was at this house – also Lazarus – they wanted to see the miracle.

People want to see how you can come from slinging dope and doing other things.

We know about Jesus, and we love Him, but let us see the

miracle.

How can I come from this hell hole and be raised up?

"But the chief priests consulted that they might put Lazarus also to death . . ." (John 12:10, KVJ). They wanted to kill the miracle again! But the chief priests plotted to put Lazarus to death also. Even after Jesus performed that miracle, they wanted to kill him again because the miracle was impacting lives. I want to see the miracle.

The miracle got shot six times in the chest and survived.

The miracle earned his GED in prison.

The devil wants to kill me using divorce and my children. He wants to kill us because we are miracles. YOU CAN'T KILL THE MIRACLE. They plotted to put Lazarus to death. "Because that by reason of him many of the Jews went away, and believed on Jesus" (John 12:11, KJV). The devil doesn't want the kingdom to grow.

The enemy doesn't want us to impact the kingdom. We have to be determined not to be fearful and realize the devil has already been defeated. But if people don't know this, he will destroy and kill. He came to kill Lazarus because he was sitting at the table with Jesus, and on top of that, Lazarus was affecting people's lives.

The Word is what heals. He sent His Word, and the Word heals. We give glory to Him.

Even now the devil is trying to kill me – and you. But we are miracles!

Did you know Paul never walked with Jesus physically? He knew Jesus better than any other disciple. In the book of Philippians 3:10-11, Paul said, "That I may know him, and the power of his resurrection, and the fellowship of his sufferings, being made conformable unto his death; if by any means I might attain unto the resurrection of the dead" (KJV). Paul's only desire is to know God. I want to know God, and I'm not stopping there. I want to know God, and I also want to know the power of Your resurrection.

It is sad how many of us walk with Jesus for years, but we don't know the power of His resurrection. God will resurrect your dreams and bring healing. Do you know how many people die of sickness because they don't believe God can bring healing to them? Why would Paul say I want to know you, God? Paul wanted to know Jesus.

Can you imagine what it was like when the disciples got together? They are the ones who walked with Jesus. But Paul felt like an outsider. It drove Paul to say, "Lord, I want to know You."

I don't preach opinions or experiences, I preach the Word of God. I'm a King James man; this Bible is what saved me in prison. Look at what Paul said. He said, "That I may know Him." Sometimes, we get busy and get too religious. It's not about religion; it's about relationships -- "That I may know Him, and the power of His resurrection." I want to know Him and experience the power to bring everything that died in me back to life. If my marriage died, whatever died in me, He can bring me back alive and renew my dreams.

It is sad we go to the house of God and live defeated as Christians. We have unresolved issues, and we have hurts and wounds and stay stuck for ten to twenty years in a church, but when you get to know Him, He will heal you of all your wounds. Jesus said (paraphrased), "I am come to set the captives free. I come to give you life and life in abundance. I am your healer; by my stripes you are healed."

Getting back to Lazarus, I love the fact these Jews knew Jesus was there. They were coming to see Lazarus because he was raised from the dead. They wanted to see the miracle. But in verse 10, the chief priests, the religious freaks, consulted that they might put Lazarus also to death. They wanted to kill the miracle, and that is you, too.

The enemy despises you because you are a miracle of life, and God is going to use your life to bring a lot of people out of bondage, so the devil tries to kill you, discourage you, and put sickness in your body.

But the chief priest consulted that they might put Lazarus also to death. You are not going to die, sir. You are not going to die, ma'am. I pray that this word will stick in your heart. "Thy word have I hid in mine heart, that I might not sin against thee" (Psalm 119:11, KJV). This is all we have and all we need. We don't need the philosophy of men. We don't need to be charismatic. We don't need you to play with other people's emotions. Just give the Word. That is all anyone needs. This is what our Savior wants.

A no-good dude, like me, needs the Word. They showed up because they heard the Word of God. They wanted to put the miracle to death. That's why you see a lot of Christians in church who are dying; their marriages are in shambles; their children are on drugs. The enemy is trying to kill the miracle because you are a miracle. It's not by coincidence that I'm writing to you today. It was ordained before the foundations of the world. I'm seeing it all come to pass.

They said they might put Lazarus to death. By reason of him, many of the Jews went away and believed on Jesus. They wanted to kill Lazarus because of his testimony, and many of the Jews believed. But you can be a miracle if you surrender your life to Christ, and if so, Satan won't be able to kill the miracle.

Chapter Two

Fitting In

I am confident of this, that the one who began a good work among you will bring it to completion by the day of Jesus Christ.
– Philippians 1:6 (NRSV)

The beautiful and unique island of Puerto Rico "is an unincorporated territory of the United States, located in the northeastern Caribbean." Puerto Rico is "Spanish for 'rich port' and "is only 100 miles long by 35 miles wide" (www.puertoRico. com). Both of my parents were born in Puerto Rico.

My Hispanic mother was a lovely light-skinned innocent girl of fifteen when she fell in love with my dark-skinned father. After realizing she was pregnant with me, she discovered this handsome Puerto Rican had deceived her. Instead of being single as he had led her to believe, he actually was a married man with several children. She was devastated. He stayed with her for nine or ten months, not even a year after he impregnated her. With marriage out of the question and her hopes and dreams crushed, my mother decided to run away to America, taking me, her nine-month-old son.

We ended up living in South Bronx, where my mother eventually married and had other children. Because my mother was light-skinned, and so were my siblings, I became the target of ridicule because I was dark-skinned like my father. I felt like I didn't fit in. All the neighborhood kids would laugh at me and tease me, telling me I couldn't possibly be my siblings' brother.

The more they laughed, the angrier I became. The kids at school bullied me, berating me with ugly and hurtful epithets.

There was a big difference between my siblings being white and me being dark. So I began hanging out with the people who accepted me. Unfortunately, they were affiliated with gangs. But I loved them because they were just like me. For the first time in my life, I felt like I belonged. This was what I'd been looking for. Finally, I fit in. When they asked me to do whatever, my longing for approval and my need to fit in was more than enough to do whatever was necessary to keep their love and acceptance.

While I lived with my family in New York, we were on food stamps and constantly hungry. There just wasn't enough food for us to feel full. One day when I was thirteen, our mother sent my younger brother to the store to purchase a loaf of bread and some potted meat. She only had a single $10 bill to her name. My brother left and after a while, we all became concerned because he'd been gone for a long time. Finally, he showed up with empty arms. As it turned out, a black kid named Elliott, who was the neighborhood menace and bully, had picked up a piece of concrete and hit my brother. He stole the $10 bill.

When I heard that, I was livid. I went crazy. As the eldest, I didn't care that everyone was scared of Elliott. Without stopping to put on shoes, I ran out the door with bare feet. Mama was screaming after me, "Get back here! Get back!" But I kept running.

When I found that Negro, I was going to kill him. I ran up to him and hit him with closed knuckles. He tripped over my foot, and his head hit the sidewalk so hard, it bounced like a basketball. Blood was spurted everywhere, but I didn't care. I started hitting him over and over again. Finally, I stopped and dug my fingers into his front pant pocket and retrieved a $10 bill. Then I found another $30 in his other pocket and took it too. My family ate really well that morning.

I hated bullies because I was a victim of bullying. When more Puerto Ricans began immigrating to New York, this began my problems with black folks that lasted for years. The black folk had been *getting it* from the white folks, so they decided to *give it* to the Puerto Ricans. But I wasn't going to have any of it. I was tired of being rejected and let everyone know it.

By the time I was fourteen, my behavior had become so erratic, my mother was concerned for my safety. Even though I never back-talked her and remained respectful where she was concerned, I was committing minor infractions and getting into trouble constantly. She had experienced hurt all of her life, and she didn't want to see me go down the wrong path. Mama worried when I fought with the black folks because she thought they would kill me one day. Something drastic had to be done to rescue me from the inevitable danger she knew I would face. Her decision was to send me back to Puerto Rico to live with my father. She believed that having a strong male role-model would help me.

For the first time in my life, I was excited to meet my real father. I felt like, "Wow, I have an identity. I belong to Jaime Torres, Sr."

But after I began working with my father, it didn't take me long to discover he was one of the larger drug dealers on the island. How could my well-intentioned mother have guessed this would be the case? Instead of saving me, my downfall was inevitable. Even though I was living in Puerto Rico with my real dad, I still felt pain and rejection. I still didn't fit in, so I became addicted to smoking weed and using cocaine to alleviate my emotional pain because the only time I felt a little bit good was when I was high.

But God watched silently, knowing He had a plan for my life and one that would allow me to always *fit in*.

Chapter Three

Slinging Dope

Let us therefore approach the throne of grace with boldness, so that we may receive mercy and find grace to help in time of need. – Hebrews 4:16 (NRSV)

Eventually, I became discouraged from working with my father and decided to move back to New York. I surmised that I could make my own money and didn't need to share my profits with anyone. In addition, I had fathered one daughter, Vanessa, when I was fifteen. Never having seen her, we had no relationship, so I left the island. It wasn't long after my return to New York when I became involved in drug trafficking.

It was easy to make $50,000 or $60,000 in one day. It felt good to own a nice car and buy named brand clothes whenever I wanted to. Besides, I craved the attention I received from the female sex. Somehow, women gave me a sense of affirmation. It was like I was fitting in. But it wouldn't last long; I'd get bored with them too. You would think that making a lot of money would make me happy, but no, I was even more miserable.

One day, my mother was walking down the street with her groceries. I drove along-side her in my brand new Cadillac. When we got to the front door, I hurried to her and gave her a wad of money. Before I knew it, she had slapped my face hard.

"I don't want your dirty money," she said through clenched teeth. "I'm ashamed of you."

Her words cut into me deeply; the pain was unreal. I'd

always counted on one person to be there for me, but now that person, my own mother, had rejected me. I immediately felt immense passion and pain and an enormous amount of pent-up anger. It was like a volcano erupting in my body and overwhelming my senses. So what did I do to release the tension? I put my fist through a plate glass window. My heart was broken. I knew I had to win back my mother's respect and pride for me somehow. But I can tell you this: My mother never accepted a single drug-earned dollar from me.

Somehow I survived being stabbed in the throat and being shot six times in my chest and leg. My life was on a downward spiral, and I didn't know how to apply the brakes before I hit the bottom.

When I was seventeen years-old, I convinced my mother to sign for me to join the Army in the late entry program. We both thought the stern discipline and attitudes of service and team work would be good for me. This was a promise for a new life. But my old ways were embedded in my skin like a tattoo; I was too weak to shake them. They followed me into boot camp and beyond.

In the Army, soldiers were paid twice a month, which meant many of the young and naïve men were undisciplined to stretch their paychecks from one pay day to the next. My devious past had taught me how to manage large sums of money and my quick-thinking mind had taught me how to take advantage of a situation in order to make money. So I quickly schemed an entrepreneurial way to take advantage of their inexperience and dire circumstances. Plus with my outside drug connections that penetrated the walls of the base, I became a loan shark and drug pusher. If a soldier didn't reimburse me for money I'd loaned him or drugs I'd advanced him, I'd take his stereo or radio or car as payment – bribery. I was wicked for money; money was everything to me.

One such soldier failed to pay me for his drugs, so I

decided I'd take his car as payment. It didn't take long for the trip to end. I wrapped the car around a tree, destroying it in the process. So I was court-martialed and sentenced to two years in Leavenworth Military Prison, one of the worst prisons in the world.

While I was incarcerated, my father had decided to leave his life of crime and drugs in Puerto Rico and come to America. By the time I was released and out a short time, my dad and I were back in business, selling dope together. Unfortunately, it wasn't long before we were arrested together and sentenced to spend two years with the Pennsylvania Department of Corrections. Dad was in cell number 118; I wasn't far away in cell number 117. But it wasn't bad. Actually, we lived like kings in that prison.

I had two girlfriends, unbeknownst to each other, who loved me and visited me religiously. I'd convinced each of them that if they truly loved me, they'd sneak dope into the prison for me. When they each agreed, I instructed them on how to do it. They were to take a balloon, cut the large rubber part off, and pack the remainder with drugs and tie it. They'd place the drug-laden balloon in their pocketbooks, but before the mandatory personal items search, they'd carefully and covertly place the balloon in their mouths. Inmates were allowed one kiss from their wives or girlfriends, so as we kissed, the balloon would be transferred into my mouth. Then I'd swallow the balloon. Once again, Dad and I were in business, slinging dope.

Now, the way inmates buy dope in prison is through a "commissary" way. In other words, they used their family gifts and trips to the commissary once a week to "trade" or "barter" for the drugs. As a result, Dad and I operated our own little store. We had generous supplies of candies, shampoos, hair conditioners, and different soaps – whatever. And we even set it up where inmates' families could send money to pay off the book. We were careful to record all the amounts we were owed and by whom. I even had my own grocery store and kitchen in prison.

On another occasion in another prison, my friend Jorge and I devised a way to bring steaks into the dormitory where we stayed. At the time, Jorge Valdes was one of the biggest drug traffickers in the United States. His influence carried into the prison system. With the help of an inmate, who worked in the kitchen, we made what was called stingers. These are plates of metal where we'd insert two wires on each side. Then we'd drape the metal holding the steak over a five gallon bucket of hot water. While the other prisoners were eating mashed potatoes, we were pigging out on steak. Like I said, we lived like kings. It wasn't always like this in prison. I recall the two years I spent at Riker's Island on the infamous C-16. This was considered the worst floor in the prison.

While there, I developed an even meaner reputation than I already had. I quickly discovered you had to fight for your life every day, or the inmates would take your sneakers, coat, or whatever you owned. Even worse, if you didn't fight, they'd make you into a woman. Determination and survival fiercely set in. I wasn't going to become anyone's woman, and no one was going to rip-off anything I had. This new-found strength resulted in my biting off a man's ear when he tried to steal my coat.

I also should mention my brief stays in county jails, of which Citrus County Jail in Lecanto, Florida, was one.

I used to own a home and sling lots of dope in Brooksville, Ocala, and Inverness. My nickname on the street was El Bori. This was slang for the Spanish word, "Boricua." But I was miserable. Sometimes, I'd drive for hours on I-95 in my nice whip, dressed in my Fresh Gear, and carrying a couple of thousand dollars in my pocket. Out of nowhere, I'd begin crying. I felt empty. I'd never known pure happiness from the minute I was a young kid. But I'd tried every way I could to find happiness in the drugs, cars, women, and money. But I had failed. As a result, I was an empty man who didn't know anything about a merciful and loving God.

Once I was asked if I felt invincible because of the money and drugs, and my reply was, "No. They only made me miserable."

In 1988, my son, Richard, was born. His birth brought me the first real joy I can remember. Two years later, another son, Michael, was born. Then I was the father of another daughter when Ashley was born. Obviously, I had not learned any societal lessons or had been rehabilitated while incarcerated in any of the worst prisons in the United States or county jailhouses. Changing my lifestyle was out of the question. Even when I was in prison or jail, I'd found ways to make my stays prosperous. Besides, I was in my late twenties and the father of five children – two daughters who lived in Puerto Rico and with whom I had no relationship. It was too late to change my ways now. I still hated bullies, especially when they picked on older folks. When they did and I found out about it, I'd shoot them in the leg as a warning not to do it again. The people I defended loved me because they knew I would protect them.

Only, no one, including myself, could predict the inconceivable downfall that was coming my way. I'd experience some of my darkest days when I was arrested for possession of two kilos of cocaine with the intent to import five hundred kilos more.

Chapter Four

Slinging Hope

What then shall we say to these things? If God is for us, who can be against us? – Romans 8:31 (KJV)

Throughout my twenties, my drug business had grown. The births of my children were what I needed to kick my own drug habit but not enough to end my involvement in the drug trade. Besides, as a father, I had more mouths to feed.

Eventually, I hooked up with some Cubans and Colombians and began receiving kilos from Colombia. This was a really strong crew, and with money being the god I worshipped, I couldn't get enough. I was determined to get money by all means necessary, no matter what it took. The more money and drugs I had, the more people would acknowledge me. They'd repeatedly say, "You my man," and I would bask in those words. Their praise for and recognition of me was nourishment for my hungry soul and a temporary potion for my longing heart. The life-long desire to fit in was still raging. But my success in drug trafficking had put me on the FBI's radar. Over time, they built a solid case against me; I was arrested in 1990 at the age of twenty-eight with the possession of two kilos of cocaine with the intent to import another five hundred kilos. I was facing a life sentence in the federal penitentiary system.

While awaiting trial, I became enraged at the disgusting antics of a certain prisoner named Gene Lawson. After spending time in some of the worst prisons in the nation and comprehending the connotative meaning behind Lawson's perpetual smile, I plotted to kill this man and rid my world of his repulsive grin forever. I was convinced the man had an angle, an ulterior motive. He was another person who wanted to see what he could get out of me. He wanted to use me. My life in the streets of the hood had taught me this: People had used me, and I had used people. I thought Lawson was weird and his actions repugnant. I wasn't used to people loving me, and I didn't love myself.

During one of my walks around the prison yard, I found a piece of metal. I hid it in my clothes. Carefully and quietly, I molded and sharpened the shank into a weapon I was convinced would do *the job*. Decidedly, I would stab Lawson while standing in the chow line. Then I'd drop the shank on the floor. What I didn't realize or couldn't anticipate was Gene was a prisoner of the Lord.

A fellow inmate had noticed my hatred for Gene, so he asked me, "Why do you hate him so much?"

"I don't like the way he smiles at me all the time. I'm not going to be anybody's woman," I answered in an adamant tone.

"That's not why he smiles," the inmate patiently explained. "He's straight. Haven't you seen his girlfriend? She visits him all the time. Besides, he's a Christian."

"A what? What's a Christian? Is that some kind of gang?"

"No. It's no gang. Haven't you ever read the Bible? Haven't you ever heard of God and Jesus Christ?"

"No not really."

"Well, people who follow the teachings of Jesus Christ are called Christians," the inmate explained patiently.

"Then why does Lawson smile like that all the time?" I asked. "He's pulling twenty-five years, too. How can he be so happy?"

"Because he says he has joy in his heart because of Jesus' love, mercy, and grace. Gene is no threat to you," he assured me.

Here I was awaiting trial. My attorney had already explained the prosecutor was asking for a life sentence based on my previous records. I couldn't sleep at night from being worried sick. I was afraid. Then I'd think of Gene Lawson, who just had been sentenced to twenty-five years. He was walking around like he didn't have a care in the world. Deep down, I longed for the peace he'd somehow found.

A few days later, Gene actually approached me and invited me to come to a Bible study. When I attended that Bible study, I became very paranoid. The man teaching the Bible study was speaking everything I was living to the point, I thought my cell was bugged. I had the urge to cry, so I rushed to my cell.

Gene began to tell me about the peace that comes from having faith in Jesus Christ. He told me I could have this peace no matter where I was. But I resisted because I didn't want the other inmates to think I was weak. But one Sunday, I found myself outside the prison chapel. Careful not to let my *home boys* see me, I discreetly entered and sat all the way in the back of the sanctuary on the last pew. The next thing I knew was when this man began speaking, everything he said was directed at me. He was describing my life, my emptiness, my misery. His words pierced my heart. He seemed to read my inner thoughts; and in so doing, he gained entrance into my heart.

That's when I allowed the pent-up tears to flow in rivers down my face. I had not cried since the day my attorney told me the prosecutor was seeking a life sentence, but I cried loud and hard – a different kind of cry – and heard my own voice pleading, praying, "God, if You are real, please give me what Gene has. I want the peace Gene has." I fell into a sound sleep. Two hours later when I awoke, I couldn't wait to find Gene and tell him about my encounter with God. I looked all over until I found him in the cafeteria. After excitedly relaying my experience, he asked me one question: "Jaime, do you want to feel this peace forever?"

Without hesitation or second thoughts, I replied, "Yes, sir."

Gene opened his little black Bible and turned to Romans, Chapter 10 and read verses 1-13 (KJV):

"Brethren, my heart's desire and prayer to God for Israel is, that they might be saved. For I bear them record that they have a zeal of God, but not according to knowledge. For they being ignorant of God's righteousness, and going about to establish their own righteousness, have not submitted themselves unto the righteousness of God. For Christ is the end of the law for righteousness to every one that believeth. For Moses describeth the righteousness which is of the law, That the man which doeth those things shall live by them. But the righteousness which is of faith speaketh on this wise, Say not in thine heart, Who shall ascend into heaven? (that is, to bring Christ down from above:) Or, Who shall descend into the deep? (that is, to bring up Christ again from the dead.) But what saith it? The word is nigh thee, even in thy mouth, and in thy heart: that is, the word of faith, which we preach; That if thou shalt confess with thy mouth the Lord Jesus, and shalt believe in thine heart that God hath raised him from the dead, thou shalt be saved. For with the heart man believeth unto righteousness; and with the mouth confession is made unto salvation. For the scripture saith, Whosoever believeth on him shall not be ashamed. For there is no difference between the Jew and the Greek: for the same Lord over all is rich unto all that call upon him. For whosoever shall call upon the name of the Lord shall be saved."

Then we knelt onto our knees, and I prayed the sinner's prayer, repenting of my sins and receiving the Lord in my heart. I felt a weight lift from my body. As it is when a blindfold is removed from your eyes, I was no longer blinded by ignorance.

I realized that even though I didn't know God, He knew me. He had waited a long time for this moment when He could free me from a decadent life of pain and misery. This was an appointment He had scheduled long ago.

You would think prison is meant for you to lose your freedom, but actually, I found my freedom in prison. That day is when my journey to follow Jesus Christ began, and I was freed from the sinful hold that had choked my life. In a matter of heartfelt moments, I was changed from a sinner into a miracle because I had received everlasting life as a result of my belief and faith in God and His grace and mercy for my soul. I now believed that God had protected me throughout my life even though I was living for the enemy. He knew my heart better than I did.

Disappointedly, I had lost my case, but somehow the judge had shown mercy, and I was sentenced to only twenty-five years in prison rather than the life sentence I had dreaded. Yes, it was a long time, and I would be an old man when I was released. But now, having found peace and acceptance through my Lord and Savior, Jesus Christ, I finally fit in. Prison didn't frighten me any longer. My focus was on serving Jesus and learning more about being a Christian. I would use my time inside these cell walls to share Christ with others.

When *The 700 Club* came on television in the mornings, I couldn't wait to find my seat to get inspired. My dedication to this show is what God used to begin my first Bible study. God was going to use me as a missionary in these prison walls. I would be slinging hope instead of slinging dope. Never would I believe I could have been so happy and fulfilled. My soul was learning to embrace a new emotion: peace.

God is awesome and powerful and has a plan for all of our lives if we just give in and allow Him to lead. Mercifully, I would become astonished to learn that God had a plan for me that didn't include spending the full twenty-five years in prison nor the twenty-three years and eight months that were mandatory for that sentence. I'd also learn that with God in your heart, no one can kill the miracle.

Chapter Five

Free at Last

You, my brothers and sisters, were called to be free. But do not use your freedom to indulge the flesh; rather, serve one another humbly in love. – Galatians 5:13 (NIV)

One day when I was praying, I told the Lord, "When I get out one day...."But the Lord halted my speech and said, "No, son, we're not going down that road. When you get out nothing . . . . You'll do it here."

I couldn't have imagined God would call me to preach and establish a church in prison. But He had, and I did, which was one of the hardest things I've ever done. If you think it's a challenge to pastor here in the free world, try pastoring in prison. You have all types of stigma. Because Christians are considered weak in prison, I did so by the grace of God. This experience would be my best training and become the best time I'd ever had preaching. God's favor was so much upon me that the Chaplain looked to me to help him do his job.

Some of the prisoners hadn't gotten to know me because they had moved me from prison to prison. They realized I was an inmate and wore the same uniform as they did, so many would ask, "How are you going to pastor me when you're in here?"

It was hard. I was told "Shut your mouth. You're a jailhouse preacher."

But when God calls you, He equips you and anoints you.

20

And that is what He did. Every night that little chapel was full of men, and they were getting saved. But the most impactful thing was they witnessed the real deal because I moved among them. It's one thing to have preachers who lives across the street or in the suburbs when you can see them on Sundays and Wednesdays. But when you live with them, the preacher lives right there, so they see your interactions every day. They respected the fact I walked the walk, and that's the greatest sermon in the world – the silent sermon. By the grace of God, I was given the opportunity to pastor men in prison.

I received my purpose in prison. What had been meant for evil was turned to good by the Lord. In Romans 8:28, we're told, "And we know that in all things God works for the good of those who love him, who have been called according to his purpose" (NIV). If it weren't for that prison experience, I wouldn't be the man I am today. I realize I may not even be alive even though God had rescued me from stabbings, my throat being cut, my body being shot six times, and multiple car accidents. I was a walking miracle because of Christ's love.

The Lord did something else that was miraculous. A high-profile firm of expensive Jewish lawyers from Miami, Florida, took one pro bono case per year. Miraculously, God ordained that they would select one file from a large stack, which was mine. Over the next seven years, Amanda Burns, Jane Moskowitz, and Janie Baker built a defense and fought for my release. They wrote motions to the eleven Circuit Court of Appeals in Atlanta. Their belief in my case gave me renewed hope of being set free, so while they worked diligently on my case, I continued setting up Bible studies and churches for my fellow inmates, and I earned my GED in the process.

In 1999, I received a letter stating my sentence was vacated and remanded back to the same judge, who had told me I'd never get out of prison. Amazingly, on July 6, 2000, I went in front of the judge, was granted a mistrial, and was released the next day on July 7. I was a free man, freed from the seventh floor of the prison on the seventh day of the seventh month. I immediately called my friend, Gene Lawson, who had gotten out of prison before me and who now lived in Boca Raton, Florida. He was delighted to hear my good news. Gene was and still is a devout man of God.

Sometimes, God has to back us against the wall. When we become lenient and rely on ourselves instead of Him, we tend to relax our morals and values. God knew what I needed, and that's exactly what I needed. I was a stubborn, hard-headed young man, and so He had to radically deal with me. In prison, I came to believe in God and to find out who I was. God used this experience to show me my purpose in life.

As a requirement of being released from prison, I had to find a job, or I'd be re-incarcerated. I felt a deep sense of guilt because my family had done without while I was in prison. Shortly after I was released, I met with a fellow believer, Brother Jones. Brother Jones would soon introduce me to Felton Burke, the man responsible for giving me my first job. Felton Burke became like a Dad to me. He gave me my first job of cleaning toilets, and I was happy to do that.

One day, Mr. Burke called me into his office. I thought I was going to get in trouble or going to get fired. He asked me, "Jaime, do you own a necktie?"

I replied, "Yes, sir."

He said, "Come in tomorrow wearing one."

I thought to myself, *I'm going to be the best dressed toilet cleaner in the world.*

The next morning when I arrived for work, Mr. Burke put me on the sales floor and allowed me to sell cars. Felton owned seven car dealerships in Georgia. I worked for him for three years (2000 – 2003). In those three years, I had advanced from cleaning toilets to selling cars. I sold cars from that day until Mr. Burke sold his dealership. Afterward, I opened up my own used car lot. Of course, I made many mistakes, and the economy went down. Then the Lord blessed me with Kingdom Builders Painting Company. I didn't even know how to hold a paint brush. The first job for which I submitted a bid and won was Burlington Coat Factory.

Then I opened up a car wash, plus I was preaching, as well. I was a pastor but received no salary. I gave my salary back to the church. Otherwise, I did everything to make money, so I could buy nice things for my family because I felt I had to repay them for the years they were without me. I bought them nice cars to drive to school, but I neglected my family by working long hours. Unfortunately, I ended up losing everything, including my family.

Now God knows I can be hot-headed and hard-headed, and sometimes God tells me to shut up. It seemed unreal to come out of prison after ten years only to lose my family. If I'd known this, I would have stayed in prison. I promise you that. Felton knew my wife and children; he knew everything about me. And he knew that losing my family was going to destroy me.

The Lord also knew my needs, so He placed a preacher in Florida in my path to send me out to seven nations: Panama, Belize, Mexico, Peru, Ecuador, Dominican Republic, and Venezuela. In 2008, I was dying inside, so God sent me to the little country of Ecuador first. And even though I was travelling abroad and spreading the Gospel, I desperately did everything possible to remain in contact with my sons, Richard and Michael, and my daughter Ashley. I didn't want to lose my children, too.

Jesus began sending me to more countries. I went to Panama, Mexico, Peru, and Venezuela. When I returned to Ecuador to preach again in 2009, I received invitations to preach in many Protestant churches all over the country to hundreds of people. They kept inviting me and repeating, "Come to my church." " Come to my church."

The people of Ecuador seemed to love me and my messages about Jesus Christ, and that made me happy.

Chapter Six

Saving Grace

Two are better than one; because they have a good reward for their labour. – Ecclesiastes 4:9 (KJV)

Grace (Jaime's Wife):
I've always loved the Lord. My mother raised my four sisters and me in a Protestant church in Ecuador where I was baptized and attended most of my life. I'm thankful God gave me a Mother who is a prayer warrior. She often told me that God had planned great things for my life. She went on and on telling me that God was going to bring my husband from another county, but I didn't believe her. I was focused on my current circumstances. We were dirt poor and living in a hut.

The first time I heard Jaime preach was in 2009, when our woman pastor had announced to the congregation that he was coming.

"We will have a pastor from the United States to preach here next Sunday," she had stated in an excited voice.

My mother and I had attended this particular church for ten years. It was a ministry we had supported for many years. I remember we fasted for three days and held a prayer vigil before Jaime arrived. Our prayers were for him.

When Jaime arrived at the church, he was accompanied by two of his freinds from Venezuela. I watched as he went straight to the pastor's office. Then he returned and preached his first message, "Love is stronger than death."

I realized that because he wasn't from Ecuador, I might never see him again. My mother and I met him that morning after the service was over. Then my mother asked permission from our pastor for us to go and hear this evangelist again that evening and in all the other churches where he planned to preach. Our pastor granted us permission, so we began showing up everywhere. I felt assured Jaime had a prophetic gift. Whenever he preached, we saw that he easily connected with the people. He was the real thing. My mother and I love the Word, and we thought he was a good preacher of the Word.

Jaime:
In 2009, I returned to Ecuador to preach. One day, a female preacher came to me and asked if I'd consider preaching at their home church. This was located in the worst place in Ecuador. My tour guide immediately whispered into my ear where we would be going and warned me that he wouldn't take me there due to lots of kidnappings and robberies. It would be a difficult journey to travel the backwoods because there were no roads. But a devout little lady began pleading for me to come.

"Please, please come!" she cried. "This is the church where I live."

I couldn't say no, so I went to the little bitty church and preached for the first time. I'd never seen a place like it. After the service, the devout little lady introduced me to her daughter, Grace, and invited me to eat at their home with her husband and five daughters. She explained it was close to her birthday, and she would be honored if I would come to their home. I agreed, but I wasn't prepared for the poverty I'd see.

Their home was a little hut with two rooms and a huge loft upstairs where everyone slept. The floor was dirt. When I sat at the table, I immediately jumped up from fright. There on the table were chicken feet with long nails which had been used to make a broth. This was my first meal in their home.

Whenever and wherever I was scheduled to preach a sermon, the little lady and her daughter Grace showed up. I had been polite but disinterested when she had introduced me to Grace. After all, I wasn't looking for a woman, nor did I want a woman. I just wanted to preach.

In Ecuador, there are native Indians, people who still carry their babies on their backs. They had asked me to come to their church and preach, which would be an eight to ten hour drive, and they promised to provide transportation. When they arrived, they were driving an old van with rotted tires and a missing door. After focusing on the bare treads, I said, "I'm sorry, but I won't be coming."

These people had driven all night long, so when I refused to come, their eyes welled up with tears. They really wanted me to preach to the natives. I was aggravated at their persistence and lack of safety consciousness.

"There ain't no way in the world that I'm riding on those tires in that bus."

Grace and her mother were there and stared at me. This made me feel bad.

"Okay, I'll go," I relented against my better judgement. Grace sat in front of the van where I was; her mother sat in the back of the van. After five or six hours into the drive, we were going down a steep and winding road when the driver of a truck filled with live chickens pulled out in front of us. The Lord used me to save Grace's life because she repeatedly had offered to change places with me, but I had declined. Before I could react, I was flying out of the doorway of the van. Blood was everywhere. I was lying in the street with most of my ear torn off. The driver of the chicken truck kept going, and the driver of the van along with several of the passengers took off after them. They left me lying in the road. Grace, her mother, and a few others had stayed behind with me. I was still bleeding profusely when out of nowhere, this car stopped. A lady inside grabbed a first aid kit and used it to stop the bleeding and repair my ear. Before I could thank her, she disappeared. I'm convinced she was an angel.

My body was sore all over and broken. We still had another hour to travel before we'd arrive at the church, so with blood all over my shirt, my shoulders and ribs hurting, we climbed aboard another bus.

When we got to the church, the short Indian pastor said, "I'll take you to the hospital."

I looked into the church, which was packed with people, standing room only. Then I noticed the fliers – pictures of me were pasted all over the walls. I couldn't think of myself and ask him to take me to the hospital. I had to preach.

"I'll be okay. I'm going to preach," I replied. "Just give me some water where I can wash."

He led me to a room and handed me a towel. I asked Grace and her mother to get a white t-shirt out of my suitcase. That night, the Lord gave me a powerful message to preach: "The kingdom of heaven suffers violence, but the violent take it by force." While I was preaching, I got lost in my excitement and became full of the Holy Spirit, which caused my ear to start bleeding again.

"The enemy will try anything powerful to keep you from making it to the kingdom. There are violent people who die serving God. You have to be courageous. People think you are not going to face adversities as Christians, but many are the afflictions of the righteous. It isn't easy being a Christian." Twenty-five Indians were saved that day.

After the service was over, several Indians brought a big pot of smelly leaves before me and placed several on my ear. The next morning, I awoke feeling "right." I couldn't believe it! The Indians certainly knew their remedies and what to do. Once again, the enemy had tried to kill the miracle.

Chapter Seven

A Partner for Life

Let the morning bring me word of your unfailing love, for I have put my trust in you. Show me the way I should go, for to you I entrust my life. – Psalm 143: 8 (NIV)

When I returned to the States, I became terribly ill and was hospitalized. The doctor's diagnosis were Hepatitis C and a bad liver, to add to my sorrow. I had to file for bankruptcy while going through a painful divorce. I had made my fair share of bad decisions.

One day as I was lying around feeling down on myself, I received a phone call with a lot of numbers displayed. When I answered, I was shocked to discover it was the devout little lady from Ecuador, Grace's mother. I realized how poor they were, so for her to purchase an international phone card to telephone was beyond touching. It had to be expensive for her; my spirit was so moved.

She said, "Son, I don't know what has been going on, but I've been feeling something bad about you. You've been on my mind for days. I want you to know I've been praying for you."

All of a sudden, these big fat tears began running out of my eyes. I couldn't control them or speak.

She continued, "I want you to know I love you." Then the call was disconnected as her minutes had run out.

I knew without a shadow of a doubt that God was working in our lives. God had moved her to call me. So after I was released from the hospital and had recuperated, I began buying phone cards to call her cell phone. Occasionally, whenever I telephoned Grace's mother, Grace would say, "Hi." At the time, she didn't speak English, so our short conversations were always in Spanish. Then I began calling Grace and her mother at the cybercafé, so we could Skype.

When I planned to return to Ecuador in 2011, it had been two years since I'd met Grace, so I asked Felton Burke to accompany me.

"Papa, I've got a girl, and I want to make sure this is a God thing, so can you go to Ecuador with me and interview her? She is younger than me and from a third-world country. I want to die preaching, so I don't want marriage to mess up my ministry.

Without hesitation, Felton bought a round-trip plane ticket for $600 and accompanied me to Ecuador. His interview with Grace was conducted in front of her mother.

Felton asked the Spanish interpreter to ask Grace, "Why do you want to marry Jaime? He doesn't have a pot to piss in. He's going through bankruptcy now. He ain't got anything to give you. Besides, he's way older than you. So why would you want to marry him? Don't you have nice young men here to marry?"

Grace had an answer for every question he asked. The last thing she told him was, "Okay, I can marry a young man here, but what guarantee do I have he won't kick me in the rear-end? In life, we have no guarantees. In my heart, I fell in love with him."

After the interview, Felton told me he felt confident Grace was the right woman for me. So I asked to speak with her father. After he greeted me, we sat and talked.

"Sir, I can't give anything to your daughter. Y'all need to reconsider. Maybe God has someone here who is way better, way younger than me. If we get married, Grace will be living in America, far away."

Grace's Dad was like any other loving father. He wanted his youngest daughter to have a happy life and future with a godly man. Grace confessed her love for me to her parents. "During the times we would speak on the phone or Skype, I fell in love with Jaime" she said.

Grace's parents had gotten to know me, and I was upfront with them about what little I could offer their daughter. But when your child is eventually leaving your home and even your country, you still wonder if she is making the right decision. Her father and mother have always honored me.

When Grace and I went to get married at the courthouse, we learned the laws were different, so we couldn't get married. In order to marry, you had to have been living in the country for three consistent months. With my job in Georgia to get back to, this would be impossible. You also had to have a bank account. Well, I had no money to open a bank account. And you had to have a special Visa, which I didn't have. Grace began crying. Secretly, I felt relieved and thanked God. "Lord, you are keeping me from making a mistake."

A lady that was sitting next to me asked, "Can I ask you why she is crying?"

"Yes ma'am. According to this paper, we can't get married," I replied while hugging Grace's trembling shoulders.

"Are you Cuban?" she asked.

"No. I'm Puerto Rican – American."

The lady picked up her pocketbook, put on her eye-glasses, and handed me her card. Then she said, "I'm an attorney, and today is my birthday."

"Happy Birthday," I said with a smile.

Then she stood, looking from me to Grace and back to me. "Do you know what I'm going to do for my birthday?"

I really wasn't curious, but I was trying to be polite. Besides, I was concerned about Grace. "No ma'am. I don't know what you're going to do."

"I'm going to help you get married. I heard you talking about a god. Well, see that young man over there?"

31

I nodded in bewilderment, still trying to process her words.

"I've been trying to get him a Visa for three months."

My eyes widened as I said, "But I can't wait that long. I only have a week of vacation. I'll have to leave and get back to my job."

She stared into my eyes and said, "I want to see if your god is real and see if you get the Visa."

"Ma'am, I'm preaching tonight. Would you like to come to the service?"

"Sure. What's the address?"

I gave her the address, but I held no certainty that she'd come. But she did, and she got saved that night! The next day, she invited us to her home for a cooked meal. Over time, this lady lawyer would become as close to me as a daughter. And in four days, I received the Visa. Felton gave me enough money to open a bank account.

On June 13, 2011, Grace and I were married in the courthouse in the capital city of Quito. Now, we wanted to be married in the sight of the Lord. Grace's uncle, a well-respected man, is a preacher of a big church. When he offered to marry us at his beautiful church, I replied, "No, sir. I want to marry Grace at her hometown village at the hut. This way, all her family members and all the children she taught at Bible study can attend."

We were especially touched to learn her mother had painted the walls of their little home in hopes we would say our vows there. We agreed. So her uncle, the preacher, married us in the hut. Our marriage was the first one to ever be held in that village. All the other girls normally leave the village with their boyfriends or just live with them in the village and without matrimony, which is the custom for poor people. They don't have money to marry. There is little hope because of the poverty.

Even though one of Grace's sisters is married, her mother told me, "You are my only true son-in-law."

After the ceremony, a little girl approached me and asked a peculiar question. "Why on God's earth did you come from America to a god-forsaken place to marry Grace?"

I didn't hesitate or bat an eye when I responded, "God did this for you, so you won't stop dreaming. Just as God sent me here, He has a place for you."

Then I smiled and caressed her little chin with my cupped hand before joining my lovely wife and her parents at the table, which was laden with all types of cakes and celebratory foods.

Chapter Eight

Postponing Blessings

But the one who looks into the perfect law, the law of liberty, and perseveres, being no hearer who forgets but a doer who acts, he will be blessed in his doing. – James 1:25 (ESV)

Just after we began eating our wedding meal, a preacher knocked on the door and asked to see me. After entering and wishing us blessings on our marriage, he asked, "Could you come to our church and preach tonight?"

Frustrated, I asked him, "Can't you see that I just got married? We're going on our honeymoon."

"But sir, you are only going to be here a short while."

Grace rose from her seat and whispered in my ear, "Forget about the honeymoon. Let's go preach."

I was touched by my young wife's selflessness on her wedding day and more certain than ever that God had blessed me with a good wife. So Grace and I went to the church wearing our wedding clothes, and I preached. That night, the altar was full, and sixty kids were saved.

Now, the churches in Ecuador don't have money to pay visiting preachers. Instead, they blessed me with livestock, food or vegetables, and sometimes chickens. On this particular night, they gave me a little goat.

"Grace?" I asked, "What are we going to do with a goat?"

She smiled and said, "Give it to some poor people."

So I did, and the little goat made them very happy. I was

happy, too, because sixty souls had been won for Christ.

On the day Grace and I were leaving for our postponed honeymoon, a man, who I had been helping when he and his wife were having trouble, called and said, "Me and my wife are about to break-up. Can you come and talk with us?"

Once again, I found myself explaining, "I'm on my way to spend a couple of days with my wife before I leave for America."

The man began crying. "My marriage is dead."

Grace interceded again, and after we discussed it, we had decided to take both of them on our honeymoon. They were delighted to accept our invitation. We travelled to Cuna Luna, where we stayed right on the ocean. Cuna Luna is Spanish for "Crib Moon" or "Moon Crib." While we were there in this magnificent place, the couple reconciled, so we all had a pleasant time on our honeymoon.

It was sad to leave my wife in Ecuador when I returned to America. But I knew we had to do whatever was necessary to get Grace to the States legally. And I needed to prepare a home for her. That's when I began saving money from full-time ministry work and whenever I preached in other churches. Often I would be given a love offering, so I would put money away or pay the lawyer who was helping with Grace's immigration.

When you want to do things the right way, the legal way, it seems you are going to suffer. I am an American citizen, but that didn't mean Grace and I shouldn't have to go through the process to get her here legally.

I was resolved if Grace couldn't come here legally, then that meant God didn't want her here, so I would have to pick up my bags and move to Ecuador. No one had placed a gun to my temple and forced me to marry her. I chose my wife, knowing she was from another country and would need to immigrate legally to this country.

While Grace and I waited for our reunification, we suffered from being apart. All we had was our computers and Skype. For two years, we did a lot of skyping and praying and watching for the Lord's time to be fulfilled. And during this time, my wife never asked me for a single dime. That's what convinced me that I had a good wife. Sure, I had doubted her and was still checking her out because, after all, I was twenty-nine years older than her and streetwise because of my past dope dealing. Just because I was a Christian didn't make me a fool. But my wife never asked me for anything.

I realized my wife was a miracle, and our marriage was a miracle, too.

Chapter Nine

Life Without Grace

I appeal to you therefore, brothers, by the mercies of God, to present your bodies as a living sacrifice, holy and acceptable to God, which is your spiritual worship. Romans 12:1 (ESV)

If I had known I would lose my wife and children when I was released from prison, I would have stayed. I always had dreamed my wife, children, and I would be together until Jesus' return. God saw the pain I was under when I lost my family.

I rented a little place in the woods where I was alone and content but closer to my children. I was doing full-time ministry and traveling to different countries to preach the Word of God, I had met Grace's mother at a crucial time in my life. Now I had married Grace. God deserved all the glory for all He had done for me. Some people talk dirt or make negative connotations about inmates, believing the only time we find Jesus is when we have jailhouse religion. I want my actions and the way I live my life to prove them wrong.

After I'd returned to the States, God told me to move because He knew Grace was coming, but He didn't want me to bring her to Georgia where there were a lot of memories and where two of my grown children now lived. So, how did I end up in Morganton? That's a powerful question.

My first cousin lives in Morganton, and fourteen or fifteen years ago, he invited me to come for a visit. It was the first time I'd ever heard of Morganton. My initial thoughts were the climate was too cold here. I met my cousin's preacher, and he asked me to preach at their church. He loved it. Another preacher had heard my message, so I began establishing relationships with other preachers in Burke County. They began asking me to come from Georgia to lead different events like youth rallies.

When I was in Belize, I received an email from a preacher named Steve Dietz from Hickory, inviting me to come and preach at his church, so after I returned to the States, I did. That's when something weird happened. After the service, Preacher Dietz asked me to come to his office because he wanted to talk to me. In my mind, I thought I was in trouble. It was like being called to the principal's office. *Uh oh,* I thought. *Maybe I did something wrong.*

Preacher Dietz offered me a chair, and I sat down, waiting for him to speak.

"I want to thank you for allowing the Lord to use you. That was a beautiful service – a most powerful service. More young people than we've had in a while were saved. But Jaime, I didn't call you into my office to tell you that. Ever since I began communicating with you over e-mail, I've had a feeling that you need to move to North Carolina. I don't know why, but I have this feeling."

Now Preacher Dietz didn't know anything about me. He couldn't have known that God was dealing with me. This was a powerful moment when I felt God's presence.

So I telephoned my first cousin, Javier Guzman, because he'd paid for me to stay in a motel room in Hickory. Javier was on my mother's side and the first Christian in my family. He had tried to tell me about Jesus many years before, but I wasn't ready to listen. My cousin had always lived in America and operated his own heating and air conditioning company. Javier took me to *Longhorn Steak House* to eat, catch up, and discuss my dilemma.

"I think God wants me to move here," I announced.

"That's great!" he said. "Do you want to move here and stay in my basement? You can have it rent free and see what the Lord wants you to do."

So even though I wasn't thrilled to move to Morganton, this is where God had led me. I moved into my cousin's basement, but I didn't obey God completely. As a back-up, I had kept the little home in Georgia -- just in case.

I continued working on the necessary paperwork to get Grace to America legally. That's when I discovered Immigration had frozen everything. It was difficult for me to find employment, so I was getting depressed.

I had gotten to know folks at Horizon Church, which gives food to the poor people on Tuesdays, so when their truck driver had been injured, they needed a volunteer to drive to Bristol, Tennessee, to pick up 12,000 pounds of food from Operation Blessing - 700 Club, and return it to the Outreach Center in Morganton. I was happy to be given this task.

I was driving a big tractor-trailer truck down Hwy. 181 on the way back from Bristol when the brakes gave out on the mountain. The truck kept gaining speed, so I tried to downshift, but the truck didn't respond. There is a curve they call "Dead Man's Curve" on Hwy. 181. As I approached the dangerous curve, I closed my eyes and thanked God.

I prayed, "Thank you God for saving my soul."

Then the truck began flipping. I felt something around my neck like a brace. It was firm and stiff. Finally, the truck stopped when the guard rail crashed through the driver's window and straight to my neck. I could smell smoke. The truck was on fire and a tire was off. I thought I was going to die.

In the distance, I heard a woman screaming and running towards me. Then I heard a man's voice shouting a stern warning, "Don't go to him!"

"But we have to help him," she appealed.

"Don't do it," the man's voice bellowed. "The truck is on

fire. Look at the smoke."

"But we can't leave him there. I have to help him."

"Think of our children."

That's when she stopped dead in her tracks, but you can't kill the miracle.

I found myself crying, "Please help me."

That's when I noticed a little white guy out of the corner of my eye. I could tell he wanted to come, but he was watching the flames.

"Please help me," I called louder. I tried to free myself, but the outside mirror was bent and stopped me. "Please run down here and bend the mirror. Run!"

The little man ran to the truck, quickly bent the mirror, and hastened back to where he'd been standing. I tried to move my legs, but they were crushed under the wreckage. It was no use.

"Please pull me out," I cried in desperation. "I can't move my legs."

He did. He ran and pulled me out. Then he dragged me to safety.

I jumped up, and a bunch of ladies saw me. "Sit down, son," Ms. Baker of Valdese, N.C., said. "You could have broken bones."

But I wouldn't sit down. I ran over to the little white man and kissed him. He smelled like whiskey; he was drunk.

"Now I know why I missed work today," he said.

When he heard the police sirens, he ran away. I never saw the man again who had saved my life.

Ms. Baker was some kind of woman. She drove a big Mercedes SUV. She grabbed me even though I was bleeding and steered me to her vehicle to sit until the ambulance arrived. Her gestures showed me love. Finally, the ambulance came and took me all the way from the mountain to Burke County.

The police, who were at the scene, came to visit me in the hospital. They wanted to see the miracle. They told Rev. Cline, who was also visiting me, the Lord must have turned me into a mouse because the window was crushed. They couldn't figure out how I'd gotten out of there.

One day when I was talking to the Lord, He spoke to me. "Go get you a place to live."

I replied, "Lord, I don't have a red cent in my pocket. How can I get a place to live?"

His reply was stern. "Do what I tell you."

So I telephoned my dear friends and surrogate parents, Papa and Mama Cline. Papa is a retired minister and a devout man of God. His real name is the Reverend Cline. His lovely wife and life's partner is Meredith Cline. I told them what God had ordered me to do.

Papa Cline didn't hesitate. "We're coming to get you and find you a place."

That afternoon, we drove around looking for a home. As the car climbed a hill, I was sitting in the back seat and noticed a little white house ahead.

"I like that little place on top of the hill. Actually, I love that place. It's beautiful!"

Papa Cline stopped the car and turned around to face me. "Yeah, it's a nice place, and the owner goes to my church. But you can forget it, son. She isn't selling or renting."

A week and a half later, Papa Cline called me. "You ain't going to believe this, son. I'm coming to get you. Remember that little house on the hill you liked? Well, the lady wants to meet you. Her name is Estelle."

Papa and Mama Cline drove me to the house where the lady met us at the door. "Is your name Jaime Torres?"

"Yes, ma'am."

"Come in. I've heard some good things about you. I've heard you go into prisons. Do you go to nursing homes, too?"

"Yes, ma'am. I go into nursing homes."

"I heard that. My husband just died, and I'm thinking of

moving to Sanford, N.C., but I'm not going to rent this place. I want to sell it."

My heart stopped beating for a second. I stood up from the chair and said, "Well, I can't buy this place now. I'm in bankruptcy. I don't have a secular job. I'm just doing ministry work now. I've just started."

She didn't seem deterred. "Let me show you the house."

"Ma'am, there's no need to show me."

She insisted. "Let me show you the house." We walked through the house; it was beautiful. Then she led me to the garage.

"This is what I'll do," she began saying. "I'll rent you the place, but I need every bit of $800 per month."

"I'm sorry, Ma'am. I'm wasting your time. I can't afford that. I'm sorry."

I went back into the house.

"Papa, are you ready to leave?" I asked.

Ms. Estelle was a stubborn lady. "Sit on down, son. What can you pay?"

"Ma'am, I can't put a price on your property. That is unfair; I can't do that. Thank you."

"You seem like a nice young man," she said. "This is what I'm going to do."

Papa and Mama Cline were just sitting there with big eyes.

"I'm going to rent you this house for $450.00 per month."

I was overwhelmed with her generosity, so I began crying. I thought Papa and Mama Cline might cry, too.

I didn't have a lick of furniture -- not a bed – nothing. Then, as if she read my thoughts, she said, "I'm going to sell you all my furniture. Can you give me $50 more each month for the furniture? That would be $500 per month."

"It's a deal!" I was beaming, and my heart was racing. God had blessed me with a home where I could bring my wife. God wanted her to have her own place. We had trusted God and His process. We had remained faithful to His timing.

The enemy is always trying to kill the miracle. When I was freed from prison, he had tried to kill the miracle with the divorce. When I was trying to help a ministry, he tried to kill the miracle with the wreck. I knew he'd never stop trying, but as long as I wore the armor of God, I would be protected.

Chapter Ten

Life with Grace

But by the grace of God I am what I am, and his grace toward me was not in vain. On the contrary, I worked harder than any of them, though it was not I, but the grace of God that is with me.
– 1 Corinthians 15:10 (ESV)

My wife has been such a blessing in my life. She is an angel sent by God.

Immigration had placed Grace's case on hold. I now realize that God did it so I would have time to get us a real home. Immigration re-opened her file on the same day I rented the house. Rep. Mark Meadows had helped me after I explained our problem. They also had kept my passport, but once Rep. Meadows got involved, I received a new passport and a telephone call where they apologized. Thank God for him.

I had been saving money from the love offerings for three years. Every time I received an offering, I'd put away $20 or $25. I needed another $1400 to finish paying my lawyer in full, so he could finish the necessary paperwork. I went to Victor, a Christian, who was having a hard time backsliding and smoking weed. But I scolded him and began loving on him.

"Victor, you are a praying man. I want you to pray for me."

He said, "You need to pray for me."

"No. God wants you to pray for me. I need $1400 as soon as possible. So Victor and I began praying.

On the tenth day of prayer, Mike Poplin of Hickory called

me and said, "The reason I am calling you is because God put this on my heart."

When I met Mike at my front door, he placed an envelope in my hand and left. Inside it was $1400, which I gave to my lawyer in Georgia. Once the necessary paperwork was completed and everything was in place, I sent Grace the air fare.

Grace was scheduled to arrive in Miami on December 2, 2013, which meant I would need to drive to Miami to get her. Fortunately, I had saved another $1400, so I planned to show her a good time. On my way to Miami, Gene telephoned me out of the blue and said, "What are you doing?"

"I'm on my way to Miami to pick up my wife."

He said, "Really? That's great. I'm going to put you in a hotel."

Gene booked us at the Hilton on the beach. Even though we didn't have much of a honeymoon in Ecuador, we did have one in Miami. How could we have known that sacrificing our first honeymoon would lead to God blessing us with a wonderful honeymoon? The first night when she arrived, I took her to Carrabba's for Italian food. This was her first restaurant in the States, and she loved the lasagna. We were able to stay in Miami for a memorable week. While we were there, I took her to the mall and bought her perfume and a pair of UGGs (boots).

When I took Grace home to Morganton, she fell in love with the house. But I explained that I wasn't going to teach her English. She didn't know a single word of English, but I expected her to learn it on her own.

"And I don't want you to come over here and become Americanized," I explained, "wanting *Louis Vuitton* pocketbooks. I'm a preacher with a modest salary. I shop at *Walmart*. I know it won't be easy to become accustomed to the language and way of life. The Lord has sent you to a Baptist country, a white church, and everyone has a Southern dialect."

Grace has done well learning English. Now she is focusing

on how to use the past tense. She can write well, but she needs to learn how to drive an automobile. It overwhelms me to be the sole driver in the family and having to get her to and from doctors' visits when I'm trying to perform ministry work. Grace loves America. She is preparing for her citizenship exam, which will have a random one hundred questions. Taking the exam will cost a few hundred dollars, but we are happy to be going through the legal process.

Since Grace came in December 2013, she has given birth to our two precious children: JonathanDavid and Isabella Grace. We may not have health insurance, but we are blessed with healthy children. We continue to Skype with her mother. Unfortunately, her parents can't afford to travel here, but they are happy when they hear how Grace lives here in America. They are relieved to know she didn't marry a shyster, or someone who would abuse her. One of our prayers is the Lord will make a way for us to go visit her family and take the grandbabies to meet their grandparents.

In the more than five years since we've been living in Morganton, God has been caring for us. He moves in the hearts of people. The other day, we didn't have any gas. Later that day, a $50 Shell gas card was left in our door. We had been driving a 1994 Toyota Camry (nicknamed the "Black Mamba") with 300,000 miles that was loaned to us by Papa Cline. When we found out Grace was pregnant with our daughter, we were nervous about the high mileage, but we couldn't afford a car. That's when Steve White of Steve White Chrysler in Hickory telephoned. He had come to know me through a relationship I had started with his son, Trey.

"Hi, Jaime. This is Steve White. Can you come to my dealership? I want to talk to you about something."

So I went. When I arrived, Steve walked me outside and behind a building.

That's when he stopped and said, "God told me to give you

this van. It is a 2012 with 120,000 miles."

How could Steve have known? When Grace and I saw the van, we started crying. The Lord places the words in our mouths and the desires in our hearts. He can and will use anybody.

One day my cell phone rang while I was driving to the prison in Albemarle with Papa Cline. I answered it. On the other end was Ms. Estelle, my landlord.

She began talking slowly. "You know how much I love you, don't you?"

"Yes, ma'am," I replied, knowing this couldn't be good.

"Well, I'm sick. I'm having problems with my eyes. I'm willing to sell you this property, and I'll finance it for you. But I can only do that for five years. I'll need $1400 per month."

I felt sick. Grace and I loved our home. "I can't do that Mama. I can't afford it," I explained.

"Well, I love you, son, but I've got to sell it. It's killing me. I have to pay all these taxes and my health is down. I can't go on anymore. I'm going to call a realtor."

"Okay, Ma'am. When do we need to move?"

"I don't want you to move soon. It could take a year to sell the house."

"Mama, we just had a baby, and my wife is nursing. I can't have real estate people coming and showing the house."

Grace cried when she learned we had to move from our little house – her first home in America. The enemy was trying to discourage us, but even so, I felt a sense of peace because I knew deep down in my soul, God had a plan for us. Sometimes, God has to move us when we become comfortable.

And I know this: God has blessed me and my family more than I could have imagined.

Life in Prison

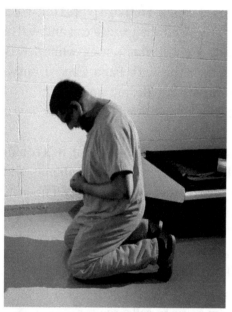

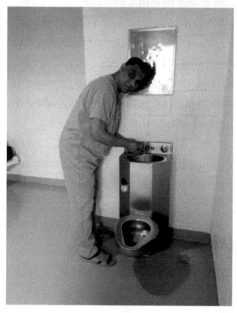

The Wreck

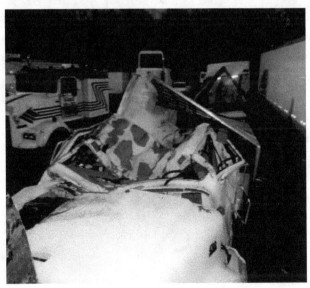

Jaime Preaching at the men's and woman's prison.

Jaime Preaching and Praising Jesus.

Chapter Eleven

Gene Lawson

I'm tickled pink and elephant proud of what he's doing.

When I met Jaime, he and I were both in prison together in the Florida Department of Corrections in Miami. I remember I first noticed Jaime as he was cleaning out his room on the second tier. It was easy to tell by his exaggerated movements he was frustrated and mad about something. A little while later, I watched him at the phone. He was excited, agitated, upset, and trying his best to intimidate the others from using their phone time, which was about five minutes long. Jaime was trying to manipulate the situation. He seemed to be angry all the time and was violent in nature. My perception was Jaime was a kid who seemed to be "lost."

At the time, I was running a Bible study, and a lot of transient inmates, who were coming in and out of this facility, would attend. On a daily basis, we had about fifteen or twenty guys attending. That's when the Lord spoke to me about Jaime.

I asked the Lord, "Really? Do you really want me to talk to this guy? He looks like he's about ready to take somebody's head off."

Of course, I knew he was Puerto Rican, and there were a lot of Latinos in the prison. Culturally, you have to be very careful when you're in prison. But anyway, the Lord was insistent. So I finally got up enough holy will to go over and speak with Jaime. He was into Santeria, Saints, and all kinds of different stuff. As I continued to minister to him, it seemed to calm him. He started participating on the fringes of the Bible study by attending. Encouraged, I continued to mentor him and help him realize there are other ways to deal with conflict.

Jaime was like a baby who had just found milk for the first time. It was quite obvious. You should have witnessed the look in his eyes. It was like he had seen for the first time. He was so inquisitive, and his eyes were yearning for more, more, more. He was star-struck and starving at the same time. He couldn't believe there was a God Who loved him. Jaime took to me and wanted to be around me all the time. When Jaime came to accept Christ, he finally found peace. Through this peace, his environment really didn't matter. When you are in peace, it doesn't matter where you are. A by product is you "fit in" – something Jaime had always wanted. When you find peace, it is a peace that surpasses all understanding. It is an amazing thing that helps your self-esteem and understanding you are in this world but not of this world. It gives you a courage and stability that other people don't have. You fit in, and because you fit in, people want you around because you possess something they want. They can't quite figure out what it is.

Eventually, Jaime and I became roommates. At the time, Jaime was a good student but not a good reader. I taught him how to read better. As a result, we developed a bond as the person who had led him to the Lord, and we became good friends. He was at my hip, my right-hand man. I watched him grow into a great evangelist – a natural. He was always talking to others and bringing them to the Bible study each day. He always cared about the people in the Bible study. It was a wonder to witness what God had done for him and how He had changed Jaime and his way of seeing God. He took away Jaime's cultic religion. I like to say, it was like a "defrosting." When you get around God's love and light, you begin to defrost all the coldness you've built up to protect yourself. It melts away. This defrosting turned Jaime into a beautiful human being.

Jaime later said, "You were always smiling when I'd see you. I could never understand why or how you could be happy in a place like this. That's the only reason I ever talked to you. I didn't know what 'this guy' was doing because he was always smiling."

Jaime came to realize as I had that when you have God in your life, it doesn't matter where you are or what you are experiencing. There is an eternal joy that isn't connected to happiness. This joy is something, which runs like a deep river inside your soul.

I had grown up in church and had always had an affinity to the Lord. At a young age, my mother had introduced me to Christ, but I had backslid because of all the things of life shining and all the stuff life has to offer. It's sort of like the temptation of Jesus in the wilderness. The evil one will take you up on the high mountain and show you all these wonderful things of life, and if you don't stay grounded, they'll overtake you. Before you know it, you're lost in a maze from where you don't know how to escape.

That downward spiral is what led me to prison. But it was in prison during the first couple of months, when I reconnected with the Lord. A wonderful man helped me to find my way back. Once I was on the path again, my relationship with God became more meaningful.

It's sort of like when you know someone as a child, that's one thing. But after you've been beat up, bruised, scuffed up, and you come back, you have more of a maturity, a deeper understanding of what this "salvation" is all about. You realize how much of a healer God can be and how much you can discern as He reveals the secrets of life. You are able to form a deeper appreciation. As a child, God doesn't reveal all of this to you, but as you go through a few things, He changes your perspective. You begin to realize how connected God is in all things of your life.

I often say you begin to see God in everything, around every corner, and in every circumstance. You can see God operate. You can't see that as a child because you're searching for solutions. You don't realize God is always the solution and the answer to every test and calamity in which you find yourself. *He is the answer.* To me, the simplicity of this is what gives you peace. You don't have to go and search for the answer – you know the answer. You just have to make yourself open to Him.

I was released from prison two or three years before Jaime. He took over the Bible study and continued the preaching and teaching. He was on his way to becoming Pastor Torres.

The Lord worked a miracle in Jaime's life when the attorneys selected his case as pro bono. It is unheard of. It just doesn't happen, but it did happen. Ever since his release from federal prison and even before, Jaime has been on the battlefield for the Lord.

Thankfully, our paths crossed again in Jesup, Georgia. Jaime calls me "Papa," and he calls me all the time. It's been good to watch him grow, trust, and accept the things the Lord has opened up for him. I'm tickled pink and elephant proud of what he's doing.

I pray this book is a great success, and it will bless some lives and maybe change some hearts – in the name of Jesus.

Chapter 12:

Dr. Jorge Valdes

He already has impacted a lot of lives for Christ and will continue to do so.

I met Jaime in prison in Jesup, Georgia, when Gene Lawson, a mutual friend and inmate at the time, introduced us. Actually, Gene was my cellmate. Jaime was a brand-new, born-again Christian. We immediately connected because we both came from rough backgrounds, but mine wasn't as gang-oriented as his had been because I had a chance to go to school and do something with my life. I found him to be a very likeable guy. One thing I remember most about Jaime at this time was he was very inquisitive about his new faith.

Jaime started hanging around with us and attending different Bible studies and different events in prison. I watched Jaime struggle with his newfound faith as he began to grow as a Christian. People think it is easy once you accept Jesus Christ. Everything in your life changes and becomes rosy, but it's not – especially in a prison environment. We were having a lot of battles with the Muslims, but even so, what ended up happening is Jaime continued to grow and grow and grew stronger in his faith. We kept in contact with each other after Jaime and I were released from prison.

I went to Wheaton College to finish my master's degree, and when I graduated, I was accepted at Loyola University in Chicago to earn a Ph.D. in Bible. It was while I was working on my doctoral studies that I wrote a book, *Coming Clean*, with

Ken Abrams, which became a best seller. When the book was released, I began to give youth rallies with members of the U.S. Congress. I began to take Jaime with me to some of those rallies as he had a very powerful story of how he grew up, was stabbed, and was shot, and yet God saved him. He has a little bit of Latin soul because he loves to dance and party and have a good time, and he brings this into his preaching. But lo and behold, he was able to change his life around and try to make different choices and decisions.

Jaime preached as an introduction to my main event, and when I finished preaching, Jaime would help with the many young men and women who would come forth to dedicate their lives to Christ. We went into high schools and brought a lot of people to the Lord. I took Jaime everywhere I went -- Atlanta, Georgia; Rochester, Minnesota; and other places. I didn't want to earn a living from preaching. I had a hard time, not with Jesus, but with Christian leaders, as I began to preach around the country. I saw a hypocrisy that really disturbed me. As a leader in a drug cartel, we were black and white, we were transparent. You knew that your yes was yes, and your no was no, yet in the "Christian world," I began to see things I did not like, so I stepped away from full-time ministry and began a local restoration company, which in ten years, had become a multimillion-dollar international corporation. I now saw what the Bible means when the prophet Joel says, "I would give you back the years the locust had eaten" (Joel 2:25a).

One day when our company was making millions, I decided that if a man does not identify when enough is enough, greed would drive him, so I told my wife we were selling our company and moving to Mexico, so our kids could see the world is not the "white suburbia" world they lived in. We lived there for five years. During this sabbatical, I didn't hold as many evangelistic events, but I kept in touch with Jaime because I believed he was a true man of God.

57

While being in business, my partners and I started a foundation, Tres Hermanos Foundation. We decided we were going to give away 10% of our gross, not our net income, and this decision allowed us to give away millions of dollars for many outreach programs with a focus on youth and the least of HIS. When we were making a lot of money, we were asked by many people to support their causes, and I know there are a lot of good causes out there, but we simply could not help all of them. So we decided to donate money to our foundation where every penny went to help someone; no one in our foundation makes a dollar off the foundation. It is important to mention this because I did make an exception in our donation philosophy, and the only foundation I support personally is Jaime's ministry. It is dear to my heart, and the brother is barely surviving. I just could not support ministries where the leaders lived a very lavish lifestyle. Out of all the preachers out there, Jaime is the only one where I give my money. I know every bit of it is going to impact the kingdom of Christ.

Even though I live in Palm Beach, Florida, and Jaime lives in Morganton, North Carolina, we are very close and talk a lot. I pray for him, as he is in my daily devotions. I love his wife and kids. He is a genuine person. What you see with Jaime is what you get. As a result of his environment and the world where he grew up, Jaime was full of hatred before coming to Christ. You can see throughout the years since coming to Christ, he is full of love. It is contagious. It is genuine love, not the love some people say they have for Christ and then live an incomplete life.

It is important to mention how I came to Christ. You see a man who taught me Karate preached the Gospel to me for three years. Three months after I walked away from being a leader in the Medellin Cartel and before I got arrested, my divorce was finalized July 1, 1990. I watched as my little daughter cried when her mother took her away. I went back to my room and basically prayed, "Hey, Jesus! I don't know if you are real or not.

If you are real, you probably look at me and don't want me in heaven. But if you are real, please change my life, and I'll die for you. I want what this guy has. He doesn't have the money I have. I can have anything the world has to offer, and I'm miserable, but this man has nothing and is full of joy because he has an intimate relationship with you."

A lot of preachers today don't seem to get it. I didn't come to Christ because of any fancy words this man said to me. Honestly, the times he was preaching to me, I probably wasn't listening. The thing that brought me to Christ was to see the way he lived his life, to see the Gospel preached without words. As a multimillionaire, I had had everything in the world I wanted. I dated the most beautiful women in the world. I owned a fleet of jets. I lived in various multimillionaire mansions. I owned more than a million dollars-worth of cars. But I was miserable, and this Karate teacher, who had nothing, seemed to be the happiest person I'd ever seen. I wanted what he had. I wanted to be happy and feel complete.

When you come to Christ, people think your life is a lot better, but things get a lot worse. Christ wants to see how real that conversion is. It's easy for someone to say, "I accept Christ." Jaime and I evangelized at events with audiences between 10,000 people and 20,000. We had thousands of people coming to Christ, which is easy when you have a charismatic speaker who moves people's hearts. It's easy to come forward and say, "I accept You Jesus Christ as my Lord and Savior." But is it real? Is it genuine?

Sometimes Christ, Who knows everything, puts us through hell to see how real our love for Him is. I lost everything after I came to Christ. I went to prison not knowing if I would ever get out again. When I came out of prison, I had nothing. I earned a bachelor's degree in Theology and started my master's degree, majoring in the Bible. Then I became an adjunct professor at Wheaton College. Finally, I went for my Ph.D. and earned a doctorate in theology. I worked and worked and worked, and He honored my conversion. Like the Bible says in Zachariah 9:12 (ESV), "Return to your stronghold, O prisoners of hope; today I declare that I will restore to you double."

I see guys like Jaime sometimes struggling and living day to day, compared to all of these mega preachers becoming richer and richer off the Gospel. I love Jaime. He is real. We need to distinguish the difference between ministry and full-time ministry. When we come to know Christ and have a genuine relationship with Him, we automatically become ministers, evangelists. The Greek word for evangelism means "one who shares the good news." It is critical when people come to Christ for them to live a life of honesty and integrity. These qualities represent Christ. At the end of the day, those who are specifically called to become a full-time minister – to live lives of the Gospel – are accepting a big responsibility in the most important thing.

I'm fed up with Christian leaders, who get up on television and support politicians who do not put any value in truth, honestly, integrity, and faithfulness to their wives. We are all sinners saved by grace. Our youth today look at these leaders and say, "They are a bunch of hypocrites because they are lying." The sad thing is in today's world, you can't hide anything. Everything becomes public.

One of the greatest preachers I've always loved and admired was Billy Graham, a simple man. But my favorite preacher is David Mainz from Canada. He was the first Christian to have an exhibit at the World's Fair. You talk about a genuine man, he lived in the same house where his grandparents lived and where his parents lived. He has the most amazing television program. He is a genuine man of God who lives a simple life.

I enjoyed planes. I enjoyed jets. I enjoyed living in a million dollar house, but I wasn't going to have all of that at the expense of people sending me $20, $30, $40, $50, $100, or whatever. I chose to preach the Gospel for nothing and decided I would support my family through my business. Now, my business –DART, LLC, a disaster restoration business.-- has given me the honor to support Jaime, to help him to do great things for Christ. He deserves a lot better. I hate to see a genuine man of God, who preaches the Gospel because of true love for God and others, struggle, but people prefer to send money to mega ministries who can't measure up to Jaime.

I was raised in a committed Catholic Christian home. My mother was a tremendous woman of faith. Our home was one of tremendous integrity and morality. I went astray, but I came back to Christ and left the world when my mother repeated, "Son, what you're doing doesn't please God. Son, what you're doing doesn't please God" several times. But the important thing is we have to teach our kids what is right or wrong. We have to teach where north is because if they go astray – south, west, east – as long as they know how to come back to true north, they will come back.

Jaime is genuine, real. I wish him well and know God has His hands over Jaime. He is an unbelievable man of God, and God is going to honor him. He already has impacted a lot of lives for Christ, and he will continue to do so.

Chapter Thirteen

Rep. Jack Kingston

It was easy to see the Lord's hand in a guy washing cars.

I attended a weekly Bible study for twenty-two years as a member of Congress. Generally speaking, we didn't allow outside guests or speakers. But if you were an outside guest or speaker, it was a very rare thing. Every now and then, we did have somebody, usually a very outstanding person, who had an incredible story or an unusual story to share. Jorge Valdes was one of the people we allowed to attend.

I had invited Jorge to come to Georgia because his story was unbelievable and clearly showed the work of the Lord. I described Jorge as "Pablo Escobar's American franchisee for cocaine in the 1980s" because Jorge was the distributor of all cocaine in America from one of the biggest suppliers in the world. I wanted him to speak to different people and especially to youth groups.

When I extended the invitation to Jorge, he said, "You know, when I come there, I have a friend who lives there now, whom I met in prison. His name is Jaime Torres, who would be great to speak, too."

We set up three or four tours around the district, so I could get the two of them in front of youth who were thirteen to nineteen years-old -- kids who were at risk. When Jaime came in, he was this huge guy. You'd look at him and think *He should be playing professional football.* You could easily imagine him as a bone-crushing enforcer for drug dealers, and if you owed somebody money, he would be the guy who would pursue the heck out of you.

So Jorge shared his story of conversion with us. He had written a book entitled, *Coming Clean,* a really great book I'd highly recommend. And as it turned out, Jaime was this loveable "teddy-bear-kind-of-guy" who had love spilling out of him. Instead of being the "wrestler type" and talking "smack," he was the exact opposite, which really was part of his charm. Even though Jaime looked like a guy who could kill you if he wanted to, he was as nice as he could be. Jaime had a great story about being in prison, similar to Jorge Valdes's story. We got to continually know each other through Valdes.

Then Jaime started a car wash in Jesup, Georgia, and was employing a lot of people who were similar to him, as well as their family members. It was like going to a fundraising event where they sell cookies or similar things to raise money for school projects. His business was like that. It had this warm, fun feeling where everybody had a job and was there because he/she wanted to be there. With Jaime being recently out of prison, he was frankly glad to be alive, glad to know the Lord, and glad not to be in prison. He had an infectious enthusiasm for anybody who came to the car wash. You could not help but think, *Hey! This is a wonderful guy. This is a special place.* It was easy to see the Lord's hand in a guy washing cars.

I've heard people say, "You can be a witness to the Lord all the time, no matter what you're doing." And here was a guy, washing cars and being a witness, not having to say a word about God. Francis Assisi has been attributed to saying, "Preach the Gospel at all times; when necessary, use words." This was the case with Jaime. You could tell by his actions and the way he went about things that he was a disciple of the Lord without even talking about it.

I would often go by to see Jaime at the car wash, and I helped him by encouraging him. It was really obvious to me he had a great talent, no matter what he was doing, but his heart was more into preaching, but he had not taken that to the Lord in prayer. I have heard many times, "If you have wandered and strayed to the extent you are a criminal and have gone to jail, anyone who hasn't walked in your shoes or down that path can't identify with you." Whereas, someone who has walked down that bleak path can empathize and perhaps say, "I was a really bad person, and I served time for it. I'm only here by the grace of God because I should have been killed long ago. I should still be in prison." That type of calling card makes you a very effective person. I saw this when we were going to the different school groups. Kid after kid who were tough, as well as kid after kid who were lost and desperate for a father figure, wanted God to love them. Jaime, who had walked in both sets of shoes, could make that presentation and build a case for them. The remarkable thing about Jaime is he is unabashed, whereas some of us native born Southerners can be.

As Georgia's State Representative, I had the opportunity to nominate Jaime for the National Hispanic Leadership Summit. This was a two-day conference, which included over three hundred Hispanic participants from thirty-six states and the District of Columbia. The Summit's purpose was to discuss various policy issues with members of the United States Congress and the Bush Administration. Some of the topics discussed were job creation, education, health care, and other opportunities for Hispanic Americans. Jaime was able to have dinner with Senator Kay Bailey- Hutchinson (Texas) and Senator Bill Fritz (Tennessee).

Jaime has since said, "This conference was a highlight in my life."

Many of us were born and raised in traditional families with traditional educations and backgrounds. We came from safe middle class neighborhoods and went to churches that were attended by our friends, school mates, and neighbors. We got used to church and worship being presented a certain way. As I grew up I learned that the Gospel is so much bigger than this. Our Lord needs witnesses and ministers of all types for all types of people.

In today's challenging, changing, and chaotic world, people like Jamie can go places that traditional ministers can't go. He has converted the souls of all types of people, regardless of their background, financial status, or position. His appeal is universal. Jamie is as aggressive in reaching people as the most persistent salesman. As a witness, he's energetic, courageous, and fearless. He makes no apology for his devotion and love for Jesus Christ. Hardened and tough people, who have hit the bottom, need somebody like Jaime who can look them in the eye and tell them, "You're on the wrong track."

If you're fortunate enough to meet Jaime and talk with him, don't be surprised when he ends the conversation with a prayer. And when he does, it's not a formality. Jaime talks to the Lord in a personal way because he truly believes in the healing power of our Savior. Jamie knows the difference it made in his life, and his mission is that it will do the same for the rest of us!

Chapter Fourteen

Pastor Terry D. Sellars

Jaime has always cultivated a hunger for God's Word....

We've had a ministry now for going on nearly thirty years at the Federal Correctional Institution in Jesup, Georgia. We are very grateful for how those doors were opened to us, and it's those opened doors which allowed Jaime Torres's path and my path to cross as a result of ministry. I preached at the prison once or twice a week in those early days. Jaime attended our preaching/teaching classes as we were going through the Bible. My first impression of him was one of joy. He had an exuberant personality that reached out and grabbed you. His kind mannerism, extension of friendship, and joyful spirit helped draw me to him. It was hard not to like the guy. I learned at the time, Jaime had been saved and had faith in Christ. He seemed hungry for the Word of God, but I believe because he was such a baby Christian, not everybody bought into his real Christianity.

Jaime has always cultivated a hunger for God's Word which was one of the key things that helped him grow and develop into the man he is today. His sincerity of heart is a tremendous attraction to people around him, enhancing his leadership abilities.

Just recently, I was sharing one episode about Jaime with our church members. In 2 Corinthians 13:12 (NIV), the Bible says, "Greet one another with a holy kiss." Well, Jaime literally practiced this verse. For about two or three weeks whenever

I came into the prison, he would greet me with a holy kiss on each cheek. Finally, I said, "Let's modernize this greeting. A simple handshake will be fine." I didn't know how seeing a guy kiss another guy might be perceived by others behind bars. To this day, Jaime and I laugh about it. It was a great time.

After Jaime transferred to another prison, I didn't see him for about a year or two. Then he was returned to Jesup before being released from prison. A lot of guys who are behind bars make commitments and promises to God. This is what some folks would call "jailhouse religion." But I knew Jaime's wasn't that at all. When he got out, he got on fire for God even more. I watched him continue his ministry in the Jesup, Georgia, area.

For thirty-three years, I've pastored the Faith Baptist Church & Christian Academy in Ludowici, Georgia, which is located about fifteen miles from the federal prison. Over these many years, I've observed how God instrumentally brings paths together and how He has intervened in Jaime's life in a unique way to give him a platform He doesn't give to everybody. Jaime preaches at our church on special days when we invite ex-inmates and their families to come and be recognized and honored. I count him as a dear friend – a faithful fellow laborer in the work of the Lord. I look forward to all the great things God has ahead for him. I could talk about Jaime forever because we have lots of stories, but I'm trying to give a panoramic view of him for this chapter.

I'd like to share my personal testimony now. My mom and dad were good folks and lived by Christian principles, but I wouldn't say we were a Christian family. We didn't attend church, and I didn't get involved in church until I was a teenager. That's when I was invited by a friend with whom I played basketball.

"Hey! Come go with me to Sunday school," he said. "Come go with me to church."

"Nah, nah!" I'd reply, trying to put him off. But between

his friendship and a few pretty girls I knew were in the Sunday school class, I finally gave in and decided to visit. I hung around, and by 1973, I was an active member of Grace Baptist Church in Valdosta, Georgia. At the time, most of my understanding of Christianity and salvation was to believe in Jesus and to do the best you could. Maybe between a little bit of faith and a whole lot of good works, you might get into heaven. I had not recognized myself as being lost as I was in God's sight. But the Word was planted, watered, and nurtured.

In a revival meeting in November 1973, I came to the clear realization that even though I was a church member, religious, and a good kid, I was lost. At the age of seventeen, I went forward to the altar. Unfortunately, the person who dealt with me at the altar didn't know how to deal with me. He only knew to talk about baptism. So I left church that night and went home. It was in my little bedroom beside my bed where I knelt and asked Christ to come into my heart. I received Him as my Savior, and my life has never been the same.

I began to feel burdened about reaching people. From reading the Bible, conversing with people, and listening to my pastor's sermons, I realized folks were going to hell. It burdened me that no one was doing anything. Seemingly, there were few young people stepping forward to fill the shoes of the older guys. My concern --something internally -- was leading or calling me in that direction.

I went to my pastor, a very wise man, and told him how I was feeling.

He asked, "Why don't you just forget about it?"

He was using reverse psychology on me and knew if I could forget about it, walk away, and go do something else, with it never bothering me again, it wasn't a call from God. It was just a personal concern or an emotional move. To withstand the test and tribulations of ministry, it had better be a call from God.

I tried to forget about it for a week or two, but I couldn't.

Every waking moment and when I tried to sleep, it was on my mind. Whenever I attended revival, the preachers' sermons were about needing more people to surrender. Every time I read my Bible, verses seemed to jump off the page: how God had called Jeremiah; how God had called Elijah; the burden God placed on Malachi's heart; or how God reached out to Paul. A combination of all these factors, along with the burden of my heart and the internal calling of God pulling, leading, and directing me in a certain way, convinced me. A year and a half after being saved, I answered God's call to preach.

I was licensed and ordained in 1976. I spent eight and a half years in Moultrie, Georgia, pastoring a church there. I came here to Faith Baptist of Ludowici in October 1985. God's done a great thing in this old sinner's life. That's all I am -- an old sinner saved by grace. I just thank Him for it. God has been so good to me and so much better than I ever deserved.

The pastor whom I sought advice is now in his eighties. We talked a couple of weeks ago which gave me another opportunity to thank him. His advice to me is something I've used on other guys: "Just forget about it." If they can forget it, it's not the call of God. God's call is something you can't forget. God will work on your heart. At least He did on mine.

***

A key event in my life was when my mom and dad got saved. It was a blessing to see Mama and Daddy come to faith in Christ. I guess your family members are the hardest to witness to, and the ones you cry over the most. I had not been raised in a Christian home, but God changed my life in a unique way through the ministering of a friend and a Bible-believing local church.

My wonderful wife and I have been married forty-two years. I wouldn't be where I am without her. We have three beautiful children: a daughter and two sons. They all graduated from Pensacola Christian College in Pensacola, Florida. My daughter is our elementary principal at our Christian school ministry here at the church. Our next child is a son who teaches at Pensacola Christian College and coaches the girls' basketball team there. After college, he worked with us for eleven years before taking this position in 2011. Our youngest son works and teaches in the school ministry. He is our athletic director. The Lord has blessed me by having my family close by, and all are serving the Lord in full-time ministry. Even though Pensacola is about six hours away, it's not too bad. We often jokingly say that we didn't mind our son and his wife going there; we just didn't want him to take the grandkids. But, oh well, you just have to live with it.

Jaime and I talk three or four times a year, especially when we are planning one of our prison ministry days. We devote the whole morning service to the men before taking them out for a fellowship meal. We try to honor them, but they often honor us. Years ago, we went to the prison to be a blessing to them. As it turned out, by trying to be a blessing, we received more blessings than we ever gave to them. I tell those guys all the time, "You've done a lot more for me than I've ever done for you." Of course, they repeat the same back to me.

Sometimes, Jaime and I talk a little more often whenever he is calling for counseling or guidance or when he just needs to talk. He has my cell phone number and can call me anytime, day or night. I try to make myself available for the guys when they get out of prison. They need a friend when they get out and not just while they are in there. Some people look at ex-inmates as "once a convict always a convict" – "once an inmate, always an inmate." My response to that is "How about giving the guys a second chance?" They made a mistake. They admitted it. They served their time. Now they are out and have been forgiven by God. It looks like folks would forgive them and give them another chance to serve God. The Apostle Paul was a jailbird, too, you know. He got out of prison, and God used him in a mighty way. Who is to say that someone who has kept a clean record may not be used as much?

In Luke 7:47 (KJV), it says, *Wherefore I say unto thee, her sins, which are many, are forgiven; for she loved much: but to whom little is forgiven, the same loveth little.* To paraphrase, he who has been forgiven much, loves much. Maybe this is an example, evidenced by Jaime's life. God forgave him of a lot of junk in his life. My, how the Lord is using him. To God be the glory!

I am thankful the Lord allowed our paths to cross, and I was able to have an impact on Jaime's life. That's the whole reason we do ministry anyway – to see the lost saved and the saved trained to become disciples. Whatever we gave, Jaime received it as it was in truth – not the word of men, but the Word of God.

In 1 Thessalonians 2:13 (KJV), we read, *For this cause also thank we God without ceasing, because when ye received the word of God which ye heard of us, ye received it not as the word of men, but as it is in truth the word of God, which effectually worketh also in you that believe.* This made a tremendous difference in how he grew, and he really grew. We praise God for that.

Chapter Fifteen

Javier Guzman
I am very proud of him.

Jaime and I grew up in South Bronx, New York City, in the 1970s. Specifically, we lived in New York's 41st Precinct, the now infamous sector, which the police, the locals, and history would call Fort Apache. This was the worst time and worst place in the U.S. for anyone to live, much less for two boys to spend their formative years of childhood. Books have been written about the history of this area, and in 1981, a movie starring Paul Newman was filmed there. This was a *very* bad neighborhood with drugs and violence running rampant – but we just called it home.

Jaime visited our home very often because we had food in the house. His favorite thing was to open our cabinet and find the Oreos. We spent a lot of time together, growing up. We were close in age, as I'm only a year and a half his senior. We didn't see each other much during the week while we were in school, but he would stay at our home most weekends. Jaime was a happy kid, and anytime we were together, all we wanted to do was have a good time. He liked to make me laugh; I think he may have used humor as a cover-up for some dark things I didn't know about, or he didn't share. Many times, our ideas of fun could have gotten us into a lot of trouble, but we didn't care.

Jaime's mother and my mother are fraternal twin sisters, which is how we are related as first cousins. In my household, there were eight of us living in a three-bedroom apartment. We were a very blended family. My mother was married three times. I was the oldest child and had three sisters from Mom's second marriage and a brother and sister from her last marriage. My second stepfather was a dear man. We all loved him, including Jaime. He was a hard worker and loved my mother until the day she died.

While growing up, there was a lot of alcohol and dysfunction in our family. Everything was celebrated with alcohol. Our family was Catholic, but none of us were really dedicated. They dabbled in Santeria, a Spanish word meaning "worship of saints." It was a mixture of Catholicism and African pagan worship. We witnessed some strange things as they practiced the rituals. My mother was known as a "seer," who would use Spanish cards, similar to Tarot cards, to tell the fortunes of family and friends. I recall the expressions of amazement on their faces as Mom would reveal accurate events she saw in the cards.

In the 1950s, 1960s, and 1970s, there had been a mass exodus from Puerto Rico because of the economy and lack of jobs. Puerto Ricans are U.S. citizens, so it was as simple as flying from one state to another. My step-father and mother packed up our things, and we flew to Huntington, Long Island, New York, where one of our aunts was renting a large house. We all lived there for about a year and a half before moving to the Bronx. Jaime's family was already living there, mainly because the rent was cheaper. Unfortunately, with lower rent and poverty came a lot of crime, and we witnessed more of it than we cared to remember.

I know Jaime felt out of place in his home as the only child from his mother's first union. Her second husband was a white Hispanic man, with whom she had four boys. As the darkest one of the five boys, he didn't feel like he fit in. Jaime called himself the "black sheep" of his family. Because my sisters were darker than I was, Jaime felt comfortable at our home. We never thought about any differences – we were just family.

We didn't have much money, so we found ways to entertain ourselves that didn't require any money. On a typical Saturday, if we wanted to go to mid-town Manhattan and sight-see, we would often wait for the train to arrive at the platform and jump over the turnstiles without paying. We'd walk around Manhattan and hang out around Times Square, looking for something to do. Occasionally, we found mischief.

Between Jaime and me, I was the one afraid to break the rules, but Jaime didn't seem bothered by it. Sometimes when we were hungry from our adventures in Manhattan, one of us would order a pizza. When it was ready, Jaime would grab the pizza and run out the door without paying for it.

After graduating from high school in 1978, I had an opportunity to move to Florida. As soon as I arrived in Florida, I knew I had to find a job, so I checked the help wanted advertisements in the local paper. I took a job as an apprentice with a heating and air conditioning company, making $2.65 an hour. With only $400, which I'd saved from working at a factory with my step-father, I purchased a used motorcycle, work boots, work pants, a work shirt, and even registered and insured my motorcycle. It was amazing to accomplish all that with just $400. As an apprentice, I had to work under an experienced installer. His name was Wayne, and he was a Christian, but I didn't like him. Because I'd grown up in a tough neighborhood, I was guarded and distrustful. However, his faith and demeanor began chipping away at the shell I had built around myself. It was part of God's plan. Eventually, as we worked together, he began to grow on me. In December 1978, he invited me to a Christmas play at his church.

"Okay," I replied and told myself *I can do a play. That's safe.*

So I went. I'd never been inside a Pentocostal church. Talk about a clash of cultures. I was a tough young man straight out of the Bronx, and here were a bunch of seriously country people. The pastor was from Kentucky, and I couldn't understand a word he was saying. I didn't know what he was preaching about because of his heavy Southern accent and Pentecostal style of preaching. The church building originally was a chicken coop, which had been transformed into the small sanctuary where I sat uncomfortably that night. But it didn't matter about the building or the preacher. It was there where I would feel a stirring and the conviction of the Holy Spirit, Who would change my life forever.

Growing up Catholic, we had gone through the motions and attended church on special occasions, like Easter and Christmas. But when I stepped into that little church, I felt something I'd never felt before. As clear as day, I felt the Holy Spirit call me to the altar. Actually, I couldn't wait to get to the altar. I was fast-walking -- almost running. When I got there, I fell on my face and wept like a baby. I didn't know how to pray the sinner's prayer. I don't remember what I prayed about other than repenting.

When I stood up, I felt the most invigorating feeling I have ever known in my life. I truly felt alive – it was like I had been awakened. My friends recall I couldn't stop smiling. I remember when I walked out into the night air, I looked towards the sky. That's when I noticed the leaves were so green. I don't know why a little thing like that sticks with me so many years later. I only can conclude that the brilliance of the green color signaled that moment in eternity when I was truly born.

Afterward, I had to share it with my family. I must have inspired them with my enthusiasm because eventually my mother and sisters came to visit me in Florida. They accompanied me to church and accepted Christ, too. Even though my mother had to return to New York, three of my sisters stayed with me for a while. I think this was the beginning of my family accepting Christ and truly learning about Christianity.

I had lost contact with Jaime, but I had a desire to see him.

I had grown up, gotten married, and was active in my church, but Jaime was on my mind and in my heart. I wanted to share with him what I had received and was feeling because I loved Jaime and wanted to reach out to him. I discovered he was in the Fort Stewart area of Georgia. The Holy Spirit was leading me to find him, but I didn't have an address. Obviously, we had no cell phones or GPS back then. So armed with just a road map and the guidance of the Holy Spirit, I drove from Florida to Fort Stewart.

When I arrived in town, I prayed, "Lord, help me find my cousin." I started asking around and finally came across someone who knew Jaime. He gave me directions to the neighborhood with some apartments where he thought Jaime might be. Ultimately, I was able to locate him. I remember his shock and surprise when he opened the door and saw me. We hugged each other tightly because we hadn't seen each other in such a long time.

I noticed Jaime had a cast on his leg and asked him what had happened. He explained he had been in the Bronx, visiting the family when one of my sisters asked him to talk to a guy who had been sexually harassing her. Jaime had approached the guy in the streets and in front of his friends and told him to back off. In the Bronx, such an action demanded a defense of one's pride, so the guy pulled out a gun. Jaime backed down, but the guy was emboldened. With a gun in his hand and a crowd watching, he was on stage. He took one step closer and pointed the gun at Jaime's head, but mercifully, he lowered the gun and shot Jaime in the leg instead.

I pleaded with Jaime to come to Florida with me. Although he resisted at first, finally, he was convinced and came home with me. There wasn't much room in my single-wide mobile home, but we didn't care. While he was there, he met one of my friends, Danny DePriest. Danny came over one day and was looking at Jaime's wound. He kneeled down to get a closer look.

He said, "You have something coming out of your leg."

I got Danny a pair of tweezers, which he used to pull a fragment of bullet from Jaime's wound.

Shortly afterward, Danny made a statement about Jaime for which he has since repented many times. "If there is anybody whom God cannot save, it's this guy."

Jaime visited my church, and I witnessed and read scriptures to him. He was respectful because he loved me. Precious seeds were planted, but he didn't receive Christ at that time. Jaime soon moved out, not yet ready to trade his lifestyle for mine.

Eventually, Jaime found his own place and got a job in a town nearby, but he soon returned to his old ways. I heard he'd gotten into a shootout not far from where I lived. I was saddened for him and hoped he would find Jesus. I wanted Jesus to transform him as he had me, but Jaime wasn't ready yet.

Once a woman Jaime was living with became enraged and slashed his throat from ear to ear with a razor. While he was in the hospital, he told the investigating detectives he had cut himself shaving. Jaime bled so much he could have died. He has a permanent scar on his neck as a reminder.

As a child of four or five years, I saw our uncle, who was a police officer in Puerto Rico, come home in his police uniform. Since that time, it had been my life-long dream to become an officer. So when I saw an advertisement for a mass hiring in the police department in Tampa, I read further. They wanted minorities who could speak Spanish. The application process required taking the civil service exam. Fortunately, I scored high enough to receive a call back. Eventually, I became a police officer. After my wife and I moved to Tampa, however, it ultimately led to a divorce.

One night in 1986 when I was patrolling in a high crime area of Tampa, I noticed a car driving slowly and suspiciously.

It was about 2:00 in the morning. I decided to pull the car over. I turned on my lights and the siren. The car pulled over. Police cars are equipped with a bright spotlight that is intended to temporarily blind the driver and passengers, so they can't see the officer as he / she walks to the car. As I approached the driver's side of the car, I could tell the passengers were hiding something – more than likely drugs. There appeared to be two men sitting in the front seat and two women sitting in the back. I asked the driver for his license and registration. When I leaned in closer, to my surprise and shock, Jaime was the driver. I had recognized him, but he hadn't recognized me.

"Sir," I ordered, "step out of the car. Let me see your hands."

He stepped out of the car but still hadn't recognized me because I had my back to the blinding spotlight

I commanded him, "Step over here, sir. Keep your hands where I can see them, and step back toward the car."

As I walked backward, he got a glimpse of my face and yelled, "CUZ!"

He threw his arms around me, but I pushed him away.

"No, No." I warned him. "Play this off. You can't do this."

He backed away. "Okay. Okay."

Then I asked him, "Cuz! What are you doing, brother? Why are you out here? I'm not even going to look in your car because I'm afraid of what I might find."

He lowered his head in shame.

"Man, you need to get out of here. Go home. You don't need this. What if someone else had pulled you?" I pleaded.

I gave him a short hug and sent him on his way. I had feared for him. When an officer pulls someone over at night, often other police cars will drive by to check on the officer. I certainly didn't want another police car to drive by and see this guy with his arms around me. It could have been misinterpreted as an attack on me.

My heart was aching and heavy because I knew he was

up to no good – drugs probably, and I could smell alcohol on his breath. They probably had drugs stashed in the car, but I didn't want to find anything. What are the odds I would pull over my own cousin? I didn't see Jaime for some time after that. He never stayed in the same place for very long

***

Jaime's mother called me from New York; she was crying and asking for prayer. "Please pray. Please pray. Jaime has been shot and isn't expected to live."

It had happened in Georgia. He had been shot six times and left for dead in an apartment. It was devastating news. I fell on my knees and face and wept for God to spare Jaime's life. He should have died, but God spared his life. The police had spoken to him, but he didn't want to share anything. When he was well enough to walk, he left the hospital before he was officially discharged.

Sometime later, Jaime called me from a bus stop. When I went to get him, it was all I could do to keep from crying. Jaime was dirty, skinny, and strung out on drugs. I took him back to my apartment and cleaned him up. During the few days he stayed, we caught up, laughed, and had a good time. He wanted to go to Miami, so I purchased a bus ticket for him. When I put him on the bus, it was the last time I saw him until I discovered he was in jail in Miami a few years later.

By then, I had been promoted to detective in the Vice and Narcotics Division of the Tampa Police Department. I also had gotten remarried to Elizabeth, who then was an assistant state attorney. Somehow Jaime had gotten my phone number and called me collect from jail.

He said, "I'm in jail in Miami. Cuz, I'm facing some serious charges."

I wanted my wife, Beth, to meet Jaime, so we traveled to Broward County where he had a court appearance on a pending state case. He also had serious pending federal drug trafficking charges. When he entered the courtroom, wearing handcuffs and a jumpsuit, his vibrant smile lit up the room. He was happy we were there. I was able to use my credentials and badge to visit him in jail. I didn't tell the officers we were related because I wasn't supposed to use my badge for that purpose, especially since I had brought him a candy bar. Based on his charges, I knew he was going away for a long time. We hugged each other and cried together. When I slipped him the candy bar, he rapidly consumed it. We talked in general because I couldn't comfort him much. Unfortunately, I had grown cold in my walk with God. There is very limited time when you are visiting someone in a jail setting – probably no more than fifteen minutes. So all too soon, I had to leave. He was sentenced to prison for twenty-five years. When I heard he'd given his life to Christ in prison, I rejoiced.

Many years later when Beth got a job as assistant attorney general in Morganton, we moved to North Carolina. I worked for a heating and air conditioning company until I got my state licenses and began working for myself.

Jaime got out of prison and was doing well. He was pastoring a church in Georgia. I visited him, and he visited us in Morganton. I was able to get Jaime some introductions into a couple of churches for him to preach and meet my pastor at the time. Unfortunately, his business in Georgia was severely affected by the economic crash in 2008 and collapsed. Their financial situation led to stress for the marriage and family. When he and his wife separated, he was very discouraged. I talked with him and tried my best to encourage him. The conversation ended with me inviting him to come and visit. He did after he received an invitation to preach in Hickory, North Carolina. We met in Hickory.

I said, "Jaime, let's celebrate."

I took him to a steak house to have a good meal and cheer him.

Jaime said, "You know, Cuz. I feel like the Lord may be drawing me this way, but I'm not sure. I don't know."

So I told him, "Look, Jaime. I have room for you. You come and stay with Beth and me."

We lived in a house with a finished basement. He would have his own master bedroom with a bath. It was ideal for someone to stay with us.

"You pray, Cuz," I offered. "If it is God's will, He will open doors for you. If not, you'll move on. Give it a chance."

Jaime agreed, and he moved in with us for several months. During that time, he was preaching, making friends, and establishing connections. In very little time, doors were opening. Jaime was preaching in jails and prisons, and churches were inviting him to speak. It was happening so quickly, we knew it had to be God. He eventually got his own place in Morganton.

Anyone can see this is truly God's work, because Jamie has impacted a lot of people here. I am very proud of him. He is a chaplain with the Billy Graham organization, a chaplain with the Morganton Public Safety Department, and a chaplain with the Burke County Sheriff's office. Who would have thought a man, who was in and out of prison and jail as an inmate for so many years of his life could become a chaplain for law enforcement, preach in churches of various denominations, and minister in prisons and jails? Only God could do this. God is truly amazing!

Sandi's Note: While I was interviewing Javier, it was apparent how much he loves Jaime; so much so, I became emotional and began crying on two occasions during our one hour interview. I believe Javier is Jaime's angel. I believe he has been the wind beneath Jaime's wings. Don't get me wrong. All glory goes to God, but we know God chooses people for different roles and to accomplish different things. It's obvious, Javier was chosen to watch over Jaime. The way Javier came into Jaime's life at certain times of need is beautiful. Because of his love and generosity and love for God, he helped Jaime to open doors and have many opportunities to spread the Word. While reading this chapter and all the other chapters, we can easily recognize God's hand orchestrating everything – even using a simple chocolate bar, which must have meant the world to Jaime.

Chapter Sixteen

Pastor Stanley Carter

Jaime is my best friend and brother. I love him, and I am blessed to have him in my life.

I grew up in a home where we attended church, but my single-parent mother didn't become a Christian until I was eighteen or nineteen years-old, but she was a woman of morals and taught my four brothers, one sister, and me good morals. We attended church like everyone else in our family, but her commitment for Christ didn't come until I was in my late teens.

My brothers and I talk about our mother all the time. Even though she wasn't a Christian in our early years, she was a good moral person who taught us the value of love. We take that love everywhere we go, especially now that we all are Christians. Every child my mother had is a Christian. My mother has gone on to be with the Lord, but God has given her children an opportunity to live out her legacy. All of our children are Christians. I have one son, two daughters, and seven grandchildren. My eldest daughter just had the seventh one -- a granddaughter. My grandchildren are Christians too. By God's grace, I am serving as pastor through New Creation Ministries Church, Inc., where my wife, Bridget and I serve together. We will celebrate thirty years of marriage in January.

But life wasn't always happy. Abusing drugs and alcohol is how I came to be a Christian. In 1984, I left Jesup and went to live in Jamaica Queens, New York, where I stayed for four or five years. I was living somewhat of a varied lifestyle – drugs and alcohol. At that time, my mother and brother, then Christians, were praying for me while I was away. I'd gotten into a lot of different things during my time in New York. Gradually, I began to feel an overwhelming fear I was going to lose my life. If things didn't change, I knew I was going to die.

I telephoned my brother and explained how I felt, so he sent for me by buying an airplane ticket. I didn't even have a way to get to the airport. After missing the first flight, I found someone who dropped me off at the airport. Finally, I came home to Jesup. Once I was home, I kept feeling in my heart I needed to make a change because I was into drugs and other things. My life was going down. That's when I met my future wife, and she and I began dating. I couldn't believe she would date me because of all the things I was doing, but she took the risk. While we were dating, I still was having some problems.

I was working at Harris Ace Hardware in Jesup at the time. If the weekend had been bad, I'd come to work late. So I got fired. That did it for me. I'd always believed in life there would be something or an event that got us to a crossroad for change. This is when the crossroad happened for me.

After getting fired, I went to one of the parks in Jesup and sat on a bench. Visions of everything I'd ever done in life began flashing before my eyes. That's when I began to sob and cry out to God. "Please put me under Your safety! Please set me free!"

After that, I went to see my eldest brother, James Carter. I was staying at his home at the time. James introduced me to Christ that day. My future wife and I went to church that Friday night. To ensure I'd done everything right, I went to the altar that night. It was amazing! While I was at the altar, Bridget came and stood alongside me. She and I committed our lives to the Lord that night. We've been saved for twenty-eight years.

Once I accepted the Lord, I was under Bishop Walter Cuthbert. I was excited and passionate about being saved. I believe out of that passion came a real conviction in my heart concerning the Word of God. I loved studying it, reading it, and being taught the Word during this time. I developed a true love for the Word of God.

When I was serving under the Bishop, I had different experiences such as a dream or a vision – encounters with God – but nothing miraculous like seeing heaven drop out of the sky. From those encounters, I felt an urge to share the Word of God and Jesus. I got my job back at Harris Ace Hardware. After making my commitment to the Lord, Tim Harris, who ran the store – his family owned the business – and I talked. I proudly worked for him for fifteen years.

At the time, I carried a little New Testament around. Everyone I met I'd do my best to explain what certain scriptures meant or what Jesus Christ had done on the cross for all of us. I felt the urge and told my Bishop, "I have the urge that God is calling me to become an evangelist."

Because he was a very strict man, he told me, "A stale evangelist. You told me God called you to preach. I didn't tell you God called you to preach."

In our culture of church, when you answered the call, the church would have you go through trial sermons. It was different from any other church to give trial sermons. Even after going through Bible school, they would have you give trial sermons to ensure you could actually deliver or present the Word of God. I did that for months and months.

Finally, the Bishop agreed I had been called to preach. As a result, he licensed me in the ministry. From there, I was ordained as a minister. There is an extension school at the Southern Baptist Church, which I attended for three years. The rest is history. Bridget and I have been in ministry for twenty-seven years and have been pastors fourteen of those years. We started New Creation Ministries Church, Inc. in Jesup, Georgia.

Thank the Lord, Harris Ace Hardware taught me how to serve the public. My first job there had been working in the lumber yard and picking up bands that were cut off bundles of lumber. I began in July when it was at least 100 degrees outside. Later I became the lumber yard supervisor. Finally, I moved inside to contractor sales. This is where I learned to become a servant to people.

At the time I met Jaime, I had become licensed and ordained in the ministry, and I was still working at the hardware store. Almost twenty years ago, we met at a church where I was preaching. From what he told me, I was the first preacher he actually heard speak after he had been released from prison. It was a special moment for him, and in hindsight, it was a special moment for me as well. After he heard me preach, we exchanged names and phone numbers. Weeks went by before we saw each other again. But one afternoon when I was getting off work at Harris Ace Hardware and preparing to head home, Jaime saw me crossing the parking lot. He turned into the lot, and we began to talk – just a regular conversation. The more we talked, we began to develop a bond. Then we began to spend time together like eating lunch and visiting each other's homes.

Jaime and his now ex-wife were living in a mobile home – very humble beginnings. When I went to visit them there, his main topics of conversation were Jesus and the Bible. As a matter-of-fact, these are the main topics of all his conversations. We began to talk and the more we met, the stronger our friendship became. From that friendship, we became brothers. Jaime is one of the closest friends in my life. He's really a brother to me; we are really close like we all should be as Christians.

Together, Jaime and I began to serve and lead different outreach programs in our community. There is a project named Briarwood in Jesup. During the summer months, Jaime and I would go to Briarwood to perform outreach services that included music, feeding those who were there, and giving a message together. People were amazed that he and I were able to preach together, which is unique in itself. Usually, when preachers preach together, one is speaking another language, and the other one is translating, but this wasn't the case with us. We would present a message for which we'd not gone over or discussed. The Lord gave us a unique way of ministering the Word of God as if it were being presented by just one person. This gift was another sign that showed us we had a real bond – a real spiritual connection. He would preach part of the message, and I would come behind him and preach another part of the message or vice versa.

We conducted several outreach programs in the community at the beginning of our relationship. Then we started holding tent revivals that lasted five days each year. We would coordinate the event together and have different preachers from the community to come and help us serve. This proved we had a connection because we were able to coordinate and use our different gifts and abilities together. Until this day, we are still able to serve with and augment each other. Our relationship is very unique and very different. You are talking about a young man who came from Bronx, New York, and another young man who came from a rural area in Jesup, Georgia. Nobody could ever have thought we would meet and come together. But God did, and He used us to do different things. And Jaime is the one to whom I confide; he also holds me accountable.

If anyone knows Jamie Torres, that person knows he is not afraid to step out on a limb in order to be honest and truthful about something you may not be doing right, or he may determine you need correction, or he believes you need to be held accountable. Not only our ministries have thrived, but our personal lives have too because we're honest with each other. We hold each other accountable. This is the only way our relationship has grown and continues to grow over the years. You may meet people whom you are able to serve with or form a close relationship with for a few years. But after a while, for whatever reason, you may go your way, and your friend may go another way. But with Jaime, not only do we share a friendship and brotherhood, he knows my family really well, and I know his family really well.

Jaime calls my children his nieces and nephews, and I call his children my niece and nephew. Our families have grown close, which is another reason I know our relationship is genuine and unique. Our families know how close we are. If something were to happen to me, my family knows Jaime is one of the first persons my wife or children should reach. That's how close we are.

Now our relationship has been tested and tried. Jaime and I don't always agree, If we don't agree, we may use the old adage, "We agree to disagree, and that's okay." We never allow our relationship to be damaged or torn apart. We work towards a resolution during the moments when we don't agree. This is why I value him, and he values me. Since being in my life, Jaime has been loyal, which he is by nature. He is the type of person who is dependable and trustworthy. It doesn't matter what I need or what I'm going through, he is in my life and has been with me through some very difficult times.

In Proverbs 17:17 (ESV), the Bible says, "A friend loves at all times, and a brother is born for adversity." This is what Jaime is to me. He is that friend who consistently loves all the time. And when I've gone through some of the most adverse times in my life, he has stood by my side and by my family's sides, too. This has allowed us to continually grow closer. I treat him the same way. Our loyalty has been mutual. He has been through some difficult and challenging times in his life. Because of God's grace, I have been able to stand beside him and be there -- not always to give advice or to tell him what he needs to do. In my opinion, when you are concerned about a person, it's not about what you say. It's about what you do – about being present. Jaime has been present in my life and has been used by God's grace. I can't do it or Jaime can't do it without God's grace.

Our relationship has been one that God has used to bring about great things, and I believe Jaime and I will be doing greater things in the future. God purposed us and ordained us to become friends. It wasn't something we did on our own or planned. It just happened. This is when the best friendships form. It's not like mutual friends knew each other and introduced us, or my mother knew his mother, or his father knew my father. It just transpired when a man from the Bronx and a man from rural Georgia met each other. The rest is history.

As our relationship continues to grow, I believe God will provide the grace which is needed for our friendship and brotherhood to continue, and I believe God will use us to do great things for Him. I am proud of Jaime, and I'm proud to call him "friend." He is genuine and honest. Anyone who knows him will attest to the same. He has this genuine aura about him.

One example I will provide is one for which I kid him all the time. Jaime literally believes that the Bible says in Romans 16:16 (ESV) "Greet one another with a holy kiss." It tickles me to watch every person he meets. It doesn't matter who it is or what position the person holds in life --whether he / she is from a humble position in life or he / she is an important, exalted Christian – Jaime is going to give the person a holy kiss. Jaime has that kind of effect on people. I believe this is a sign he is showing his genuine concern about the person and really cares about him or her. If he cares about something or anyone, he shows it.

Jaime doesn't meet strangers. We can be in a grocery store or walking in a mall. We can be anywhere, and Jaime is going to treat the people he meets like he has known them all of his life. That's just who he is and how God made him, and he's like that all the time. I'll say this about Jaime. Others who know him will say the same. Jaime is loving, genuine, and passionate about everything he does. As a man I can respect him being a passionate person, especially regarding his work for Christ

Jesus. He puts his entire heart into everything the Lord gives him an opportunity to do.

Jaime is my best friend and brother. I love him, and I am blessed to have him in my life. I believe and know he always will be a part of my life and my family's lives. I am grateful to God for giving me the opportunity to preach and for Jaime hearing me as the first preacher he'd heard after being released from prison. I'm thankful he stopped at the hardware store that afternoon, and we had the opportunity to talk and build a bond and relationship. Here we are today, close to twenty years and closer than we were the first time we met. That's what I have to say about Jaime Torres.

This is not the last book for which Jaime will be a part. I believe he has many more books inside of him as there are many things God has done in his life and so many more things God is going to do.

I tell Jaime all the time, "I don't know how you do everything you do. You're amazing in being able to do all you do and have the effect on the people as you do."

But this I know. Because Jaime Torres is alive, this world has an opportunity to hear God's message which will influence not just a few people, but the masses. This is what I have to say about my brother.

Chapter Seventeen

Sara Watson

Jaime has been like a father to me.

I met Jaime when Mama and Papa Cline (Meredith and Rev. Larry) introduced him to the family. My grandmother, who was Papa Cline's eldest sister, was sick and bedridden at the time. Jaime came to visit her, prayed with her, and sang songs to her. My grandmother loved his visits and she loved him. I got to know Jaime a little bit then, but I was deep in sin and suffered a really bad addiction to pain pills. Whenever he came to see my grandmother, he'd try to encourage me, but at the time, I didn't want to have anything to do with what he was saying.

I was born and raised in Lenoir, N.C. My parents had divorced when I was seven years old. Since then, my father hasn't been in my life. As a result, I was very close to my grandparents. I came to know God when I was nine years old. One day when I was visiting my grandmother, we were talking about God and praying together -- something we always did. However, on this particular day, I felt as if God were calling me to Him. After accepting him as my personal Savior, I proclaimed my faith and was baptized in church soon after.

My grandfather was like a dad to me. When I was just sixteen years old, he suddenly got sick. Three weeks later he passed away. I felt a terrible void in my life because he was the only father I had ever known. At that point, I'm not sure if I were angry with God, but I do know that I had lost all care for life.

Thanks to my mother, I went to church, was involved with our youth group, went on mission trips, and attended Sunday school. However, I slowly became uninterested in those things. Instead, I began hanging out with a bad crowd in school, experimenting with drugs, smoking weed, drinking alcohol, and partying. Things took a turn for the worst when I was introduced to pain pills because they numbed all my feelings. I didn't care about school anymore. Actually, I hated it. I missed a lot of classes, and when I did go, I slept through or was high during class.

Once I turned eighteen, I signed my drop-out papers and got a job waiting tables at Hooters, making a lot of money. The money sent me even more deeply into sin and led me into a party scene where I was hanging out with the worst people, doing more drugs, drinking more alcohol, and enjoying the nightlife.

For the next eight years, I was addicted to pills and men, constantly seeking love in all the wrong places. I found myself in numerous abusive relationships where men physically and mentally abused me, even putting guns to my head. I got to the point where I believed all the lies the enemy was telling me. "You are no good. No one will ever love you. You can't do any better than this."

Drugs and pain pills had become my identity. My life spiraled out of control, and I lost my grip on reality. Things continued to get worse, becoming so bad I went from weighing 125 pounds down to 90 pounds. My appearance changed drastically, and I even had holes in my face due to the effects of these drugs. I couldn't hold down a job. At this point, I had become a manipulative liar who would do anything to get my fix. From sun up to sun down, all I did was chase pills. I had to have them, or I'd be sick.

I lived next door to Mama and Papa Cline. One day when Jaime was at their house, he asked me to come over and talk to him. When I got there, Jaime sat me down, looked into my face, and read my life to me like he'd been watching a movie. I know now God was speaking through him to me. That happened a little over two years ago -- August 2016. From that day forward, I began attending his weekly Friday night Bible study, which is entitled, Real Faith, Real Talk. Jaime and his wife, Grace, invited me into their home, embraced me like family, and showed me the love and mercy of Jesus Christ. However, I was still getting high.

One night, Jaime sat me down in his living room and said, "This is life and death. You are going to have to make a decision because you're going to die or end up in prison for the rest of your life."

I realized I needed help. Jaime found me a rehabilitation center called Grace Home in Santee, S.C. However, there was a waiting list to get in, and I had to call every Monday for over four months before there was finally a bed available for me. This place required you to be clean from all drugs when you arrived; this was very scary for me. They drug test you even before they carry your bags inside. This was a huge challenge for me, but I knew I was going to die if I didn't clean myself up and go.

Jaime, Grace, my mom, and I drove four hours to Grace Home where I would start my new life. At this rehab, it is required to start your day in the Bible. You're in the Word all day when you're not working. Daily chores included yard work, cooking for the house, doing laundry, vacuuming, working in the garden, and tending to the chickens – one of my favorite things to do. I loved the chickens. We were not allowed to leave the grounds except to attend church events as a group. With the help of the amazing staff, I was able to get myself on a regular schedule and back with God. Going to Grace Home was the best decision I ever made.

When I returned from Grace Home, I put all my energy into

serving the Lord and working with Jaime Torres Ministries. Jaime and my Real Faith family surrounded me with love and began working to strengthen my faith. It was shocking for me to be out in the real world again after leaving rehab. But for the first time in a long time, I was completely clean, and I felt really good.

Since losing my Paw Paw, Jaime has become like a father to me and has been the only consistent man in my life. I trust him. And like Jaime always says, "Consistency breeds trust." Grace is a wonderful godly wife, mother, and friend. They have a beautiful marriage, and they practice what they preach. They never left me and are still challenging me to grow and be the best person I can be.

Currently, I'm working on my GED and excited to see what God has planned for me. I'm considering going into ministry or possibly drug counseling. I have learned when you live through something and are vulnerable enough to share your story, you draw people toward you because they can relate. It is easier for people to open up to someone who has been through some things. I want to be this person for the lost and hopeless. I have had the opportunity to share my testimony while ministering with Jaime Torres Ministries inside jails and prisons. The impact Jaime has on these men and women is remarkable. I've also volunteered for Forgiven Ministry's One Day with God.

Now I can see how my selfish ways hurt my family and me, especially my mom. But through it all, she never gave up on me and stuck by my side the entire time. For her, I am forever grateful. I want to let people know there is hope, and Jesus is the way to bring people out of darkness.

I also want to ensure people understand how important Jaime is to me. He was used as a tremendous, mighty vessel to change the course of my life. Jaime, Grace, JonathanDavid, and Isabella are my family as ordained by God. With them, I have been blessed.

I have also forgiven my daddy and pray for his soul. I have let go of the anger and hatred I felt toward him. Now I'm praying for God to make a way and restore our relationship someday. With God, anything is possible. There is nothing He can't do. I rekindled my relationship with God, and by His grace, I am still clean.

Chapter Eighteen

Amy Kincaid

He was a guardian angel for our marriage and for us individually.

I met Jaime in January 2013 when my husband, Charles, and I had recently separated. Victor Salvat, whom we refer to as "bruuuder," and Charles had grown up together in the North, and together relocated to the South. Charles and I owned a coffee shop at the time, and we hired Victor to manage the shop. Victor met Jaime shortly after our closing, and they began holding a Bible study in my "brother's" living room. Victor kept asking me to join them on Friday nights.

I asked my "brother," "Who is going to be there?"

"Just me, my roommate, and a couple of other guys."

"Well, I'm not coming if I'm the only girl. I don't want to be the only girl." I was adamant.

But Victor said, "I think you would enjoy it. Besides, it's okay for you to be the only girl."

I kept putting him off and didn't go for a while. But one Friday night, while I was driving down the road, I thought, *I'll just stop because Victor keeps asking me to come.* So I went in and immediately enjoyed how they were just sitting around and having discussions about the Bible. That night Jaime asked me if I'd keep coming.

When I assured him I would, he also asked, "Do you still love your husband?"

"Yes," I replied. "But he hurt me so badly, I don't want to be with him anymore."

"You keep coming, and we will pray for your husband," he promised. Then he asked, "Would you want him to die and go to hell?"

I said, "No! I wouldn't want that to happen for my worst enemy."

"Well you commit to coming on Fridays, and we're going to pray for a change," Jaime said.

My husband, Charles, kept noticing I was attending a Bible study on Friday nights. I invited him to go with me, but he never would give an answer. One Friday night, he appeared at my "brother's" door and began coming regularly to the Bible study each week. After a few weeks, Jaime invited Charles to accompany him to church the following Sunday because Jaime was going to be preaching nearby.

On Sunday morning, Charles appeared at my home and was dressed for church. I will never forget it because he was wearing the same suit he wore for our wedding.

"Are you going with me to hear Jaime preach?" he asked.

"I had planned to go to my church," I answered.

But I went with Charles, and he got saved on that Sunday morning in March. We waited until August to begin living together. During the time while we were living apart, Jaime met with us and counseled with us. We became close friends with Jaime, and he and Charles formed a bond like brothers.

The Bible study continued to grow, and other women began coming. The Friday night gathering went from having five or six people in the apartment's living room to having twenty or more. We were packed! Soon we had people sitting on the floor, so we moved to another location, and the Bible study kept on growing.

Because Jaime's full-time job was ministry, he needed someone with financial security to sponsor his wife, Grace, to come to the States. At the time, I worked for an attorney and was able to assist him with the completion of the legal immigration papers. I also was honored to sign the paperwork to sponsor Grace so she could come here and join her husband. That instantly sealed and bonded us as family – no longer was the word "friend" used. We became family.

Jaime wanted to form a ministry because he didn't want anyone to question the receipt of donations and fear they would be mismanaged or used inappropriately. The answer was to form a 501-c3, so there would be accountability. We began talking with other friends and family and formed a ministry with a Board of Directors. I was one of the original board members, serving as the secretary, then the treasurer, and finally holding the position of president for a year.

I grew up in the Lake James Community of Morganton where my mom ensured I attended church every Sunday. When I was twenty-years-old, I married and had my first child. But Sunday after Sunday, I kept feeling as if something were missing. I was just going to church, but I didn't read my Bible or study it. I knew there had to be more for me spiritually.

One day I telephoned my pastor, and she met me at the AME church. I explained how I was feeling -- like there was more to religion than just coming to church each Sunday, so she talked with me, prayed with me, and asked if I'd personally accepted Christ as my Savior. I told her no, but I believed in Jesus and had never made a personal commitment to salvation. We prayed together, and that following Sunday, I went before the church to let them know I had accepted Christ as my Savior. Still nothing changed. I continued to attend church each Sunday, but I wasn't a disciple.

I was married for ten years and had two children from that marriage before we separated. After I remarried, my new husband, Charles, and his family belonged to the Baptist faith, so I began going to the Baptist church. I renewed my vows to God there and was baptized in 2010. There I worked in various ministries, attended church each Sunday, but still I didn't feel I was growing in my relationship with God. From the time I'd gotten saved, I felt I should be doing more. I began praying and asking God to show me what it was He actually wanted me to do. What was my calling? What did God want me to be in ministry?

I can honestly say that until I met Jaime and started attending the Bible study, I never had a close and personal relationship with God. I lacked the connection of God being my Father until Jaime began pouring that into me spiritually and encouraging me to know God fully for myself by forming that personal relationship with God.

***

I fell twice within two years and broke the same ankle. While I was out of work, I kept praying and crying out to God to show me what He wanted me to do and where He wanted me to be. I knew He had set me apart to have this time of stillness for a reason. One night, I awoke and began writing what appeared to be a sermon. I felt like God was calling me into ministry. In my past, whenever I attempted to do anything, I always wanted to know the reason why. I always desired to understand the purpose for doing it.

I was moved to enroll in divinity school. I'm finishing my last year at North Greenville University in Tigerville, S.C. I'm still praying for God to lead me through this entire process. I feel like my calling is evangelism and unity. In anything I'm involved in, I want to connect people and bring about unity. I believe the denominations have divided the church, and we need to come together in one accord. I don't know where this is going to lead me, but I always find myself wanting to unify the body of Christ --- for all to come together in love for the glory of God.

I prayed for God to open the door for this opportunity to go to school; and when He did, I stepped down from being on Jaime's Board. After my second fall and ankle break, I was unemployed, and I prayed earnestly for the Lord's guidance and direction for my life. One day, I believe I'll have an opportunity to serve in this ministry again. But right now God has set me apart. The ankle breaks helped me to discover my separation was needed at this time.

In addition to attending divinity school, I work as the program supervisor for the Guardian Ad Litem program in Morganton. We serve as advocates for abused and neglected children in Burke County. Initially, I began as a volunteer, and during my time out of work, the district administrator offered me an opportunity to work as the program supervisor.

I know I can speak for my husband when I say we both feel like God specifically brought Jaime to Morganton for us because he'd just moved to the area when we met him. He was a guardian angel for our marriage and for us individually. And Jaime didn't just pop in and pop out. He stayed with us. He called every day to check and be sure we were okay. We had dinners together in our homes; we bonded. And he holds us accountable for our relationship with God, so we stay on track.

Charles and I are blessed with three children: Ikea, Andrew, and Alana, and consider JonathanDavid and Isabella are our nephew and niece. We are like family. That's how our Friday night Bible studies are. With Mama and Papa Cline, we're all just one big family. It's a family where we hold each other accountable for Christ. We want each other to grow and have that relationship with Christ and be obedient to God and His Word.

I thank Jaime, and I'm thankful for Grace. She is just pure love with a sincere love for Christ. Grace is the same age as our son, Andrew. But she is the mother of this ministry. She ensures everybody is okay and feels loved. We share the same blood of Jesus Christ, and this love we have can never be broken.

Chapter Nineteen

Kesha Nichols

*He made me believe there truly was hope
for everyone who believes.*

Jaime Torres came into my life about four or five years ago through my cousin-brother, B.J., while I was living in New York City. Every time I came home to North Carolina, which was pretty often, B.J. would invite me to his Bible study. He kept telling me about this guy named Jaime, saying I absolutely would love him and the way he talks about the Lord. B.J.'s persistence paid off. I finally was able to go and see what this Friday night Bible study was all about.

I felt love and the presence of the Lord as soon as I stepped into the room. Everyone greeted me with acceptance and kindness. I instantly knew I was right where I needed to be at that exact moment in my life.

The evening began with a married couple singing a beautiful, acoustic version of a song called, "Rescue," which I'd never heard before. As soon as they began to sing, I felt the Spirit move. Something was stirring in me that I hadn't felt in a long while, if ever. The lyrics of the chorus were, "I need You Jesus, to come to my rescue. Where else can I go? There's no other name by which I am saved. Capture me with grace. I will follow You." Those words penetrated my heart and opened up my soul to receive the message Jaime was about to deliver.

The moment Jaime began talking, I was connected to him. I believed him and every word he was saying. I trusted him. He was speaking directly to me about everything that was going on in my life at that time: my broken heart, my worries, my insecurities, and my deepest fears. It felt like he already knew me, the real me, even though I had never met this man.

Jaime called God "Big Poppa"; that was definitely something I'd never heard before. He talked about not having a religion, but a personal "relationship" with Jesus Christ. I had never considered it that way. His delivery, his vulnerability, and his transparency about his regrets and past mistakes really touched me. I never had heard a preacher (or anyone for that matter) be so honest about his own shortcomings and failures. And I had never heard someone give such a powerful testimony about the love of Jesus and how by having faith in Him, anything is possible. I never had heard of such miracles the Lord worked in Jaime's life. He made me believe there truly was hope – for everyone who believes.

Later, I asked B.J., "Did you tell Jaime my whole story?"

He replied, "Nah, man! I didn't tell Jaime anything about you except you were my cousin who lives in New York! That's what is so crazy because I know you felt like he was talking right to you." B.J. was right. Jaime was talking straight to me, and I needed to hear more. I needed more of this Bible study. I understood why they called it "Real Faith, Real Talk." And I needed something REAL in my life.

I began flying home to North Carolina more and more often, purposefully on Friday night, so I could attend the Bible study. I was travelling all the way from New York City to attend this little study group that was beginning to change and shape my life. It was everything I didn't know I needed.

Then, my grandmother (Maw) and my mom began going to the Bible study with me. They fell in love with Jaime and the "Real Faith, Real Talk" experience just as I had, and they even kept going on the nights when I wasn't in town. They would go in my absence and fill me in on everything that was discussed each week. I was hungry for more and eager to learn more about this Jesus Who Jaime talked so wonderfully about.

Fast forward about a year. As my personal relationship with Jaime grew, I got to see the Lord work a miracle through him, and it just happened to involve my grandfather (Paw) and a close family situation.

I came home to care for Maw during her hip surgery and recovery. During the six week process, Paw wasn't doing a good job at accepting and adjusting to the fact Maw was out of commission and wasn't able to wait on him hand-and-foot. She had him spoiled, and he never had to go without her for a long period of time. He had a bad attitude and wasn't being nice or supportive during her time of need. So I (unable to stop myself) decided to tell him I didn't like the way he was treating Maw, and I asked him if he could be a little nicer and more considerate of her feelings. He did not receive this request very well. It turned into a huge fight which led to me not speaking to him for the next six months. It was pretty bad and extremely sad.

One day, Paw got to the point he couldn't take the silence between us anymore and asked Maw, "What can I do? I've got to make this better. I want to sit down and talk to Kesha."

When Maw told me this, I responded, "The only way I'm going to sit down with him is if Jaime is present."

My grandfather is a very difficult man and has a hard time communicating his feelings without being harsh and making the women in his life cry. So I knew the only way anything positive could come out of us sitting down and talking was if Jaime were present.

Paw had never met Jaime and didn't know much about him. However, he was willing to do whatever it took to make amends with me because he was really sorry for what he'd done and our not speaking was hurting Maw. So I asked Jaime if he was willing to come with me and talk to Paw, and he agreed to come. So we planned a meeting during my next trip home. The craziest part of the whole situation was Paw had been a captain at the local prison for twenty-five years. He was a really tough man. And Jaime, as we all know, was in prison for many years. Just knowing my old, white Southern grand-paw was open to having this black Puerto Rican, blended, ex-convict stranger come into his home to work out family issues was a miracle in itself. But what transpired in our meeting was the most beautiful thing I have ever seen.

Jaime arrived, sat on the couch with Paw, gently held his coffee mug, and carefully spoke with my grand-paw man-to-man.

Jaime said, "Mr. Nichols, you were the captain at the prison for many years. I know you were in charge of a team of men who, through your leadership, kept you and each other safe from harm. If one person on your team was out of line, the entire team was at risk of being hurt. Sir, this is your home, your sanctuary, and you are the captain of this family. If you aren't leading your team and running your home correctly, you all are in harm's way. You have let the enemy in, and he is winning. Sir, you have to step up and lead your family in a godly, respectful manner if you want to keep them safe."

It was like a light bulb came on. Paw got it! He said, "You are right, Jaime. I am the head of my family and haven't been doing what is right!" At seventy-eight years-old, my grand-paw finally got it! He vowed to do better and be more loving and understanding to his family. He promised to work really hard and try to soften his heart. He said he wanted to be more like Jesus. And to top it off, my Paw Paw made a profession of faith that day. He rededicated his life to Christ.

It was beautiful to see my Paw Paw allow Jaime to love on him and kiss on him, while they both cried happy tears. That day, Jaime showed me he can reach the unreachable, touch the untouchable, and even kiss the un-kissable. If Jaime can help

Captain Luther "Buck" Nichols find the Lord at seventy-eight years of age, he can do anything – in Jesus' name. Now Paw is a regular at Bible study, and it's my favorite thing we all do as a family.

***

Now, I'd like to tell you a little about me. I was born in Morganton, North Carolina, to a white mother and black father in 1978. Mom was around sometimes, but Dad was never in my life. Then Maw dedicated her entire life to me and made me her world. In return, she became everything to me – my best friend and the light of my life. I had no idea that love like that could exist, but she showed me the true meaning of unconditional love.

While growing up, I attended church with Maw. I learned about Jesus, got saved, and was baptized when I was twelve years-old. I'd always considered myself a Christian, and the Lord was a part of my life, but I wasn't seeking Him; I wasn't hungry for the Lord and had no personal relationship with Him. I was simply going through the motions of what I thought a Christian was supposed to do, but I never really knew Him.

After college, I moved to New York City, where I lived for thirteen years. There were some good times, and there were some bad times. I was spiritually lost most of the time. My city life was a series of the highest highs and the lowest lows, with nothing in between. There were two events, which stand out as particularly traumatic and life-altering during my time up North. One involved a high-profile wedding that didn't happen. The other event involved being bullied on national television. Both events were extremely hurtful and humiliating but were magnified because they happened in the public eye. I'm not sure if you've ever lived out your most embarrassing moments on TV before, but let me tell you, it's awful. Watching my worst nightmares play back live and in living color, along with the rest of the world, is something I cannot fully express with words.

I'll just say it was upsetting, uncomfortable, and downright horrifying.

I couldn't understand why those awful things were happening to me or how I had gotten myself into these situations. I realized the things I thought were blessings and life-enhancing opportunities were actually big mistakes. I was chasing worldly desires that had nothing to do with God. I had no foundation to stand on; I had no solid ground. I had no real focus, and I found myself alone, depressed, and far away from my family and friends. I isolated myself and hid from the world for a long time. I was embarrassed, and I felt like a failure. I had lost myself.

Somehow, even in my darkest, loneliest moments, I still knew the Lord was out there. Somewhere. I knew God was watching over me. I knew He was protecting me and preparing me. For what, I had no idea. But I knew His plans for me were better than any I could make for myself. I had tried it on my own and failed. Then one night I began to pray. In the silence of my room, I began to cry out to the Lord. "Please help me. Please guide me out of this darkness. Please show me the way back to You."

It was then I heard the Lord speak to me for the first time. It was a faint whisper, but I heard it. He gave me two choices: I could allow myself to stay in a place of depression and sorrow, or I could choose to use those experiences as leverage in my next stage of life. He told me if I chose to follow Him, He would make all things work together for His good. And I believed Him. That night, I made the decision to live for the Lord. Then everything started falling into place. The very next day, I met someone on the subway who told me about Hillsong Church. I began attending Hillsong and became very involved with the "Connect Group" in my neighborhood. Those people became my support and helped me to begin building my foundation of faith.

This is around the time I met Jaime. He came into my life at a time when I needed him most. I had been betrayed by those who were supposed to love me, abandoned by every man who was supposed to love and protect me, and envied and belittled by those who were supposed to be my biggest cheerleaders. I've had to lean on the few humans who actually love me for me, and Jaime Torres is one of those people. He loves me and encourages me. He cheers for me when things are good and cries with me when things are bad. He's my spiritual father, mentor, and my best friend. He is the only father-figure who has ever been there for me. He is my "constant" and has been since the day we met.

I decided to move back home to North Carolina a few years ago. It was the best decision I've ever made. Coming home is a perfect parallel to coming back to the Lord. Just like my family, the Lord welcomed me with open arms. He saw me from a long way off and was just waiting to welcome me home. I learned that it makes no difference how you get here – it only matters that you came. I learned that "home" is meant to be a place where you find peace. Wherever you go, Jesus is within you. You just have to seek Him.

It's taken baby steps, but I'm finally ready to be seen again. I'm ready to stop hiding. I'm ready to use my testimony to bless others. I'm ready to use my talent and passion for dance to worship His name. I'm ready to lead by example, empower women, and let others see Him in me.

Of course, there will always be hard times. It is difficult trying to figure out how to exist in this world when so many things are pulling me in every direction. But I now find my focus and identity in Him. He is my everything. God always steps in and makes me feel like I am enough. He speaks the truth to me. He loves me for me. He has taken away the confusion of being mixed or "mixed up" and has shown me that I am a beautifully-blended Blen Diva, who belongs to Him. He has given me a steady foundation to handle the continuous ebbing and flowing of life. I know who I am no matter how high or low the tide may be.

My scars tell a story. They are a reminder of times when life tried to break me, but it failed. They may not be visible to the world, but they are etched into the fibers of my being. God restores. God is amazing. He gives me EVERYTHING I need. I choose to love who I am every day, flaws and all. It may not be easy, but the Lord tells me it will all be worth it! God offers peace as a gift, and all we have to do is receive it.

Thank You, Jesus, for being my personal Lord and Savior. Thank You for sending Jaime and my Jaime Torres Ministries family into my life. I don't know what I'd do without them and without YOUR love. I am truly blessed.

Chapter Twenty

Mike Poplin
God is using Jaime mightily.

My parents raised my brother, sister, and me in the Charlotte, North Carolina area – close to Matthews. I didn't grow up in a home where we attended church, but I had a grandmother who always prayed for me and invited me to attend church services with her. So the only times I actually attended church were when I visited my grandmother. I had always believed there was a God, but I didn't know Who He was. And I always had questions, like this one. "If God is real and He knows our future, then what is the point in even trying? He knows where we will end up anyway." It's a huge question. "If God understands where you're going to end up anyway, what's the point in believing in Him or not believing in Him?" Besides, I always felt if you didn't harm anyone or do bad things to people, all was well.

After I moved to Hickory, some friends invited me to attend the Christian Outreach Center in Morganton, North Carolina, with them. I went and kind of liked it. I had attended a Wednesday afternoon church service, which was a good service, as I recall. It was around 9:30 p.m. that Wednesday night in November when I was relaxing with a glass of wine and watching a television show. That's when God began dealing with my heart. It felt so heavy, I thought I could possibly die. I began feeling anxious. Even so, for the entire night, I was in God's presence, and He was dealing with me.

I found that I could ask God any question I had, and He was

able to answer it. I had all this newfound wisdom that He was giving to me. Obviously, the first question I asked Him was, "If You know how I'm going to turn out and the roads I'm going to take, then what's the point?" His response was immediate and profound: "I know all ways that you could take." That stuck with me, and I thought, *Wow! No matter what road I take, He knows my outcome.* It was very powerful and true to me at that moment.

God even gave me a glimpse of something I wouldn't wish upon my worst enemy: The moment when you would be cut from His presence. Everybody on this earth still has a chance to find peace with God. You're in His presence, but being cut away from that, the darkness and loneliness you feel is the worst thing you could experience. I felt that. God showed me that. It's as real today as it was then. I stayed up the entire night. The next morning when the sun came up, I was extremely glad to see the sun. I was glad to be alive.

I had this energy about me – even though I'd stayed up all night, I didn't feel like I'd stayed up all night. I called people and told them about my testimony. I told my friends, "God is real." I couldn't wait to get back in church. Looking back, I often wonder, *God, who am I that you would share this experience with me and show me what being cut off from your presence is like? You had so much compassion on me, You allowed me to experience that awful void without dying first.*

I feel very privileged God shared this experience with me. I don't know if He shared this same thing with everybody, but obviously, this is what it took for me to turn my life around. By far, I'm not a perfect man, but that experience really impacted me.

I initially met Jaime when I moved to the Hickory area from Matthews, where I'd grown up. As a fairly new Christian, I enjoyed attending the Christian Outreach Center. This church is where I met Javier Guzman, whom I loved right away. Javier always talked about his cousin, Jaime, who lived in Georgia, so I was happy to finally meet his cousin when he was coming to our church in Morganton to preach. Actually, I was able to meet Jaime at Javier's house prior to the service. Jaime and the two gentlemen who accompanied him had stopped there first. That night, I heard Jamie give his testimony. That's when I knew he had a special spirit about him and an openness I've really never experienced with anyone before. I can describe him as being an open book type of person whom you immediately are drawn to.

Another thing that intrigued me about Jaime that night was the fact that when the service was over, we had planned to go to dinner afterward. That didn't seem to matter to Jaime because he was about the Lord's business. He stayed and prayed with people until the work was done. Hanging out with his cousin and his new friend, me, were not a priority. At that point, I realized he was about doing the Lord's work. That was the most important thing to him.

Because of our shared love for music, cars, and God, it was easy for a relationship to occur and our friendship to grow stronger. As a drummer and a singer, I've played for my church when I'm able. I've grown up with worldly music, but it's good. We have some wonderful Christian music we can listen to. Jaime likes to sing, and with his Latin heritage, he enjoys playing the bongos and maracas. Whenever his father comes for a visit, we play and sing for him.

When we first met, Jaime was going through a lot in his personal life, but he'd come over and pray for my businesses even though he had two businesses of his own and still lived in Georgia. We couldn't wait to see each other, whether he was coming up for a visit or just driving through. We hung out and shared our own experiences and things we'd heard about other people's lives changing. At the time, he wasn't doing a lot of evangelism, so I was able to help him financially. I told him, "Jaime, I think God wants you here in North Carolina. I think this is where He wants you to be." Jaime and I didn't know how that would ever happen. When he finally did move here, he lived with Javier for a period of time. That's when God started opening doors for him. After meeting Pastor Cline, he began doing more evangelistic work. His life has changed.

When Grace was still in Ecuador and Jaime was trying to get her to the United States, I remember he was worried about the attorney's fees. Because crunch time arrived, he wanted her here more than before, and I did, too. I had been witnessing a level of unhappiness in his life. Each night, Jaime and Grace would get on their computers and Skype. Sometimes the connections weren't good. One night I was sitting there thinking, *She is his wife. Why are they apart? Why are they only seeing each other's face?*

I learned the attorney needed $1500 or $1600 (I can't remember the exact amount) by a certain date, or Jaime was going to have to wait longer for Grace to arrive in the country. I thought to myself, *You know what? I have that money. He needs his wife.* I remember when I handed the money to him, he was ecstatic and called Grace on Skype. When he told her about the money, she was so happy. So I was able to help God bless him and get his wife over here. Now he has two beautiful children.

There are amazing things God has restored in Jaime's life. Looking back, sometimes a person doesn't realize the blessings until you talk to somebody about them. Our God is a God of restoration. In many ways, I've witnessed Him restoring everything the devil took from Jaime and Javier, too -- new cars, places to live, children, and finances. It is amazing to look backward and see all that He has done in their lives and in mine.

Jaime is the most special person I have ever met in my lifetime. His love for God is special as is the way he is able to express that love to other people. Jaime doesn't always notice the many things God does in his life because he struggles with different things. Even now, he is going through some health issues where God has always been there for him. God is using Jaime mightily. His reward is not here even though he gets rewarded here. Jaime has a huge reward waiting for him in heaven because of all the souls he has touched, and he has really touched mine. I love him with all my heart and would not trade any time we've had together for anything in the world.

Unfortunately, I went through a divorce. It's been a tough and trying time for me. But I continue to pray about it, and God is restoring things for me. I don't share a lot openly, which I believe irritates Jaime about me. I tend to hold things back or inside when I should be sharing them with him, especially. He is always sharing things with me. I just don't want to be a burden on somebody. It's probably a pride thing getting in my way, too, but I think that's something we all deal with. Sadly, I lost my father in April of 2018. But the wonderful thing is my parents turned their lives around and became Christians. Today, my mother is a very strong Christian and quite a prayer warrior.

The one thing I tell people is this: God restores things. He always knows a better outcome for you. Unfortunately, you have to go through the tough times to get to the outcome, but the tough times are what make you a better person.

Chapter Twenty-One

Ectohedobanny (Hector) Garcia

You don't get to know or meet a Jaime Torres just anywhere.

I was experiencing my worst moments ever when I met Jaime. I just had gone through a painful divorce, and I was feeling really low, knowing I was not going to be able to raise my children under the same roof. That was killing me and my ministry, too, because I was on fire for the Lord and could not believe this had happened.

I had to go and pay a friend, Darvin, who had helped me to do some work.

That's when another friend invited me to accompany him to a church service in Winston Salem. I was running late, and there was no point for me to go to the service other than to pay Darvin. My friend convinced me to go.

That's the night I met Jaime, who was a Spanish guy. He was translating for an African preacher. I noticed whenever the preacher was explaining something or being really animated (even rolling on the floor), Jaime was mimicking him and being animated (even rolling on the floor, too). They were connected in Spirit. I could tell the translator had more energy than the preacher. Maybe this is why my friend says he was crazy. He was spinning around on the floor and doing everything the other man did. But I was impressed with Jaime, thinking, *Wow! I enjoyed this sermon and laughing while watching "my man" doing his thing.*

After the service that night, he came to me, introduced himself, and kissed my face three times. He relayed a powerful message about something I was going through. I'd never met this man.

Amazed, I asked, "Are you a prophet or something?" I thought, *Wow! Who is this guy? I don't know him, but he seems to be a strong and powerful man of God.*

I spoke with my friend about Jaime, and he asked, "Have you ever met a crazy person about Jesus?"

"I don't know. Not really," I said.

"Well, you just met one tonight."

We began joyfully laughing. He shared a little bit of Jaime's testimony with me. I was shocked and couldn't believe some of the things he told me were possible. On my way home, I kept thinking about Jaime's life sentence and being shot six times in the chest, having his throat cut and needing two hundred stitches. Only God Almighty could save anyone from those tribulations.

That night at home, I couldn't get Jaime off of my mind. That's when my phone rang. Somehow, he had found my phone number. We talked for over an hour.

I told him about the divorce and how it had been hard on me. Try to visualize these two strangers crying together. He felt my pain. That's when I fell in love with the man that night. I recall crying and praying to the Lord to send me somebody to help me. God answered my prayer by sending my spiritual father, my best friend, and the one who helps me whenever I'm in a hole, no matter what. I can begin crying just thinking of that.

Then Jaime called the next morning, the next afternoon, and the next night. I was thinking, *God still hears me. He sent this beautiful man into my life.* As Christians, we're not used to having someone love us without knowing us. But he continued calling to check on me three times every day, even though he had a busy schedule. Jaime invited me to come to his Bible study on friday nights. He explained his ministry had a program where they worked with people who had drug problems and tried to help them. So I thought, *Okay. I'm going to the Bible study to see my new friend.*

When I arrived at the Bible study that first night, he was already teaching. But as soon as I entered the door, he stopped, hugged me, and kissed me. He made me feel like I had come home. And I really was home but didn't know it – jajaja. I saw Kesha and thought, *Wow! That girl over there is really pretty.* I don't know if my next thought was me or the Holy Spirit because I heard, "You just met your future wife tonight."

I continued attending each Friday night, and Jaime kept supporting me because he recognized I was in a hole and needed help. God and Jaime gave me the major support I needed – not my sister Karina or my cousin Maru. But God and Jaime were there 24 / 7 for me.

That same Friday night, he invited me to his house after Bible study. He didn't want me to leave. "You're going to spend the night at my house," he stated matter-of-factly.

"No, I can't," I said. "I have to work tomorrow."

He wasn't fazed. "Yeah, you're spending the night here."

I was shocked he was allowing me to sleep in his home. Our relationship started to get stronger and stronger, and I can tell you he is the most amazing man of God I've ever met. It is a cool thing because I'm living it. It is incredible! He's been there for me ever since.

He is always checking on me and my children. Earlier this year, Jaime officiated at our wedding when Keisha and I married. It was amazing to marry the woman of my life, my best friend, and my life partner, but Jaime didn't stop there. My spiritual father continues to counsel us. When I am around him, my spirit grows. He pushes me and challenges me to be better. He is full of love and compassion for everybody, and he's real. When I listen to his testimony, I am so impressed, I can't help but wonder, *How is this possible?* I'm proud to have Jaime in my family's life and to be in his life. You don't get to know or meet a Jaime Torres just anywhere.

I've always been the person who, whenever I go to a different church, the preacher will look at me and say, "Hey you. Yes you. Get up. You're the guy." Then the preacher would confirm things about me and tell me God had spoken to him about me or share things God had spoken to me about other people.

***

My father was electrocuted when he was forty-three, and I was fifteen years-old. I lived in the Dominican Republic where I had been born on March 16, 1977. I used to convert those numbers to John 3:16. I have one sister and two half-siblings from another marriage my father had. My dad had gone on vacation in the countryside and was watching television. For some reason, probably because it was raining, the television began having a lot of static. So Dad climbed onto the roof to adjust the antennae in the rain. He was a smart man and could handle live electricity well. But there was a cable with high voltage, and one of the wires was uncovered. It seems ridiculous for him to have died that way.

As a young boy, my dream always had been to become a professional baseball player. I was one of the best players in town. My father, who was my favorite person, was always pushing me to become a ball player. But after he died, I lost all motivation. He had been my idol. I know you're not supposed to have idols, but he was so special to me. I went into retirement after his death for a year and a half. When I heard my back-up at short stop had gotten hired by the Seattle Mariners, I thought, *Oh, well. What about me? If I begin playing again, I'll get signed, too.*

One day when I was wrestling with someone -- something

you should never do when you are pursuing a baseball career -- my shoulder popped out of socket. When I got home that evening, the first thing my mama told me was to forget about playing baseball. I thought, *Wow. Really?* I'd lost my father; and now I was losing my dream of playing professional baseball. This was really hurtful and frustrating– but the Lord had something better for me.

***

I became a Christian when I was twelve years-old. I had gone to church with one of my neighbors. That night the preacher said, "If you were to leave this place, and you were to die without knowing Christ, you will go to hell."

Right then and there, the lights went out in the neighborhood. I told myself, *I don't want to go to hell.* So I received Jesus as a little kid. I didn't know much about being a Christian because my family's background was more Jehovah Witness.

My mom began mocking me and asking me, "Why are you walking around the neighborhood with a Bible tucked under your arm?"

Imagine a twelve year-old kid who used to be a little bully. Not a bully with the definition that is common today, but someone who wouldn't back down from a fight. If someone wanted to fight, I'd fight. Actually, I used to fight a lot because I was fired up. But at this point, I was fired up for the Lord until my own mom made fun of me. Then I gave up and went astray for twenty-one years. I was never angry with my mother; she did what she did out of ignorance.

When I was thirty-three years-old, I attended a random church with a friend, where they prophesized the Lord was going to give me a son. I was delighted and wanted to reconcile with God and did. Then I began attending another church in my town. My pastor at the time advised me to go to the theological institute, so I immediately enrolled.

Then my beautiful daughter, Samara, was born, and I wanted to have a son. My wife at the time stopped taking birth control pills, but nothing happened after several months. We had been listening to preachers who were talking about the end times too often, and we became scared. My wife said, "I don't want to bring a child into this world now." Out of ignorance, we believed the preachers. "I'm going to begin taking the birth control pill again to prevent us from getting pregnant."

I pleaded, "No. No. Let me talk to God first. I'm going to tell Him what is going on. Just let me have another month."

She agreed.

I began praying to God in my praying spot. It was a Wednesday afternoon. "Lord, you told me you were going to give me a son. I truly want a son to carry my name. Send me a prophet in the spirit of Elijah to conquer nations for your kingdom. The lost and poor need to hear the Gospel. Open doors for the captive. I will call him Elías (Jehovah, my God in Spanish). I will also call him Josué (Jehovah saves) because Elijah was one of the mightiest prophets in the Old Testament and Joshua was a mighty conqueror who destroyed thirty-one kings. Please give me a son, and I will give him this name.

When we were at church on Saturday night of the same week, my wife pulled something out of her pocket that indicated she was pregnant. It barely showed the pregnancy, so she'd just gotten pregnant. I was delighted and began testifying it was a boy. I told everyone in the church God was giving me a boy.

When my wife went to have the required sonogram, she asked me to go along, so we could see what the baby's sex was.

"No, I don't want to go. I already know it is a boy."

"Let's find out for sure."

"I'm a man of faith. I believe God heard my prayers. I wouldn't expect anything else." If you are a person of faith, you believe. I knew it. So I named him Elias Josue, as I had promised the Lord.

Then a few different preachers started picking me out of the crowd and telling me about the Lord having a ministry of miracles and wonders and blessing me with wisdom and knowledge. The Lord would perform amazing things through me. But I had no clue what they meant.

One time my mom broke her wrist, so I went to see her at my sister's house, where I found my mom with a cast on her arm.

I said, "Mommy, I'm going to pray for you, and I have this anointing oil that I will place on you to heal you." My sister was being used by the enemy and followed me to the door as I left.

She asked, "Why do you want to pray for her? She is an old lady. It takes time to heal."

My response was, "I don't care what you think. I know what my God can do when we believe Him." I started praying for my beautiful mother, and I felt and saw in the Spirit, two giant hands over my hands and over her whole body while I finished praying, without even touching her body. She began crying because she couldn't believe what was happening. She said she literally felt two hands inside her bones, rubbing, massaging, pulling, and touching her.

"Somebody was touching me!" Mommy said. "I couldn't believe it!"

I cried all the way home because God confirmed my calling that day.

Then another time, my mother was going to have surgery on her shoulder. She asked me to pray for her.

"Mommy, I will pray for you." But in my mind, I knew these surgeries happen all the time. I knew the Lord would take care of her. So I prayed for her on Sunday. When she went to the doctor on Tuesday, he told her there would be no surgery because everything was healed perfectly. God is a great God.

Although my mom has received Jesus, she doesn't attend church and isn't a church member. I tell her, "Mommy, God has things for you to do. You need to go to church. Besides, what can you lose?" I know she will one day believe in the name of Jesus! Now, I understand why the devil always tries to break families apart and derail us from God's purpose, so His will might never be fulfilled in our lives.

Humbly, I want to say this. Jaime is a man of God. I'd never lifted a man higher than another man. He's teaching me how to trust God no matter the situation and has helped me open my eyes and heart again to the Lord through his testimony and love and wisdom from God and the Holy Spirit. But I pray to God to give me a heart for people like Jaime. I want to reach people and help others like Jaime does. He is bold and like a modern Apostle Paul when he goes to visit the jails, knowing he is not getting money for doing it. He does it out of love. And he travels with no money. Not everybody can do that because most people nowadays love money and recognition more than they love God.

I thank God for the most beautiful and amazing wife a man can ask for – my precious and lovely Kesha, who loves Samara and Elias, as if she had given birth to them. She is the future mother of my children to come soon. I pray God will keep us strongly united in one flesh, one soul and to keep us happy and in peace with each other. I pray we can do the Lord's will and together, speak life to the needy and broken. No matter the situation, no matter what you are going through, God always has the answer. Through love and faith, we will conquer the world for the Lord in the name of Yeshua Ha'mashiach ben ELOHIM. Shalom!

Chapter Twenty-Two

Robert Colbert

Jaime has been a dear friend and influence in my life.

I met Jaime around five years ago when he came to visit Victor Salvat who worked for me at my car dealership, Colbert's Auto Outlet in Hickory, North Carolina. Jamie and Victor had just recently met, and Jaime would often stop by to see him. After their visit, I would talk with Victor about who Jaime was and what was his purpose living in Morganton. At the time, I didn't know Jaime's testimony, but my desire was to learn more about him personally, so I kept watching and checking him out. Over a period of time, I began speaking with Jaime and hearing about his heart for ministry. Finally, I realized Jaime was real.

I began to invite Jaime into my office with the intent to learn more about him and his ministry. He freely shared his story, his love for people, and his love for preaching the Gospel to those who are lost and without Christ in their lives. I was intrigued with his methodology and how he preached the Gospel within the prison ministry and to people he met along his walk of life who were far from God. Our relationship developed through our one-on-one conversations and discovering more about each other through Christ. We discussed the many things God had done and was doing in our lives.

Over a period of time, Jaime got to know me, my story, and my testimony of faith as I began to open up and share with him.

***

I was born and raised in Hickory, North Carolina. I have

four siblings, two older brothers and two younger sisters. We grew up as unchurched children. Our father was an alcoholic, and my mother had removed him from our home. She raised us by herself. So from the time I was in the fourth grade on, there had been no father influence in my life.

Mom would not accept government assistance – no welfare and no food stamps. This meant working two jobs seven days a week to support our family. Her first job was from 8 a.m. to 5:00 p.m., and her second job was from 5:30 p.m. until 11 p.m. With Mom working 105 hours a week to support us, I had no accountability in my early life because no adult was home. But I knew I had to be home by 11:15 p.m. every night; that's when Mom got home. Following normal predictions, the odds for a person like me to make it or to become a Christian were zero, especially without any kind of Gospel influence or a church background.

In 1980, I started working in the new car business as a salesperson. I had been successful in my career and even had purchased my first home when I was nineteen years-old. My god was the influence of money and the desire to become successful. My motives were to have both because we didn't have money when I was growing up.

My life changed drastically when my sister invited me to accompany her to a revival at Winkler's Grove Baptist Church. So I went and ended up hearing the Gospel for the first time in my life in a clear way that helped me realize I was a sinner. The date was November 14, 1981. That night when the altar call was given, I didn't respond to the Gospel. Instead, I went home. My heart began burning, as if it were on fire. Now I know, I was under conviction, but I realized the stark truth that night: If I died, I would go to hell. The scary truth and I wrestled all night long.

The revival was meeting each night for the rest of the week. I began telling people, "I'm getting saved tonight." I really didn't know what the word "saved" meant; I didn't understand its profound meaning, but I knew God was working in my life. I was a sinner. I would go to hell if I died. So that night – November 15, 1981, -- I couldn't wait for the preacher to stop talking because I wanted to surrender my heart and life to Christ.

I became a member of Winkler's Grove Baptist Church and worshipped there for ten years, becoming active in the church. In February 1982, I was invited to go to the Holy Land with a tour group my pastor had gotten together. I saw where Christ walked but never really understood its importance because I was new to the Bible. That is when and where God really started working on me. After the trip, the desire to know the Bible better was realized. So now, whenever I read the Bible, the scripture comes alive because I can visualize it. God really did work in my heart. I also went to Rome to see some of the prisons where the Apostle Paul was imprisoned and wrote some of his epistles.

"So Jaime, after all these weeks and our intimate conversations, you now know my story," I concluded, "I was born again on November 15, 1981, which is the day I now call 'Testimony Day.'"

Through Victor's attendance and commitment to "Real Faith, Real Talk" Bible study on Friday nights and his interactions with Jaime, I learned how Jaime Torres Ministries (JTM) was growing. So I began investing more time in Jaime. Whenever he walked into my office, he brought with him that infectious zeal he has about God – a zealousness that few men I've ever met have possessed. Jaime has a passion for the Gospel, a passion to preach the Gospel, and a passion for the Word of God. At the end of our visits, Jaime would always say, "I want to pray for you, and I want to pray for your business." Later I would learn that Jaime had been driving from Morganton to walk the car lot and pray over it at night when the office was closed. He had been praying for God to prosper the business and for God to bless and put His favor on me. Little by little, the Gospel linked our relationship together, along with Jaime's love for the Gospel and his love for people.

As our relationship continued to grow, Jaime and I, along with our families, would break bread together. I became interested in some of the things Jaime was doing. I attended several JTM Board meetings to see how the ministry worked. During it, I gave a little counsel and began investing monetarily in Jaime. Jaime and I came from two different places and had two different backgrounds as far as the world would say. Our relationship is an amazing story of how our connection was orchestrated through the Gospel. We had never met and had no reason to meet, but we had been linked together in life because of the Gospel. Our relationship became like that of Jonathan and David. We have kindred hearts.

Jaime got to know my good friend, Steve White, and together, we introduced Jaime to other prominent leaders in social circles and to people who led ministries in Hickory. Through these connections, Jaime had the opportunity to speak at Brotherhood, which is a gathering of men that meets on Thursday nights. He really challenged and inspired the men. Some of the attendees even began donating to JTM. Then Jaime was invited to preach the service on "SPREAD Sunday" at Corinth Reformed Church in Hickory, N.C., which is a large church with predominantly white, affluent members. This was amazing! Only the Gospel could have opened the doors for Jaime to preach there. Jaime's passion for the Gospel, his testimony, and what God was doing in and through Jaime's life are why he was able to do what he did. Jaime is real. If you don't want to hear the truth, don't call Jaime.

Jaime has been a dear friend and influence in my life. Jaime and I talk regularly. We sharpen each other with the Word and end in prayer. I pray for Jaime every morning, and I know he prays for me and my family every morning. Among other things, there is one thing Jaime and I have. Since I've known him, we have grown together in our relationship. We've also grown to understand we will encounter some things we disagree on, but our love for each other will overcome any barrier between the two of us. We have not always agreed about the methodology and how God works, but because of our respect for each other, that keeps our differences from becoming a barrier. I love that about Jaime. Jaime's grace and mercy, which he is full of, is so beautiful. Just observing Jaime for as long as I have, I've watched how he can go into different circles and whether he agreed or disagreed with the methodology or doctrine of the circle, it never stopped him or prevented him from going because he was focused on the message he had to preach. From his example, I've realized we need to lessen the importance of "what I believe," "what you believe," or "what they believe." It doesn't matter! The Gospel is what matters and what breaks down barriers.

There are so many stories and testimonies I have seen happen by being around Jaime, but I don't want to crowd the book. There have been many tears that we've cried together. And we've celebrated, and laughed, and fellowshipped. It is a beautiful friendship and a unique relationship. As I mentioned earlier, Jaime calls it the Jonathan / David relationship. I agree with him.

Part of who I am today is because of Jaime coming into my life. He can see my growth. As I am a word guy, I enjoy doctrines, apologetics, and an expositional style of preaching and teaching. I like a studied person to whom I can listen. This caused me to have a stigma that I didn't realize I had within me. The stigma could be "I may be right, you may be wrong." When Jaime came into my life, he helped me even without my knowing it as the Holy Spirit was using our relationship to change me. What I believed four years ago or two years ago or even one year ago is not what I understand now in the person and the work of the Holy Spirit. That is powerful.

Jaime and I had to learn each other and recognize love was the key ingredient. Because of love, when I hear his testimonies of how God is working and what God is doing, I know they are true, and he wouldn't mislead me. If love were not the key ingredient, I might ask, "Is God really doing that?" "Does God work like that?" "Did God heal that person?" "Does God heal like that?" If I heard them from someone else, I might not agree or believe or be moved to investigate it. My love for Jaime makes me want to know more. That is the biggest way God has used Jaime in my life. Jaime has allowed me to see more of Who God is than what I used to see. This is truly powerful. There are not enough words to describe and explain how God has used Jaime in my life.

My influence on Jaime has been to let him know he is more valuable monetarily than he sees himself. This is why I went to JTM Board meetings to see how Jaime was being compensated. When Jaime's influence had reached a broader level to preach at different church denominations, I told him he needed two new suits, so he would feel confident by looking good. I took him to the men's clothing store where I purchase my dress clothes. I instructed the salesman, "I want you to take care of my man here. He's an evangelist and loves the Lord. I want him to look good and feel good today, so please take care of him."

And he did. He treated Jaime like a king. It was so beautiful to watch. Gradually, another store clerk was attracted by Jaime's personality. He came to add his assistance especially with tie selections.

Jaime would smile and ask me, "What do you think, Papa?"

I'd say, "Man. I think you look awesome!"

He was pampered that day, and I loved seeing him in that realm where he was allowing God and me and the salespeople to pamper him. Before we left, he had everybody in the store standing in a circle, holding hands. He prayed for them. It is easy to see how God has favored Jaime's life. It was an honor to pay for his suits.

I lost my mother December 4, 2016, but all of her children are born again Christians regardless of not being raised in church. We all attend church now. Mom loved the Lord and used to tell me she'd talk to the Lord and say, "You are going to have to raise my children and protect them because I have to work." So God was faithful to my mom and her prayer. Thankfully, when she moved out of Hickory and only had to raise my younger sister, she didn't have to work so hard. She had worked a season of life, putting in 105 hours a week. My mother instilled in me a strong work ethic. She was a beautiful lady. Because of her example, I will never complain about hard work or the faithfulness of God. He provided for my family in many ways in Mom's absence. It is a beautiful thing to know all of Mom's children are saved.

My life and journey began on that November night in 1981 when I was twenty-two years-old. I'm fifty-seven now, and I love Christ today more than I ever have before. I have seen the faithfulness of God measured throughout my life and my family. I have a wonderful wife, Renee, and two beautiful daughters, Paige and Madison. Paige was recently married to our son-in-law, Daniel, who is a pastor at Harvest Bible Chapel in Chicago. Jaime loves my children, and I love his.

Jaime – God has used you through the power of the Holy Spirit to help me to continually grow in grace and truth. For that, I will be eternally grateful.

Chapter Twenty-Three

Steve White
He's the real deal.

One night around 9:00 p.m., my twenty-six year-old son, Trey, was the only employee left at the dealership. Everyone else had gone home for the night. That's when Trey noticed a tall man walking around, looking at some of the vehicles. Trey went outside and approached the man he considered to be a potential customer.

"Hello! Can I help you?" Trey asked.

"Hello," the man said in response and smiled. "I'm just here praying for your parking lot."

The man's response, of course, intrigued Trey, so they began talking. At the end of their conversation, the man, Jaime Torres, asked if he could pray for Trey.

My Christian son later told me, "Dad, it was such a sweet prayer. It made me cry."

After that prayerful night, Jaime and my son developed a friendship. Jaime has been a strong influence in Trey's life to remain on the right path. Invariably, after Jaime came to the dealership another time or two, I was happy to meet him. That's when we began developing our own friendship, as well. Then Trey and I began listening and learning more about his ministry and the work he was doing.

One of my friends, who has a keen business acumen, decided he wanted to travel to Morganton and attend one of Jaime's Board meetings as a visitor. He was intrigued with

Jaime and wanted to determine if anything was less than above board. I really had never considered that it would be, but my friend wanted to be sure.

He telephoned me after the Board meeting and said, "Hey. I went up there, and this Jaime Torres is the real deal. He has a Board of Directors that handles all his money. He doesn't touch the money. When people give him donations, he turns them over to his Board."

When my friend relayed his experience, I repeated his words. "He's the real deal." I've never hesitated to support Jaime in his ministry.

Over the past year, I've gotten to know Jaime better. He came and spoke to a men's group called "Brother Night," and gave an unbelievable presentation. It was such a special night. "Brother Night" is a non-denominational organization that isn't affiliated with any church. Men meet one night a month (there is one held in Hickory and another one held in Granite Falls) for prayer, fellowship, and someone usually shares his testimony. That night, Jaime shared his story. Since then, we've become close friends, who don't always get to see each other often, but we text and telephone each other. Jaime is all about relationships.

***

When I was twelve years old, I became a Christian at Concord Baptist Church in Granite Falls, North Carolina. The events that led to my salvation were difficult to live through as a young boy.

My dad was in the car business, too. For reasons unknown to me, he experienced a nervous breakdown and was resolved to commit suicide. He planned to end his life by pulling in front of a speeding train. On the designated night when he'd decided to end his life, he was sitting at a train crossing in a brand new car. As he attempted to pull the gear shift into "Drive," the lever wouldn't budge. He tried several times, but the brand new car's gear shift wouldn't budge. He watched as the train barreled past him. Dad broke into a cold sweat, realizing he needed help. Somehow the gear shift changed, and he drove himself straight to the hospital where he was admitted. Obviously, he knew he wasn't in a good place mentally.

My brother and I knew what had happened. As a result of Dad's hospitalization, we were sent to stay at our parents' friends' home for a few days. This was a scary time in my life, but it has become a miraculous memory. While in the hospital, Dad accepted Christ, and it dramatically changed his life and ours forever.

Four days later when he was released from the hospital, he came home. My mother, brother, and I were thrilled to have him with us again. God had protected my father. God had jammed the gear shift. God had guided him to the hospital for help. And God had saved his soul.

Dad immediately told us, "We're going to start going to church," which we did. My mother had been raised as a Lutheran and was a good wife and mother. She still is. But this experience had transformed her life and ours. When we began going to church as a family and heard the Gospel preached by Pastor Roy Collins, my mother, my brother, and I accepted Christ as our Savior and were saved. My father's mental anguish and survival had led our family to Christ. There is no better legacy to leave this world than to lead others, and especially beloved family members, to God.

Fourteen years later, my parents blessed my brother and me with two more siblings, whom we love and treasure. Throughout the years, Dad talked a lot about the train crossing and the gear shift that wouldn't work. Unfortunately, he passed away, but we are assured he's in heaven with God, and we will see him again one day. Dad never had the pleasure to meet Jaime, but he heard a lot about him from Trey and me.

We have a friend, an employee, who is an alcoholic and just

came out of alcohol rehab. As a friend and employee, we care about him and had sent him there to get healthy. When he was released in April 2018 and had been out of rehab for ten days, I invited him to come with me to hear Jaime preach.

Afterward, he said, "Wow! What a story. It just helped me so much."

Here we are in September, and I asked him yesterday how he was doing. His response was, "I'm doing great!" I truly believe hearing Jaime's testimony so soon after leaving rehab helped him.

I believe in Jaime Torres. Whenever you meet someone in life who is that "sold out," for God and who shoots you texts that say, "Hey, I'm thinking about you;" "Hey, Brother. I'm praying for you;" "Have a wonderful day;" and "God bless you," then you know he / she is someone special and sent by God. I enjoy the times we've travelled to Charlotte and other places together, and I can tell you, "Jaime is the real deal."

Chapter Twenty-Four

Victor Salvat

He took me to the next level.

Five years ago, I was operating and managing a coffee shop/café, The 109 A Café, in Morganton, North Carolina, for Charles and Amy Kincaid. Charles and I grew up together in New Jersey. On several occasions, a local minister, Pastor George Logan, came into the café, and after a short while, we became friends. He listened while I shared my story and testimony. Afterward, Pastor Logan asked me if I knew Jaime Torres.

"No, I've never heard of him," was my reply.

"Well, he travels from Georgia to Morganton from time to time and preaches at my church and other places. The next time he comes to town, I'd love for you to meet him because you guys have similar backgrounds. You both came from the inner-city, had similar lifestyles, and are Puerto Rican.

Not giving it much thought, I said, "Cool." Then, I forgot about it as life has a way of consuming you. A few months later, my roommate, Sheldon Tate, invited me to his church for a youth service. I recite poetry and write spiritual Christian-based Hip-Hop music.

Sheldon asked, "Hey, why don't you come to the youth event, and start the event off with a poem or an encouraging word?"

"Sure," I said. "I can do that."

So I went to his church, and on that day, the keynote speaker / preacher was none other than Jaime Torres. When

133

they announced his name, I said to myself, *Man, that dude might be the guy Pastor Logan was telling me about.* At the end of the service, people gathered around the guest preacher to shake his hand, thank him, and converse with him. During that time, we looked at each other. Finally, there were only a few people left in the church.

He looked at me again and said, "Man? What are you doing?"

"Heck. I'm not doing anything. I'll probably go home from here."

That's when he threw me the keys to his car and said, "Man, let's go get something to eat. Drive me somewhere you think would be a good place to eat. I love rice."

"Okay." So I drove him to a Mexican restaurant, La Salas.

Jaime and I literally sat in that restaurant and talked for hours. I'd never met this man, but it was like he had known me all of my life.

"Man," I said, "Pastor Logan told me about you."

His reply was that Pastor Logan was a great friend and consistently spoke truth in his life.

Also, it seemed as if Jaime knew my struggles. By this time, I'd already given my life to the Lord and was active in my church, but God had spoken to him, so he dug deep and was able to address some things I was battling with and other people didn't know about. It was amazing! I'd never heard a man or anybody speak to me about God like he did. He made it so relevant and pertinent to our similarities. We'd both come from a life of drug dealing. We'd experienced lots of pain and brokenness in our families. We'd lived a lifestyle of being addicted to drugs and fast money. Jaime was the first guy who referenced the Bible in a way that related to that lifestyle. He had a great gift of making God seem relevant, especially in the streets. For example, there is a scripture in the Bible where Jesus is walking with his disciples, and he asks, "Who do they say that I am?"

134

Jaime is the first guy in the mix of dinner to say, "Man, it's like Jesus. One day Jesus is walking with his boys. You know. They were chilling, man. He asked them dudes, 'Listen, who do these people say I am?'"

He was sitting there breaking down the scripture, and he was making it sound like we were talking about a guy up the street. It was amazing. We talked for three or four hours with him being able to speak directly into my life about the issues that had been weighing me down.

Looking back at that night in the café, I know for a fact this was an absolutely divine appointment. God had laid our meeting on Pastor Logan's heart for a reason, and He had put it in play months later. Pretty much from that day on, Jaime and I went through a roller coaster of ups and downs. You know, any true friendship is going to come with disagreements and arguments, but he became one of my closest friends and mentor. I've been right by his side ever since.

Some of the difficulties we experienced were because I'd never been held accountable the way he was holding me accountable. And to be flat-out honest, I just couldn't handle it. I was learning that he is so rare. This man can love you and give you his last dollar, but two minutes later, if you do something sinful, he's not going to co-sign it. As a matter of fact, you could give Jaime $5000 to begin his ministry, or you could give Jaime $50,000 on Monday to build a drug rehabilitation program, but on Wednesday, if he learned you'd cheated on your wife or disrespected somebody, he wouldn't care and would hold you accountable like you had never given him a dollar in your life. I have never been around anyone like him.

Jaime is passionate in a different way. He knows I'm a single Christian man, and he doesn't play games. We can be watching a boxing match, and he will turn around and ask me, "Hey man, that girl you had lunch with yesterday, you ain't sleeping with her are you?" Jaime is just raw like that only in a loving way.

He earns the right to talk like that. He's not disrespectful or imposing, but when he becomes a friend, he's a true friend. He loves the correct way. If we look at the Biblical definition of love, it's not just about hugs and kisses and talking nice. There is a verse in the Bible that says if you love a friend, you are not going to stand for unrighteousness. We have been friends ever since we started hanging out and having lunch together.

Jaime introduced me to one of his friends, who was like a spiritual son to him, and even though the guy had gotten off task a little, Jaime still loved him. He tried to encourage the guy to return to doing ministry and being strong spiritually. He and this young man had even discussed starting a Bible study at the man's house because he had a nice basement – lots of room. Soon, they'd set up the first Bible study, but the day before it was scheduled, the young man reneged and backed out.

Jaime was upset and driving from Georgia when he called me. I could tell he was really down and sounded depressed.

"Man, we're not going to have the Bible study. It's my fault. Maybe I was rushing things. Maybe it wasn't God's will." That's when I felt God tug at my heart.

"Man, don't worry. Let me talk to my roommate. Maybe we can have it here."

"Man, don't worry about it. You know, maybe I was jumping the gun. I was doing it to encourage him. Maybe my motives weren't right."

"Let me talk to my roommate," I insisted.

So I did. Sheldon worked a second job a couple of nights each week, so his response was, "Sure man. I don't care."

A week after that, we held our first Bible study in my living room. It wound up being the beginning of "Real Faith, Real Talk." In my opinion, it was the beginning of Jaime Torres Ministries. Jaime, B.J. (the guy who I play music with), Charles, another friend (Buda), and I were the only attendees. From there, it grew with Jaime and me becoming closer. We invited more guys to the Bible study. I talked Amy into joining us, even though she was reluctant to be the only woman there. But soon Amy brought her husband, Charles, with her. She was the only woman attending with six or seven guys. So Amy began inviting other women. Before long, we had twenty-five people in my living room, in the kitchen, and sitting on the stairs leading to the second floor. It was just amazing.

Today, Jaime orchestrates the "Real Faith, Real Talk" evening Bible studies and handles the preaching / teaching aspect. Our agenda is after his arrival, we pray. Then he simply asks the people, "Is there anything anybody has on his/her heart?" He asked this question when there were only three attendees, and he asks it now when there are fifty attendees or more.

Sometimes, the response(s) will dictate the whole evening. For example, if someone says, "I've been dealing with forgiving my husband," or "I've been dealing with addiction," then this becomes the subject of our discussion, which is always Bible based. Everyone has the opportunity to share thoughts, give ideas, and ask questions. Jaime never preaches his personal opinion. If attendees aren't talkative, he'll just begin preaching in a structured kind of way. But we always begin by giving the people an opportunity to set the tone or to get something off their chests, whether it is good, bad, or whatever. Since we've been holding these Bible studies for five years, if he has to go out of town and preach, then sometimes I lead, or Papa Cline leads, or someone else for whom Jaime feels comfortable leads.

***

I was born in New York, but I grew up between New Brunswick, New Jersey, and Highland Park, New Jersey. At first I lived with my grandfather and two aunts and an uncle in the projects of Spanish Harlem. After a while, my mom came down. She had been in the process of separating from my dad and met a Caucasian man in New Jersey who became my step-father. I didn't grow up in a church or a home with a Christian foundation. Most Spanish / Puerto Rican families in the New York and New Jersey inner city area are mostly Catholic, but we weren't practicing Catholics. We didn't attend church. There was only a small presence of God in our home.

I gravitated to the streets at a young age; I began leaving home and coming home late. I had a mixture of friends – the guys who were really in the streets, selling drugs, smoking weed, and drinking and the guys who were good athletes. As a result, I played baseball and basketball in high school. But I'd also be with the street hustlers, so I bridged those two communities together.

In the mid-'90s, we began selling drugs on a bigger scale. A friend of mine went to prison for shooting someone while I was still in high school. When he was released and came home, I was already in the streets selling drugs. He travelled to North Carolina to visit his father and paternal family because he hadn't seen them in the four or five years while he was incarcerated.

When he returned to Jersey, he gathered another childhood friend and me together and said, "Listen, I just came back from North Carolina. You can sell an ounce of cocaine in North Carolina for $1200."

At that time, we were able to get cocaine by the ounce in New York for about $500 or $600 an ounce. Now you were talking about street guys who could instantly visualize a way to start selling cocaine on a bigger scale and at a faster rate. So we put our money together and went to North Carolina, beginning a whole new lifestyle of trafficking drugs back and forth from New Jersey to North Carolina and from Florida to North Carolina.

During this time, I was in a Sprint store getting a cellphone turned on. While the clerk was setting up my phone, I went next door to Tony's Pizza where I saw an attractive young lady, whom I approached. We talked for a while and exchanged numbers. The next thing I knew, I was hanging out with her. I would come from New Jersey with drugs, distribute the drugs to a couple of guys I trusted, and hang out with her while I waited for the guys to return with the money. Then I'd head back to New Jersey for a couple of weeks before returning again. We began a relationship with each other.

She had three daughters who were young at the time. I began to enjoy the "family lifestyle" even though we were living in sin. I still didn't know anything about Christ. Even though I was selling drugs, there was something about the family feel I liked. So I continued to come and stay with her. The youngest daughter was in the second grade when we realized how good she was in basketball. (She eventually won a basketball scholarship to a university in Tennessee.) So here I was – selling drugs, doing the street stuff, and then coming to my girlfriend's home. It was like living in a fantasy world. Man, this was the American dream! She knew what I was doing and didn't like it, so we often argued about my lifestyle.

Very rarely was I with her on the weekends – just during the week. But on one particular Sunday morning, I was still at her house, waiting for guys to bring me money.

She said, "My girls and I go to church. You should come with us."

"Cool," I replied. Then I thought, *I'm not going to argue. I'll sit in the back, throw $20 in the plate, and get home before the football game starts. She can't say that I didn't go to church with her.*

Man, I walked into this church, and it literally changed my life – not overnight and not instantly -- but over time. I'd never been to church and knew nothing about prayer and the Holy Spirit. I walked in the predominantly-black, non-denominational church and sat on the back row. The pastor at the time was a short white guy. After watching for a while, I said to myself, *Man, they say I'm a drug dealer. This dude's got the best hustle going. He's sitting in front of a room full of black people, and they're giving him their money. This is crazy. This is what I've seen on T.V.*

Now, mind you, I grew up in the inner city where there was a heavy Muslim influence, so the Muslim brothers had told us, "Christianity is the white man's slavery religion. They use it to enslave the black people."

I was witnessing this short white dude and all these black people bringing their money to him. I said under my breath, "This is what they were talking about."

By the end of the service, I knew this man was speaking truth. His words did something to me, and these Conover, North Carolina, people were showing me a lot of genuine love. Here I was in a church where everybody was giving me love, and I was coming from the streets where everybody was manipulative and trying to get each other.

So I continued coming back and forth from Jersey, but I began feeling this weight, this heaviness in my soul. Every time I came, I wanted to return to this church. I found myself asking my girlfriend, "Are we going to church?"

There was this young man at church whom I noticed every time. Because I always sat in the same place, I had a direct view of this guy. He was a young black guy about my age – late twenties or early thirties –who looked like me and dressed like me in the Hip-Hop culture with a Polo shirt and Nike shoes. But he was always smiling. He had a wife, daughter, and a little baby boy. I was drawn to this guy named Johnny McGiver. After services, he'd always come to me and ask me how I was doing, and we'd talk sports. The next thing I knew, he introduced me to the associate pastor. This is when I began having a relationship with these guys.

I hadn't seen my mother or talked to her in five years because I was running so fast and so hard in the streets. I'd begun dealing drugs at a level where I didn't want to bring any harm around her. There were times when I owed people $40,000 to $50,000 because I got kilos on consignment. You had to bring the money back to them to pay for the drugs they'd loaned you. I was wrapped up in a drug-trafficking mess. And I was embarrassed – deep down inside I knew I wasn't raised by a family who did this. Do you want to know something? Sin separates you. It separated me from my family, but I didn't understand yet about sin.

That's when I began feeling and thinking, *Something is going on.* Here I was bringing drugs here, and it was taking me forever to get rid of them because I didn't want to sell them. I wanted to hang out with my girlfriend and these guys at church.

One day I was attending basketball practice with the youngest daughter who by this time was on a traveling team with older girls because of her excellent skills. The only other person in the gym besides the coaches and parents was Associate Pastor Ron Carson. Suddenly, I was so convicted and wanted so badly to vent.

"Pastor, I have half a kilo of cocaine in my girlfriend's house. I'm confused. I don't want to sell it. I'm hearing all this stuff from church. I'm starting to feel some kind of way. I'm so confused."

He seemed sympathetic and replied, "You're involved in a lot of stuff, aren't you, young man?"

"Yes sir. Unfortunately, I am."

Then he said in a calming voice, "I need you to get those people whatever money you owe them. After you do that, then let me help you find a job."

And that's what I did. Because of Johnny McGiver and Associate Pastor Ron Carson, I gave my life to Christ at church in 2006, and it's been a process ever since. I don't have one of those testimonies where people say, "I gave my life to Christ, and the next day, the taste of alcohol made me sick." I don't have one of those. I have grinded out every aspect of my walk, grinded out every test and temptation put in front of me, and grinded out every sin that had become a way of life. I've had the faith to hang on.

I stopped selling drugs, shacking up with the lady, and doing a lot of other things, but there were still issues I had to face. My church had learned about my reputation for rapping, so I was working now, serving my church, and creating and performing Christian Hip-Hop music and poetry on special occasions. But occasionally, I would drink a beer, smoke a joint, or sleep with a woman. This is why I know God put Jaime Torres in my life. Here he came with that extra bit of tough sandpaper, and he began to wear away, soften, and smooth out my rough edges. Jaime is really the guy who made me say, "There is a calling for my life."

When Jaime came into my life, he took me to the next level. That first night in the restaurant when I met him, he warned me. "Listen man. You are part of a church. I don't want you coming around me or doing anything unless you have the blessings of your pastor. You aren't going to start leaving your responsibilities and running around with me. That's your church. That is where God planted you. I love you. I'm here for you. I'm going to help you, but I don't need you to do anything without your pastor knowing."

I have had beautiful relationships with my pastors. Johnny McGiver is now the Associate Pastor at my church. They know all about Jaime's and my relationship. It has been God sent. My church has never dealt with insecurities. They know God put Jaime in my life. I still attend the same church, Covenant Christian Church in Conover, North Carolina. On some Sundays, if I want to go with Jaime, I ask my pastor first. Sometimes if they need me, I can't go with Jaime, but if they give me the green light, I travel with Jaime.

But this is what Jaime told me that first day in the restaurant, "Man you're not going to be running around with me without your pastor knowing." Jaime is a man of order.

God has shown me the power and necessity of real accountability to men of God. He put Jaime and my pastors in my life, and together, they hold me accountable for my actions. There was a time when I slipped and had an encounter with a woman I shouldn't have had. We went to Jaime and confessed our sins. Jaime called Johnny McGiver who by now had become my Associate Pastor. Johnny drove me to Jaime's house. We sat in Jaime's living room where they gave me Biblical discipline and five things to do. Two of them were for me to get off of social media for a while and step down from Jaime Torres's Ministries' Board of Directors. This was real Biblical discipline, and they loved me through it – truly. They walked with me during a time when I had to face what being a single Christian man meant and coming to terms with the sacrifice that comes with it. No longer was I in the streets and in the world where if your flesh needed to be fulfilled, you just went out and filled it. But as a man of God, the Bible teaches you should have no sexual relations until you're married. These men continue to hold me to these standards to this day.

At the age of forty-three, if I even go out and have a slice of pizza with a woman, I let Jaime know beforehand, and I let Jaime know when I get home. This Biblical accountability is one of the main things God has shown me and has used to speak to other people through me. Everyone has one or two things in his/her spiritual warfare he/she uses to minister or talk about. Where Jaime can talk about prison, I can talk about the power of being held accountable to biblical men. Jaime is a huge part of that.

Johnny had led me to Christ, I had gotten saved, and I was still a baby in Christ. A month or two after I had given my life to Christ Jesus and had gotten a job, the FBI came and picked up one hundred guys from the surrounding area: Morganton, Hickory, and Lenoir. These were guys they had been watching who they believed were selling drugs. In the late '90s or early 2000s, there was a conspiracy law, which stated if people were arrested and admitted to getting drugs from a named person, that person went to jail.

This is when I told Johnny, "Man, this is crazy. I gave my life to God, and now I'm going to prison."

Johnny said, "Why are you putting God in a box? Why can't you be the guy who goes around talking about His grace and mercy?"

His response surprised me. I thought, *This church guy is a cute dude, but he doesn't know how this works. He is supposed to encourage me, but he doesn't realize what the chances are out of a hundred people who are incarcerated in the federal building in Charlotte, North Carolina, that three or four of those guys won't say my name. Besides, I know for a fact there are four or five down there to whom I have dealt drugs.*

***

I accompanied Jaime Torres to Statesville, where we told people about God's grace and mercy. God does things all the time for me. You know, He knows us all so intimately to the finest details because He created us. God knows Victor Salvat was not this big street tough guy. I had a gift for gab. I was around the right people. I was a good negotiator. I was a connector. I was able to facilitate the guy who had drugs with the guy who had money because I was friends with both. God broke me down by showing me what He'd saved me from. He tenderized my heart when He could have split my head open.

I want people to know Jaime and I grew as real friends. Sometimes when you deal with spirituality, people place you in a different category. There seems to be no realism. People assume that when you're dealing with two men of God, then everything is hunky-dory, but it's not true. Jaime and I grinded our friendship out. We grew like friends by having arguments, verbally fighting, and having misunderstandings. We've cried and apologized to each other. I admit to being immature about a lot of things, but Jaime loves me so much, he doesn't compromise his beliefs and sticks to his guns. He holds me to the fire in a loving way.

Jaime believes in my gift and helps me grow by taking me to prisons and schools to perform my Christian Hip-Hop music and poetry. He encourages me and allows me to introduce him before he speaks. He has shown me I have a role in ministry by placing me on his Board of Directors and encouraging me to speak in meetings. When he calls on me, this gives me confidence to know I really can be a ministry man.

Jaime has been a great disciple to me. To this day, I'm more obedient, and God is dealing with me on pride. God placed Jaime in my life for a reason. We've grown to be real friends, and he is my mentor.

Chapter Twenty-Five

Pastor George Logan
He's a real friend.

Javier Guzman, Jaime's cousin, had contacted me about having Jaime come and speak to our church congregation. I didn't know Javier well, and I definitely didn't know Jaime. But Javier gave me one of Jaime's business cards, along with information about him and his background. I sat on it for a while – I can't remember how long -- and when I revisited it again, I was led to invite Jaime to speak to our congregation. I felt at peace with my decision and thoroughly enjoyed his ministry. From the beginning, I felt a kindred spirit with Jaime. I enjoyed learning about his background and hearing his testimony – all about where he'd been and where he was at that time.

My own background involved prison ministry for over twenty-something years, of which four and a half years were in Los Angeles, California, prior to returning home to Morganton, North Carolina. Although I was never incarcerated, I had done a good bit of prison ministry, which is where I cut my teeth in jails and prisons in California and Nevada. I'd always felt strongly about this type of ministry. So in this regard, Jaime and I related well with one another.

I'd always felt strongly about the need for incarcerated men, in particular, to come to the knowledge of Jesus Christ. That had always been my leaning – to go into jails and prisons and bring men to the forefront as far as their faith was concerned and get them to live from a Biblical perspective. To me, Jaime was a living example of everything I had been teaching. He was the prototype – what you desired to happen to anybody who came in contact with the Word of God and accepted Jesus Christ. Seeing Jaime was like seeing the fruit of what could happen when someone brought the Word of God behind walls. This meant a lot to me. It was like a bottle for me of what the Word could do in a person's life who is in a dire situation.

Since our first encounter, we stayed in contact. With a little hard work we figured out how to relate to one another and become friends. I feel like we had a true kindredness. It was like we walked through spans of time when he'd come to our ministry for several occasions and then spans of time when he was in Jesup, Georgia, and we wouldn't see each other. But always, if Jaime called me, or I called him, it was an immediate catch-up conversation. We never missed a beat.

Throughout the years, we've experienced occasions when we have been a source of encouragement for one another. It seems we've called the other at just the right time. I would receive a phone call and ask him, "How did you know to call me right now?" I think the same was true for him at times when I was led to call him. It's not like we talk every day. It's not that type of relationship where we are constantly on the phone with one another. But it's similar to two guys riding down a highway.

Let's say these two guys in my example are traveling from Morganton, North Carolina, to Los Angeles, California. These two friends say few words until it's time to say something. Then they engage in conversation for an hour or so. Afterwards, they continue their journey for another five or six or eight hours. Finally, they continue their conversation and catch up.

It's a relationship that says Jaime and I are connected, not always with words, but in some way. Our relationship has always been meaningful, supportive, and encouraging. And at times, it has been correcting, when he's called me on something, or I've called him on something. For example, I might say, "I

147

don't know if that settled well with me," or he might say, "That scripture didn't seem to be in the correct context."

We have had good confrontations which I believe are the marks of a good friendship. Having confrontations and still being friends is how I view us. It has been one of the most valued relationships I've had in relation to people.

***

I well remember when I became a Christian. I grew up in a two-parent household in a wonderful community in Black Mountain, North Carolina. My mother and father raised me in a Baptist church and taught me to revere God and all things of God. In that regard, I was tremendously blessed to really respect the things of God. I was one of those kids who was always in church, other than when my family was out of town. Missing church was not an option in our home. We didn't miss church, but in many ways for me, it was more of a religious act. I don't speak of this disdainfully, but I didn't have a relationship with Jesus Christ. Our family had some wonderful people around us who were committed to Christ as they knew Him, and some great people who were committed to the church. It was a good wholesome environment all around, but for me at the time, it wasn't sustainable.

When I left home for college at the University of North Carolina in Chapel Hill, I began attending church less and less. Church had less of an appeal for me. But I still had reverence for God, especially around exam time. This is when I would attend church as a religious act to appease God and hope He'd help me pass the exams. I remember the religious side of me doing this when my internal little boy would say, "I need to go to church now."

In my senior year of college, I went to a service that was upstairs in the same building where I went to party – Upendo Lounge. I don't know if it still exists, but on Saturday night, you'd go downstairs to have a good time partying, but on

Sunday mornings, there was a church that met. One day my friend and I decided we'd go to church. When we arrived, there was a guy who was speaking in a way that touched me. He was talking like the Bible was real, and it really could affect our lives. He said, "God wants to be in your lives. God wants to talk to you." I don't remember what the message was about even though it touched my life at that point, but I didn't give my life to Christ at that time. I now believe that God began the wooing process for me.

There were several friends of mine who attended those church services. One friend was Karen. There was something different about her because she was always kind. Actually, I couldn't understand why she seemed so wonderful and giving and was such a joyful person. I can't remember Karen witnessing to me about Jesus Christ; her witness was her lifestyle. She had this friendliness about her. She was a non-condemning person – someone who was merciful. She was a reference to God for me.

Jerome was another guy who attended the services. He is a pastor today. Whenever I'd see him on campus, I'd turn and go in the opposite direction. You see, I did this because of what was going on within me at the time. Jerome was another of my references to God. I've since seen Karen and Jerome and have told them what was going on with me and that unbeknownst to them, they were witnessing to me and didn't even know it.

After I graduated from college, my parents offered me an opportunity to travel to Los Angeles or to get a set of golf clubs. At the age of twenty-one or twenty-two, I chose the trip to Los Angeles. Can you imagine in what interests a young man heading to Los Angeles might have? Already, I'd dreamed about the big time I was going to have. Back in those days, the television program, *Soul Train*, was a popular show.

I'm going out there and meet a Soul Train *dancer,"* I promised myself. *That's my goal.*

I left North Carolina on a Tuesday morning in January 1987. When I arrived in Los Angeles, the weather was nice and extremely pleasant for January, and to top it off, my aunt was waiting to greet me and treat me to lunch in a restaurant. Because my aunt and uncle were Christians, they said we were going to church that evening.

I told myself, *Well, I guess I have to do what I have to do.*

So I went to church with them. Let me tell you this. God's wooing process, which had begun in the latter months of my senior year in college, and my attendance at the Bible study that night all came together. After the Bible study was over, I gave my life to Jesus Christ and also received the baptism of the Holy Spirit. Even though my plans for Los Angeles were ruined, the most wonderful thing in the world happened to me: I had received Jesus Christ and the baptism of the Holy Spirit.

During the same period of time while I was in Los Angeles, the spirit of God spoke to me about being in the ministry. It wasn't an audible voice. It was like when I used to be a kid. I would have thoughts and dreams of being in the ministry – being a pastor. These were not good thoughts and dreams. They were scary. At that young age, I had thought, *Maybe this is how God scares people. Every kid must be having these same thoughts and dreams.* But after I experienced this divine intervention, this divine interruption, I knew that what I'd experienced as a child of five or six was the beginning of God wooing me, and it had continued into my college years and culminated in this trip to Los Angeles.

I remember getting off the plane in North Carolina where my mother and father were waiting for me. Excitedly, I told them about my whole experience and how I'd received Jesus Christ and the baptism of the Holy Spirit. Then I told them I believed God had called me into the ministry. I believed God had spoken to me. That began my journey of seeking God and defining what this call would be like. God was wonderfully patient and persistent at the same time.

***

In my personal life, Jaime has been a blessing to me because we speak a common language. I don't find it difficult to understand Jaime, and I believe he would say the same about me. I consider Jaime as a brother in the truest sense – not just a brother in Christ – that is certain. But I see Jaime as a brother from the standpoint of his loyalty to me. He is a very loyal individual. He has been loyal in our friendship through the years. Jaime has been a tremendous source of encouragement and support for me.

There have been times when he's come to our church and has given a specific word for me that was right in line with what God was doing at the time in my life. We have different backgrounds as relates to our family lives and our personal lives, and I've never been incarcerated. But these opposites have attracted us to each other. There is an edge, a rawness about Jaime that I really enjoy. And I would say there are things he enjoys and agrees with about my personality and the way I function and operate. The way we get along and know thoughts without saying words are proof we have a truly divine match up.

I believe God put Jaime in my life, and I believe Jaime may have the same feelings, as well. We were matched, so as to speak, in heaven. We don't know what that means for the future as far as how God will use us together in some capacity. We are intentional and deliberate about our activities with one another as pertains to God's will and what He wants us to accomplish together. We don't want to get ahead of God that way, so we're really intentional that way. But like I said, the greatest gift anyone can have in human relationships is a friend. That's what Jaime is to me. He's a real friend and personally speaking, I enjoy every aspect of our friendship.

Chapter Twenty-Six

Pastor Barry Camp

He knows from where God brought him.

I am the senior pastor of a nondenominational church in Morganton, North Carolina. We started the church in January 1999, which was called Harvest Praise Church. Two years ago, we merged with another church and changed the name to The Rising Church.

Ministry is a totally different calling. As senior pastor, I'm a business man, a spiritual leader, a confidant to many people, a comforter, a life coach, and even a dart board for some. A minister has to have a determination for survival. It happened to the Apostles and the early founding fathers of Christianity. But the good news is God gives us good people to help us carry our burdens.

I received a phone call from Javier Guzman, who was working for a heating and air conditioning company. At the time, he was in the office of one of my church members where he had been sharing information about Jaime Torres with this gentleman. The gentleman gave Javier my phone number and told him to call me because he thought I'd be interested in meeting his cousin, Jaime.

One Saturday morning, when my wife and I were going on a picnic, Javier Guzman called and invited us to his home to meet Jaime. My wife and I accepted his invitation and met Javier, his wife Beth, and his cousin Jaime – all for the first time. We sat in Javier's living room and had a good talk.

Jaime had a beautiful spirit and smile. (He's always smiling.) He just opened up his heart. He didn't try to hide anything and wasn't asking for anything. He just wanted to meet me. I felt impressed by the Holy Spirit to allow him to open the service the next day, so I invited him to come and speak for us. He came and gave an awesome word, sharing his heart. This was the beginning of having Jaime come to our church frequently.

Jaime and I were able to talk some more. Other than the Holy Spirit linking our spirits together, the one thing that drew me to him was the fact he wasn't proud of what he had done in the past and wasn't sugar-coating it either. He knew from where God had brought him and was using his experiences as a testimony and for good reason because God has done so many great things for him. His transparency is what I really admired. When I preach, I lay my life out there on the line too; it's not that I try to hide anything either. You don't witness many people doing this, or if they do, they will use their past to make you feel sorry for them. Jaime didn't do this. He used his past as a testimony which was all about from where God had brought him, and that is really impressive.

We stayed in touch even though Jaime was living in Jesup, Georgia, at the time. I'd call him, and he'd call me. So we'd invite him to come and speak a couple of times each year. He'd come and stay a few days, and we'd have fellowship. He always was willing to go with me anywhere. I can remember having a member in the hospital during one of his visits. Jaime asked to go with me, so he could pray with this member. That impressed me because this truly is our mission as Christians to go and pray. It shouldn't be left up to the pastor. Jaime was doing the work of a true evangelist. So we began to share stories and share our hearts with each other – we just had kindred spirits.

I introduced Jaime to several pastor friends. I guess the story opens from there as to how God moved in his life through many circumstances. He would call me many times, asking for me to pray for him when he was at some of his weakest points or going through difficult times in his life. I would request the same of him. I'd call, and he'd pray for me. Then there were times when he'd call, and, of course, it was because he was being led by the Spirit right when I needed an encouraging word the most. He was there through several low points of my life in ministry and was able to pray with me and give me encouraging words.

Jaime and I have shared moments when I felt the Lord was leading me to go to the mount to pray. I'd call him to ask if he wanted to go with me; he never hesitated. We'd be there when the sun rose and have an awesome time in prayer and in fellowship. I can say this about Jaime: He's after the heart of God. It doesn't matter if it is inconvenient for him. If it is something for God, he's going to do it.

You don't meet many people like Jaime. There are lots of great ministers, each one having his/her own gifts, callings, and places. But in this life and in ministry itself, you have only a few spiritual connections. For ministers, it is even more rare. You can have lots of acquaintances but few spiritual connections, which I can count on both hands -- really just one hand. I know lots of ministers and have lots of minister friends, but it is special when you have those connections where you are certain no matter what happens, these friends are going to be with you during the low times and the high times. You know you can rely on these individuals. In ministry, this is far, few, and in between. I consider Jaime one of these, and I think he considers me as one of these in his life, too. Because we have had some very special times in the Lord – just praying – we don't have to say a lot, but we can go together and pray. He's opened his heart to me, and I've opened my heart to him in sharing our frustrations and hurts, as well as the good times. That's why when Jaime feels like a dart board, he calls me for encouragement. When I feel like a dart board, he does the same for me. But that's life in the ministry. There is no way around it.

***

I surrendered my life and received Christ as my Savior when I was twelve years old. Also, I was baptized in the Holy Spirit at twelve, which was very unique. I always had a heart for God, but as I grew into my teen years, I didn't always live for God. I guess that is one way I can relate to Jaime because I backslid in my teen years although I wasn't living life like he was. I didn't get caught up in drugs and criminal activities as he did, but my life was still a mess because I was trying to live for myself. But deep down in my spirit, I knew I had committed my life to God. And I knew He had placed a calling on my life early in my life, but it was something I ran from for many years.

My father was a minister. Unfortunately, he died on a mission trip to Haiti when I was six-years-old. I didn't have the luxury of having a father during my impressionable years, but I could recall him a little bit and remembered some of the things he did. My father owned a small grocery store, so I spent time with him behind the meat counter cutting meat. But everybody told me what a good man he was. And they always compared me to him. "Maybe one day you'll grow up to be a minister just like him." "This is Dwight's son." "This is Pastor Camp's son." "This is Reverend Camp's son." With all those accolades about my father, I experienced difficulty developing my own identity.

As I grew into my teenage years, it wasn't that I was ashamed of my dad, I was honored to be his son. But I didn't believe I could live up to all the expectations. This was my own thinking – planted by the enemy to destroy me. In my own mind and thoughts, I allowed the enemy to manipulate me. I turned my back on God and said, "You know, I can't be as good as he was. There's no way. I've already messed up way too much, more than he ever did." But I didn't know this. I have no idea what my father was like as a young man. I'd never heard his story. I just formulated these thoughts on my own.

155

I began doing things I knew were not of God, and my father wouldn't have approved of. When I began drinking, I liked the taste of certain alcohols. After I graduated from high school, I began social drinking. This led to a lot of different things and relationships that were not of God. I knew in my soul were not right. But in every instance, God was there; I just wouldn't listen. I went to clubs, but I was surprised when everyone I met wanted to talk about God. Have you ever been around drunk people, and all they want to do is talk about God, Christian stuff, Jesus, and being saved? I couldn't run from it.

Right before I had a life-changing encounter with God, I went to a club in Greenville, South Carolina, with some friends, expecting to dance and have a good time. I was the designated driver that night, so I wasn't drinking. I met a girl who was a designated driver for her group, and we began talking. Come to find out, she was running from God, too. She felt her calling was to be a missionary to the Indians. That night, we looked at each other and asked, "Why are we here?"

It wasn't too much longer after meeting this young woman when I had the encounter. By the time I was twenty-three years-old, I had been running for five years. One night while I was out, I had a couple of drinks – nothing major – just as I normally had. I went to bed thinking everything was fine, but it wasn't. I had what some people would call a dream. For me, it was an encounter with God.

I found myself in the pit of hell, a literal place and not somewhere you can imagine. I literally could feel the heat, smell the stench of what death really is, hear the screams and groans, which were sounds you've never heard in your lifetime. I knew where I was, and I knew I didn't belong there. The Bible says there will be gnashing of teeth because of torment; truly, that is the way it was. It was a place of torment – not a partying place like the world wants to promote it to be. It was a place of constant torment and darkness. It was dark; the sense of darkness was so overwhelming, it was painful to be in that darkness. All I could remember was *I don't belong here. If I can get to Jesus, I'll be okay.*

Suddenly, I could see a light shining around and under a doorframe. I knew if I could get to that light, I would be okay. I started toward the door, yet every step I made towards the door was a struggle; I was being pulled back. *I have to fight to get to the door. I have to fight my way out of this pit, out of this place. I'm not staying here. I need to get to the light. I have to get to the light.* I continued fighting my way toward the door and the light and out of this pit. Immediately, when I grabbed the knob and pulled the door open, there was a strong vacuum, which sucked me out. The next thing I knew I was completely awake, out of my bed, and standing upright. My body was soaking wet from head to toe. Even my bedding was wet. Before I could return to bed, I had to change the sheets and my clothes. When I was fully awake and in my natural mind again, I hit the floor with my knees and repented to God.

"Please forgive me, Father." Then I made a covenant with God. "I will never again turn my back on You if You will receive me back."

That's been thirty-three years ago, and I've kept that commitment. I told God I might fall, and I might mess up, but I'd never quit and turn my back on Him. Many times I have felt like quitting because things got tough, but I have never quit, and I've been serving God ever since. In 1987, I accepted my call and was ordained into the ministry. I've been ministering the Gospel ever since. My encounter with God was life-changing.

I've shared my encounter with other ministers. Of course, some didn't believe in things like that. Some said, "It was just a bad dream," but I know I've had dreams, and I know the difference between a dream and a live encounter. If people don't believe, that's fine; they don't have to. The encounter wasn't for them; it was for me. When I shared this story with

Jaime, he actually cried. He's one of my close-friend ministers who believes me and rejoices with me in how God brought me back, received me into His kingdom, and established my way as a minister. One reason the church as a whole isn't living up to its potential is because we don't believe in what we can't physically hold, touch, see, or smell. Faith relies on the ability to be ridiculed, and many Christians are not willing.

Some people ask me why God took me to hell. I have asked the same question, and my only explanation is I heard God say, "This is your chance to come out." I had to make a choice of what lifestyle to live and whether I wanted to live in the world and end up in hell or live for God. That is why I believe God took me to hell. He knew I couldn't see what I was doing to myself. I had to go to hell to know I wasn't created for that place.

Jesus never would have fulfilled His mission if Judas hadn't betrayed Him. We all have the same choice Judas had. We can either deny Christ or receive Him. When we make mistakes, the enemy comes and fills our heads with destructive thoughts. "You ain't worthy." "You ain't good enough." "You can't go back." "Everybody is going to look at you." "God doesn't want you." "God doesn't love you." "You're a failure." "You betrayed Christ."

So many times in Jesus' own teachings when Judas was present, He told listeners about the love of God. Jesus' messages about forgiveness and grace should have been embedded in Judas's heart so he'd know, "Yeah, I betrayed Jesus, but God will forgive me because He loves me." Unfortunately, Judas listened to the voice of the enemy rather than listening to the voice of the Holy Spirit.

Christianity is Christ likeness. In order to become like somebody, you have to be around the person, so you can imitate him/her. If you're not around the person, then you can't emulate him/her. The more time you spend with God, the more you get to know Him. And the more time you get to know Him, the more you get to know God's people. There is no successful

Lone Ranger in Christianity. The Lone Ranger wasn't alone. He had Tonto and Silver, or he wouldn't have become as successful. If he didn't have them he'd just become a dead dude out in the desert somewhere. It's the same with your walk with God. He puts special people in your life, so you can know Him more.

Each relationship, each person God connects you with is there to grow you. The Bible says the iron sharpens the iron. If we can learn to use each other to the betterment of our own walk, knowing we are different, recognizing our differences, and embracing these differences, we can become more successful in our walk with God and our walk throughout life. Everyone has something to give you if you're willing to listen.

Even though we don't always get to see each other, Jaime and I still have a wonderful connection. He lives here in Burke County now, but we don't get to see each other as often as we'd like to, but I know if I need him, he is a phone call away, and he knows the same about me. We have a good, interesting relationship and friendship.

Chapter Twenty-Seven

Reverend Larry Cline "Papa Cline"

I will love him unconditionally until the day I die.

My mother's first two babies died. She experienced a difficult time in her life. She had a nervous breakdown and attempted suicide. I always wondered why my mother had to go to the hospital so often when I was little, but she became a wonderful, tremendous Christian example for her five children: Shirley, Gail, me, Barbara, and Richard. I remember as a kid, she used to call us to the make-shift family altar. There our mother would read scriptures to us and pray with us. I didn't like this time of the day because I wanted to play or do something else. So I was glad when she finished.

I once had a man tell me, "I used to see your mother walking to church with your two sisters. She was pregnant at the time (with me), and she'd walk a mile to Central Baptist Church in Whitnel, a little community between Lenoir and Hickory. This man was lost and never got saved, but his words stuck in my mind. Whenever I reminisce about childhood memories and think of what the man had shared about my mother's dedication to her faith, I realize how God had placed that man in my path, so I'd be aware of my mother's Christian example.

My father was in the Navy during World War II. He and his brother dared each other to join the Navy as they were certain they would be drafted into the army anyway since the War was on. So at the age of twenty-nine, he enlisted. Mother took us to

Norfolk, Virginia, to see him, and we got to ride a ferry boat.

After the War, my mother worked in a mill, and my father worked in a furniture factory for the rest of their lives. But we did have something to eat, a little something to wear, and what we needed.

Daddy didn't get saved until I was eleven years old. We were having revival at church when he accepted Christ. He became a great Christian man.

I remember going into the ninth grade. My mother had bought me three new shirts that cost $1 a piece. I was absolutely proud of my new shirts. When I went to orientation the first day in August, I wore one of them. It was so hot, I almost died from heat stroke, but I was determined to wear that long-sleeve shirt because I didn't get many new clothes. Back in those days, you got one pair of shoes. You wore them until you wore them out. When holes appeared in the soles, you placed pasteboard in them. I had attended grammar school in overalls – whatever you wore back in those days. I had two wonderful parents, and when I reminisce about my childhood, I realize God stood all that up in my life.

Meredith and I got married when we were eighteen years-old. I placed everything I owned in this world in a brown paper bag called a "poke." We lived with Meredith's parents for eight years before we built our own home. When I was twenty-three years-old, I went to work at the Coca-Cola Bottling Company in Hickory. I wasn't a Christian, and because the rest of the fellows enjoyed drinking, I started drinking and became a heavy drinker even though I'd never tasted alcohol when I was in high school or the years prior to working at Coca-Cola.

On Mother's Day in 1964, my mother wanted her children to attend church with her. I complained to Meredith, "Well, Mother wants us to be in church with her on Mother's Day. I don't care anything about going; I don't need to be in church." Then I thought to myself, *That's the last place I need to go on*

Mother's Day. But I went and got saved that day. The Lord changed my life and has been in my heart and life forever.

I remained at Coca-Cola until the end of 1968. In the meantime, I kept getting promoted and eventually became a sales manager. Then the Lord called me to preach.

It is one of the most difficult things I've ever tried to explain. Later when I was pastoring Pleasant Hill Baptist Church, our local association had an ordination committee, which was responsible for questioning prospective or new pastors before referring them to their own churches for ordination.

One of the first questions we ever asked was, "Tell us about your salvation experience." The second question we asked was, "Tell us about your sense of call to the ministry." The second question is a difficult thing to explain. It's something that won't leave you. Now, there is an old saying among preachers. "I woke up one morning and had a craving for chicken and didn't want to go to work." But that isn't so. It is just something you know you have to accept.

Of course, I didn't go into it immediately. I told Meredith about receiving the call, and we prayed about it, but we didn't share it for a while. Then we tried to explain it to Meredith's parents. I told them I felt the Lord was calling me to preach. I don't think they understood it either because I didn't even understand it. I'm not sure I understand it to this day. But it wouldn't leave and stayed with me until I answered that call. I finally made my public announcement the Lord had called me to preach. It was probably five or six years or more before I began pastoring my first church. But I knew this is what I had to do.

When God calls someone, I don't think He ever withdraws His call. You may not be obedient, but it is never withdrawn. There was a man in our church, who shocked me one day. It had taken him years before he could tell me, "God called me to preach when I was a young man, but I never would do it." He never provided a reason as to why he didn't answer God's call to preach. He had to be miserable because you can't get away from it. It stays with you. You can't have full joy and peace until you do. In all, I pastored for forty-seven years until I retired two years ago at the age of seventy-five. And to be honest with you, I wish I hadn't retired.

I left the bottling company at the end of 1968 and was called to my first church where I was ordained to preach in January 1969 to a small congregation of fifty. My whole package was $120 a week. I went from being a sales manager to being a pastor. Fortunately, at the time we owned our own home and Meredith worked.

I had graduated from high school, but I had not gone to college. When I began pastoring, the small church congregation allowed me to enter Fruitland Baptist Bible College – in Hendersonville, and they paid my way. After I graduated from there with an Associate's Degree in ministry, I went on to Luther Rice Bible College and Luther Rice Seminary. I was able to do this because the next church I pastored, Pleasant Hill Baptist Church, paid my way. This was a blessing because Meredith and I weren't making a lot of money and had two children, a daughter, Caron, and a son, Chris.

In 2008, I was diagnosed with cancer. I underwent surgery, took radiation treatments, and then was placed on different medications. The doctors' prognosis was I had three to five years to live.

In December 2012, I was inside a tire store in Morganton. There was another preacher there, but I can't remember his name. Anyway, Jaime was talking with him. The preacher informed Jaime that I was a local pastor, so Jaime came inside the store to speak with me. I didn't know him nor had I ever met him, but he handed me a brochure about a state representative or senator in Georgia who had sponsored Jaime to go to Washington, D.C., and represent a Hispanic event.

When he showed it to me, I read the brochure, which included his story. Within a few minutes, something about him grabbed me spiritually speaking. It was like an instantaneous "God thing" as to why the Lord had put us together. I began to ask him questions. Within ten minutes, I had invited him into my car and took him to meet our Director of Missions at our local Baptist Association in Burke County. Then I returned him to the tire store.

Before he left my car, I asked Jaime if anyone was sponsoring him financially; his response was "No."

Then I asked, "What brought you to Morganton?"

He said, "I felt led by the Lord to come to Burke County. I moved what furniture I had into a church in Hickory and am living in my cousin's basement in Morganton. His name is Javier Guzman."

I heard my voice asking him, "Do you have any money in your pocket?" I have no idea why I asked him that question.

He said, "No, sir. I don't have any money or anyone to sponsor me or any means of getting money."

The Lord pressed on me to give him some money, so I handed him a hundred dollar bill.

At the time we met, Jaime had been coming to Morganton off and on for about ten or twelve years and had preached in the CoMMA (City of Morganton Municipal Auditorium), but for whatever unknown reason, I hadn't heard of him. I was a little skeptical. I talked to a lot of people in Jesup, Georgia, where he had lived who knew him personally. I talked to the chief of police. I talked to the man who gave Jaime his first job out of prison. I talked to the woman who rented to him before he came to Morganton. Then I began to call around to preachers in our community when I received a wonderful report from every single one of them who knew him personally. He'd even preached in their churches – Pentecostal, Hispanic, African-American -- but not Baptist churches. Why I hadn't heard of Jaime until I met him in the tire store is something I can't explain.

Later when Jaime discovered I'd followed up on some things he'd told me, it hurt his feelings. He didn't think I trusted him to tell the truth. I explained I just wanted to be sure. But I knew meeting him was a God thing I can't describe or explain. It was spiritual when the Lord hooked me up with this young man, and we've been hooked up ever since. I'm sure a lot of people don't understand it, and I'm not sure I do myself.

January is when we have Baptist Men's Day in accordance with the Southern Baptist State Convention. I was talking with my wife and said, "I'm trying to find out who I can invite to come and speak for me on Baptist Men's Day." The custom was for us to get an outside speaker to come in.

Meredith didn't hesitate. "Why don't you call this Torres fellow and see if he'd be interested?"

Jaime had gone back to Georgia for whatever reason when I called him. I explained the nature of my call, and he graciously accepted the invitation, happily stating, "Well, that's going to be on my birthday!"

He came back but he didn't preach per se. Instead, he gave us his testimony, which he'd already shared with me. Everybody loved him. His testimony blew everyone away. Afterward, we invited him to our home at the parsonage for lunch. While we spoke, he shared with me that on the day he'd met me at the tire store, he'd been so hungry he'd gone straight to a restaurant and bought two or three hamburgers after I gave him money. I felt led to give him another hundred-dollar bill out of my pocket for speaking that day, and the church gave him a small offering, too. From that point in time, we began to build a relationship. Jaime and I became closer than brothers.

As a matter of fact, after a short period of time, Jaime began to call Meredith and me "Mama" and "Papa." He told everyone we were his mama and papa because he'd never had a good relationship with his own parents. So to be honest, we happily took him under our thumbs. Everywhere we went, whether it was to revivals or when Meredith and I were able to attend some of his events since I was still preaching, we told people Jaime was our adopted son. Because he was dark, he'd always chime in, saying, "I'm the black sheep of the family."

I told Jaime about my cancer and the doctor's warning in 2008 that I had three to five years to live. He prayed for me and told me, "Papa, the Lord is going to heal you." It's been almost eleven years since the prognosis, and I'm still making it. I've fooled the doctors. Now Jaime tells me, "The Lord preserved you and let you live because he wanted you to meet me."

We learned his wife, Grace, was still in Ecuador. Jaime was having a difficult time getting her here legally. He was having to pay his lawyer in Georgia lots of money. From the time he officially moved to Morganton until the time Grace arrived in the U.S. was about two years. During the time we were going through the immigration process, our church and other people collected money to assist Jaime in getting his wife here.

In the meantime, to prepare for her to come, Jaime was searching for a place to live. Now, this story isn't all about me, but I knew a lady in our church who owned a house. I began mowing her grass because her husband had been in an automobile accident and was broken up a good bit. Then he got cancer, so I continued to mow their lawn until he died almost two years later. And I continued the mowing another year until she decided to move to Sanford, N.C., to live closer to her daughter.

We had been looking for a home for Jaime to rent. When I discovered her plans to leave, I called and asked if I could come and speak with her. She agreed, so I took Jaime with me to look at the house. Unfortunately, her homeowner's association didn't allow residents to rent their homes; they could only sell them. But she went out on a limb and rented Jaime the house anyway because I'd been faithful to mow her grass for three years. And she wanted to help Jaime.

***

Neither of our children ever married, so we didn't have grandchildren. Our son, Chris, lives in Raleigh and works with the state. He went to N.C. State University, and Caron went to Appalachian State University. Chris got his Master's Degree at UNC-Chapel Hill. Both of our children have good educations and great jobs. Our son, Chris, told us he didn't want a woman telling him what he could do and couldn't do and how to spend his money. He loves to travel and has been all over the world to China, Japan, Europe, Australia, Yugoslavia, and South America several times. He loves to go, which is another reason for not marrying. He says, "I go where I want to go and when I want to and don't have to ask for anyone's permission."

Once Grace arrived and their baby son came along, we called him our grandson. Meredith actually named their baby JonathanDavid, one word. Then came Isabella Grace, who is our granddaughter. They are the grandchildren we never had. We have bought just about every piece of clothing they have ever worn, and I've bought JonathanDavid enough toys to fill up a panel truck. He calls me "Papa" and Meredith "Maw Maw."

It was my idea for Jaime not to hold a regular job because the Lord had blessed him with such a spiritual mind and a great ministry. He's on the go constantly. He visits ten or more prisons each week. Actually, he goes too much, and I fuss at him because he doesn't rest enough. Like now, he and his family drove to Tampa, Florida, to visit his father, and then they were coming back to Georgia to preach a revival. He'll get home on Friday and then turnaround and head to Raleigh to the women's prison the next day.

My wife and I have helped him – not to brag – financially, and we still do so he doesn't have to hold down a job. To this day, some of the little churches where he goes to preach don't give him anything or give him very little. He has to have money from somewhere, so we have been helping him since we met him. And at the church where I pastored, Pleasant Hill Baptist Church in Morganton, my wife had an idea of asking everyone to give $5 a week ($20 - $25 a month) to help support him. Probably half or three quarters of the congregation began to financially support him, so he could go and do and not have to hold down a steady job.

But he did try to find a steady job. There were some people who accused him of not wanting to work, but he turned in about twenty-five applications in Burke County. I know because I helped him complete some of them. Unfortunately, there is a place on an application. If you are a felon, you had just better forget about getting hired because employers will not even look at the application. Job after job after job and application after application after application – not one single soul would hire him as he was a former felon. That's part of his story, his testimony. Jaime has always said it was his own fault. He has never blamed anyone else or society. He made his own mess, but the Lord saved and delivered him from prison after ten years.

Jaime has such a unique gift for touching young people's lives that only God can give. As I'm cleared to go in some prisons with him, I observe as he ministers to the people in a way that I couldn't because he has been there and has done that. When he was fourteen or fifteen years-old, he belonged to a gang in New York. He was into drugs and an addict himself. His conversion was dynamic as he came to know Christ as his personal Savior. So he visits the Gang Unit in Morganton every Wednesday morning and has been doing so since he came to Morganton. He can identify with those young men and has them eating out of his hand. You'd have to see it to believe it.

One day as we were leaving, I told him, "Jaime, I could go and preach to these kids all day long, but they'd never listen to me because I've never had that kind of experience. You know their language."

Jaime is especially good with young people because he was a youngster when he got into trouble. You can't believe the number of people he has helped by being invited to high schools and different places where young people are. He has won so many young souls for the Lord in addition to adult souls. Right now, our Jaime Torres Ministries' Board is trying to collect enough money to someday build a home called "Grace Place" for young men and women, who have gotten hooked on drugs. It is unreal how Jaime helped my niece, Sara. She was addicted to drugs and near death. Our family thought she was going to die. She'd lost weight and weighed only ninety pounds. But you should see her now. She's gained all that weight back and then some. It's hard for me to explain how he has touched so many people in the short time I've known him.

Jaime and his family rented the house for several years until the owner notified him a few months ago that she didn't need the house any longer and intended to sell it. Sadly, Jaime and his family would need to move. They did and are currently living in a small apartment, but now we're searching for a larger home for him and his family.

A lot of people don't understand my relationship with Jaime, I know. We have a special relationship. Something I tell Jaime is, "My love for you is unconditional." And it is. It's not based on what he does or doesn't do, and that's the way it's going to be until the day I die. I don't know when that will happen. My father's death came at the age of seventy-three. I've outlived him now. My cancer has jumped up, and I'm on chemotherapy for that. I don't know how much longer I'll be around, but I will love Jaime into eternity.

Chapter Twenty-Eight

Chaplain David Turbeville
My prison ministry would be totally different without him.

Jaime and I met quite a few years ago after a volunteer at the prison asked me if Jaime, a former offender, could come to the prison and work with the inmates. I said, "Okay. He'll have to complete an application." When Jaime came in to fill out the application, I met with him. As we talked, I realized he was a man who loved the Lord and had a passion for prison ministry. After he passed the background checks we performed, he met with our assistant superintendent. All of this entailed a period of weeks.

When we began having services and Jaime came in, he was a natural -- an immediate success with the inmates because he knew what they were going through. You could hear a pin drop while he spoke. Jaime knew what it was like to be in prison and away from family. His testimony reverberated with all the inmates. They understood his background and how it was to grow up as he did. They also understood the change in his life and how it was brought about by another inmate at the federal penitentiary.

At Foothills, we have a unit for our gang guys, which is called The Security Risk Group Management Unit (SRG). It is a nine-month program, broken into three different segments. Each segment lasts three months. When the guys get to the final segment, they are allowed more privileges and can come to the chapel to participate in programs and so forth. Jaime leads the Bible study for them on Wednesday mornings. Every three months a new set of guys come in, so Jaime is always introducing himself to the guys. Once when a new group was coming in, several of them told him, "We already know who you are because the other guys have already told us."

Jaime possesses an ability to reach these guys with the Gospel of Christ that is so beautiful. They hear his message and respond to him. The guys always want to see him and have the opportunity to talk with him. Sometimes, if schedules permit and we can arrange it, Jaime will counsel with one or two of the guys. He has gone to segregation to minister to guys in the restricted housing unit. He's gone to SRG to meet with guys. He's talked with guys in regular population at the minimum custody unit. We allow him to meet wherever he wants to.

One Wednesday the guys were anticipating his arrival. Unfortunately, Jaime had a conflict, which caused him to arrive late. When he walked through the door, they all began clapping because they were so excited for him to be there.

Jaime is a wonderful person to have as a friend, as someone to pray with, and as someone to pray for me. Having Jaime around is uplifting and joyful. He challenges me to become more of the person God is wanting me to be. I've always liked being around people who are brighter than me because it makes me look good.

I enjoy helping people advance or find new outlets for ministry. But I don't recommend everyone who comes and asks me to because it is my name and reputation that is on the line. From an early age, I've always been taught what the Bible says about your reputation and name. "It is more precious than gold," so I'm very particular about whom I recommend for certain things and certain places. If they know me and trust me, then I've been able to help. Don't get me wrong. My name isn't well-known or valuable, but whenever you hear "Turbeville," it's a name you don't easily forget. Jaime's name is right there at the top of the list of those I've endorsed who have done well.

I've been at the Foothills Correctional Institute for twenty-three years, so I do have credibility with other organizations. With my connections, I have been able to recommend Jaime for certain programs and different institutions. I consider myself being used by God to spread the ministry to other places because they don't always know Jaime. By doing so, I have helped him get his foot in the door. From there, he's been able to do whatever is necessary to expand his own ministry.

Jaime continues to do a remarkable job here at the Foothills Correctional Institute in Morganton, N.C. and in other prisons for which he is involved. The guys continue to respect Jaime and listen to what he says. His impact has been tremendous.

***

I was raised in a Christian family in a little town named Childersburg, Alabama. We attended the First Baptist Church of Childersburg. One thing that always fascinated me as a child was the Lord's Supper. I didn't understand the meaning behind it at first or why I couldn't have the juice and whatever they were eating. So I discussed it with Mother, and she explained what the Lord's Supper meant. I began listening closely to our pastor at the time. One Sunday after we'd had a Communion Service when I was eight years-old, I'd paid especially close attention that day and understood as much as an eight year-old could understand. It was enough to know that God loved me, and I needed Christ in my life for the sins I had committed. On the way home, I remember speaking with Mother about the Communion Service. I accepted the Lord that day, and a few weeks later, after meeting with the pastor and my parents, I professed my faith in Christ at church and was baptized.

As a teenager, I later learned that when a little child would come forward, they had to meet with the pastor and their parents. After the pastor was assured the child understood the ideas of salvation and forgiveness, Christ's death on the cross for our sins, and resurrection on the third day ensured we have life not just for the future but for the present, then they'd bring the child back to church and he / she was baptized. It was important the child understood what he / she was doing. If the child didn't, the pastor wouldn't baptize the child at that time. Instead, he and the church would help the child to grow and mature and study. They never put anyone off to the side and forgot about him / her. They always wanted to ensure the child grew into the faith and understood the decision and promise being made.

As I grew, I became active in our youth group at the First Baptist Church of Childersburg. Rev. Vess was our youth minister and our music leader. He was a tremendous mentor for me, along with Mr. Cannal, Mr. Fleming, and Mr. Chapman. These wonderful gentlemen worked with the youth and taught Sunday school. Sadly, all these men have passed away, but I know one day I will see them again. Along with my parents, my brother-in-law Jerry, had a great impact on my life. For me to see the man he is, to watch how he has raised his family, to witness how he's taken care of my sister, who is a few years older than I, and to observe how they work together has been a strong Christian influence in my life.

During my teen years, there was a lady in our church, Peggy, who worked at the Alabama School for the Deaf – now the Alabama Institute for Deaf and Blind. I was a member of our puppet ministry, so Peggy would take our group to the school for the deaf where we conducted a Sunday school class for them. We'd place our puppet stage on their stage. Then she'd stand below to interpret the different parts for the kids. This is how I was introduced into the deaf ministry. With an ease for "picking up" things, including a natural knack for learning how to sign, I enjoyed working with the deaf kids.

As I neared high school graduation, I'd planned to attend Auburn University to study history and pre-law. Then I wanted to go to Samford University's Cumberland School of Law and graduate as a lawyer. But at the age of sixteen, the Lord called me to be a minister. I remember to this day when I received the call.

One thing Rev. Vess had done for the youth was to organize mission trips in which we could participate. Our youth choir would go and sing; we also had a hand-bell choir. Now, whenever I sang, it was very unique from the aspect people began crying and asked me to stop singing. It's true! When my own children were little, and I would sing to them, they'd place their little hands on my mouth and say, "No." This is not made up. It's true! My wife Lisa can verify it.

Well, even though I couldn't sing well, I could participate in the hand-bell choir, of course, by setting up the bells. But Rev. Vess helped me to find two things I really enjoyed doing – working with the sound equipment and performing drama. I was responsible for setting up and breaking down the sound equipment. I enjoyed working with the mixers, mics, and speakers. I could help load the sound equipment and ensure we had everything ready to go to our next church. I also enjoyed the drama/speaking parts in our church youth musicals. So everyone had a place to fit in on our mission trips.

We were on a mission trip to Rehoboth Beach, Delaware, to conduct Vacation Bible School. We'd have one session in the morning, have a Bible club, and then we'd have another session in the afternoon. I was working in the Bible club with younger children, and we'd gone outside to the swings. As I was pushing this little kid on a swing, God used this moment to speak to me. I can still hear His voice today.

"David, this is what you need to do. I'm calling you to do this if you'll accept it."

God's voice wasn't audible to anyone else, but it was audible to me.

"Yes, this is what I need to do."

At the age of sixteen, I had accepted God's call to the ministry to become a full-time minister. I went to Samford University in Birmingham, Alabama, a four-year school. Karl Ray Minor was a year older than I at Samford. We became good friends, and to this day, we are still close friends. Karl has a tremendous mind and a tremendous love for the Lord. We've gone on several mission trips together. We went g to Wales to conduct Vacation Bible School for kids and preach at night. He is a good influence on me even to this day.

One of the greatest positive influences in my life is my wife Lisa. We met at Samford University. She had her two-year degree from Samford in nursing and was earning her Bachelor's degree in nursing. She was a junior, and I was a senior. Lisa graduated in May of 1984, and we married on August 11, 1984. After our honeymoon to Destin, Florida, we moved to Ft. Worth, Texas, on August 18, 1984, for me to attend Southwestern Baptist Theological Seminary.

While I was at Samford, I still worked with my congregational youth group, but I also became a deaf youth minister at a little church in Talladega, where I volunteered for deaf youth camp and preached some when the pastor was away. I kept up with the sign language realizing I was being called to work with the deaf. After graduating from Samford, my plans were to attend seminary at the Southwestern Baptist Theological Seminary in Fort Worth, Texas. Before I left for Southwestern, the minister at the church in Talladega contacted someone in Texas and explained there was a young man who was coming there to attend seminary who worked with the deaf congregation. The North Irving Baptist Church in Irving, Texas, had a deaf ministry and was looking for a deaf mission pastor. So I answered the call for it. I would sign for my own sermons – never having an interpreter.

I graduated from Southwestern in May 1988 (I was able to take a three-year program and squeeze it into four years – yes you read that correctly). In November 1988, the First Baptist Church of Morganton in North Carolina had a deaf ministry and called me to be their pastor. So my wife, son, and I moved from Texas to North Carolina. I was pastor there until November 1993 when the funding ran out.

The deaf ministry had been funded by the church, the state convention, and the national convention. For a while, I became bi-vocational, working at the church part-time and at the School for the Deaf in Morganton. Eventually, I resigned my position at First Baptist because I was preaching on Sundays and supervising my congregation, and I was working at the School for the Deaf during the week. It just wasn't working out.

In the meantime, I had helped my good friend, Karl Minor, distribute his resume around here. He accepted a call nearby, and my wife and his wife became good friends. One day when our wives were shopping at the local mall and my wife Lisa was wearing an Auburn sweatshirt, a gentleman walked to her and said, "WAR EAGLE!" (As a side note, that's how Auburn fans greet each other.)

"WAR EAGLE!" Lisa replied.

Then he introduced himself and his wife to Lisa and Sonja.

"My husband is a minister," Lisa said, "but he is working at the School for the Deaf."

The man, Chaplain Ted Swann, said, "Well, I have a chaplain's position open and would like to know if he could apply for it."

So I did. I knew working at the School for the Deaf wasn't what I would be doing forever. The monetary circumstances at the church had led me to the School for the Deaf. But I was a minister and wanted to be a full-time minister.

In May 1996, I began working in the prison. When I walked through the door, it felt like home. Don't get me wrong. It's not like I wanted to move into prison or commit a crime. Coming to work here in prison was a fit for me, like a hand in a glove.

I've always worked with people who were out of the mainstream – the deaf, the blind, and the imprisoned. I can look back and see that all the positions I've held and all the places I've worked were preparing me for this ministry. I believe everyone's call can change – not because you're doing something wrong or because there is nothing to do. I believe God is willing to use people if they are willing to serve in whatever capacity it might be. If God wants you to serve in one place and go from there to another place and from there to even another place until His ultimate goal is to get you to your final place, then He will call you to learn certain things. If I hadn't worked at the School for the Deaf, I couldn't have gotten here. Because the applicants for this job were all equal, I had an advantage because I had time built up with the state, and no other applicant applying for the position had state time.

Getting back to Jaime, he is one of my most favorite people in the world. I enjoy his company and his family. When he was trying to get his wife here, I gave him a couple of dollars to help pay for the expenses for the lawyers and everything else she had to do to get here to the States. I support his ministry, and I served on his board for a short time. Unfortunately, my work schedule here at the prison and commitments at my church caused me to miss meetings. I wasn't able to fulfill all I wanted to do for the board, so I resigned. I still support Jaime and what he does. I believe in him. My prison ministry would be totally different without him.

Chapter Twenty-Nine

Dixie McDaniels
He was God's light for me.

I've known Victor Salvat since I was a teenager. Victor had been attending Jaime Torres Ministries' Bible studies on Friday nights and had invited my sister, Allie, and me to go several times. On May 2017, Allie and I went to the Bible study for the first time. On that night, Sara Watson had returned from Grace Home, a Christ-centered addiction recovery ministry in Santee, South Carolina, and was giving her testimony. Afterwards, Jaime discussed two themes: 1) What is your purpose in life? 2) Ensure God is working in the forefront of everything you do. Even though I'd never met him, his preaching spoke volumes to me. Right away, Jaime captivated me with being well-spoken and close to the Lord. He made me hungry to have that same closeness with God and a relationship with Him as well. Within seconds of the first hour I knew him, Jaime made me feel like I had been in his life for twenty-plus years and was a part of his family.

When I first began attending the Bible studies, I was addicted and low on myself. I didn't know how to approach the many people who already loved me. But Jaime taught me that even though I was going through this addiction, I was loved, and it wasn't just God who loved me. Through Jaime's testimony and all that he had gone through, he helped me realize this wasn't the purpose of my life or what it was going to be. I was assured God had a purpose for me.

Throughout my childhood, my parents, older brother, Ramie, and older sister, Allie, and I were constantly attending our Southern Baptist church in Morganton, North Carolina. My parents weren't the type to send their children into Sunday school, so we had to sit with them during the worship service. I remember one Sunday night when I was eight, we were at church. The preacher was talking about getting saved and what hell really was. Even as a little kid, his message stuck in my mind. When we returned home, and I was in bed, I kept thinking of it and went to my mom and dad and told them I wanted to be saved.

"I believe in God and believe Jesus died on the cross for my sins," I said.

Then as Dad prayed for me, I immediately felt something change inside my body. From that night forward, I was in church and eager to learn more about the Lord from an eight-year-old standpoint.

At the age of thirteen or fourteen, our family brought dad's mother into our home to live with us. We slacked off going to church on Sundays, and around this time, I began to backslide in my relationship with the Lord. When I was sixteen, my maternal grandmother passed away, which took a toll on the whole family – especially me because I was so close to her. This is the time when I began using drugs, smoking marijuana, and drinking. I was doing the whole nine yards.

It started when I began hanging out with the wrong crowd and began smoking marijuana, which I considered myself to be a social smoker. Maybe this crowd thought that since I was smoking, they'd offer me pills. When someone finally did, I accepted them, again thinking it was recreational because I didn't do them all the time – only when I was around these people. But I guess the void left by my grandmother's passing resulted in me developing an "I don't care" type of attitude. It wasn't long before I'd become sick if I didn't have the drugs. Then it got to the point where I was searching beyond these friends and calling people I didn't necessarily have a relationship with just to find the next pill.

As a result, I hid from my family and became distant. It was a dark time in my life. I struggled with my addiction until I turned twenty. Even though I'd backed out of it a little bit, I still dabbled in it. When I was twenty-one, I got pregnant and had my daughter, Porter, when I was twenty-two. During the time I was pregnant and delivered Porter, I was completely sober, got involved in church, and read my Bible. I was trying to work back into my relationship with the Lord. I felt like I was getting to a point where I was ready to give all this up for Porter. I guess this is where I went wrong. I wasn't giving it up for myself; I was giving it up for my daughter. That sounds like a good thing, but at the same time, if you're not giving it up for yourself, you're going to slide backward. That is something I learned at Grace Home. You can do this for your daughter, your family, your friends, but if you're not doing it for yourself and for the Lord, then you won't succeed in breaking the addiction.

After Porter's birth, I began working at a job which was difficult for my body, so I began dabbing in drugs again. My body was hurting so I'd take a pain pill here and another one there to ease the pain. I used the pain as an excuse. Before I knew it, I was back into drugs, full-force into my addiction again. I began using heavier drugs, became distant with my family and daughter, and sunk into a deep depression. The darkness was overwhelming. Satan was pulling me further and further into his plan to destroy and devour me. By May 2017, when I attended the first Bible study, I was as far into my addiction as I'd ever been.

I was extremely uncomfortable going into this Bible study because I knew what I'd been doing, and it felt like people already knew even though I hadn't told anyone what I was doing and going through. But Jaime just reached out to me with open arms. It's like he knew right away I needed that hug and reassurance. Even though I was there with all those people, I was okay. At the time, it seemed ironic that I'd be attending for the first time, and Sara would be giving her testimony the first Friday night after returning from Grace Home. But as I reflect, I know it was God's plan. When Sara gave her testimony, I knew then and there Grace Home was where I needed to go. God had put me in this Bible study for that very reason.

It wasn't quite two weeks later when I knew I had to go to Grace Home. There I faced my demons and faced my addiction and all that comes along with it. In October 2017, after staying the required ten weeks, I graduated from Grace Home.

By December, I didn't have a job, didn't know what I was going to do, and became depressed again. But during that entire time, Jaime was there. He was God's light for me. I was young and getting back into my relationship with the Lord, and he reassured me I was going to succeed and make it. But I relapsed and told Jaime in a meeting with him and a couple of other people from Jaime Torres Ministries. I was so ashamed of myself. Jaime shared the Word of the Lord with me and advised, "You don't beat yourself up. You move forward again."

It finally came to my mind: *You don't need this. God is all you need. No matter what kind of day I'm having or how hard the week seems, the fact I can fall back on God and know He has me no matter what is the most uplifting and relaxing thing I can ever feel. I can sigh in relief because I know I am taken care of – no matter if it is money, a relationship, a job – as long as I am faithful, focused, and obedient, God will get me through.* When I realized this and let everything go, man, it was the best feeling in the world. Although this was one of my lowest points, from that moment forward, my relationship with the Lord has thrived. Now, I am as close to the Lord as I've ever been.

When I learned to put God first above even my daughter and myself, I think that is when it clicked for me: I was putting the drugs down. Jesus had died for me because He loves me; He wants the best for me. So at that point, it was simple for me to put them down. And I haven't looked back. Sure, there were temptations in the beginning, but when I got with the Lord, I didn't even think about them.

When I first went to Jaime Torres Ministries' Bible study and heard Jaime speak about how God could free you from addiction, I didn't believe it at first. I thought in my heart, *Once an addict always an addict. I may get clean and healthy, but I'll never be free from it.* After going to Grace Home, getting back in the Word, working on my relationship with the Lord, and going to hear Jaime preach at different churches and other functions, it really clicked with me.

Ultimately, it has been my hard work. It is not easy. People think when you're walking with the Lord, it is an easy walk. But it is hard because the closer you try to walk with the Lord, Satan tries to do every single thing he can to get you. But my walk has been so well worth it. Getting my daughter into church and attending Jaime Torres Ministries' Bible studies have completely changed my entire life. God really did free me from that addiction. I'm no longer an addict. When you commit yourself to God, He really does free you from addiction. It's an awesome feeling. I just can't wait to see where God takes me from here.

Porter just turned five in August. She is the light of my world. I have full custody because her biological father is not in the picture. Another thing that has happened since I've gotten closer to the Lord is I used to be bitter and angry with him. But now it is so easy to pray for him and hope he gets his life right. I would like for Porter to have a healthy relationship with her father. I wish the best for him and hope one day he can get right for her and himself.

I do have to thank Jaime and Jaime Torres Ministries. The people working in that ministry do a lot of work, as well. But if it weren't for Jaime, I would never have had faith in myself to go get the help I needed. I thank him for giving me that "umph" and "push" to realize it. Yes, I may have been scared, but once I got beyond the addiction, the depression, and the anger I held toward myself, God has taken me so far. He will take me farther. It is nice to be excited about life because when you are an addict, all you feel is misery and regret. You don't look forward to the future. But to be able to anticipate everything to come is a hard and wonderful feeling to explain.

Chapter Thirty

Alex Semande

He is absolutely my spiritual father.

I'll never forget the first time I met Jaime Torres. My friend, Sheryl, had extended an invitation to me. "Alex, I'm going to a Bible study Friday night. Do you want to go with me?"

"Sure," I agreed. I had no idea where this Bible study was being held or who was holding it.

When we arrived at a little coffee shop at 7:00 p.m. Friday night, there were about eight attendees. So we sat down among the other attendees, and immediately, I felt uncomfortable. Why? The man who was speaking and teaching began to stare at me. Even though I was walking with God at the time and had begun teaching the youth at my church to get my foot in the door with ministry, I was under attack spiritually. As I always taught the youth on Friday mornings, it seemed that every Thursday night, I would fall to temptations or begin thinking negative thoughts. It was just awful. My parents raised me and my younger brother in a Baptist church, but the Baptists never really talked about what in-depth spiritual warfare is. So I was oblivious, ignorant to it and what had been happening in my life.

While I listened to the teachings of the Bible study that Friday night, I noticed this man – Jaime Torres -- solely spoke about how the enemy tries to get in and penetrate our lives. And he continued staring at me the whole time. I'd never experienced this feeling – this confirmation -- in my whole life.

When I use the word "confirmation," I mean God speaking a direct word to me, but I realized He was.

This may sound crazy; I haven't told many people this because they look at me like I'm crazy or as if I'm making it up. But while Jaime spoke and taught and stared at me, everything was transformed to black and white. Literally, my vision only saw people and things as black and white. I couldn't shift my eyes away from him. Honestly, I was intimidated and scared. I thought over and over again, *How in the world is this happening? It seems like he has looked at every area of my life and has begun teaching about it. It is like he knows me inside and out.*

For a full two hours, I stared at him, and he stared at me while he was teaching. I was totally engulfed in what he was saying. I was amazed. Afterward, he came to me and asked, "How did you like it?"

My response was, "Dude, can you see right through me? Did I come in here looking a certain way? Did Sheryl tell you something about me?"

"No, man," he said. "I didn't know you were coming."

So I explained what had been happening to me on Thursday nights and how his teaching had been directed to me. "Dude, I'm telling you this is insane!"

I had been a dedicated football fan and attended games every Friday night, but after Jaime's Bible study, I began coming to the study and didn't go to another football game.

I was talking to my girlfriend at the time and told her about the Bible study. "Hey, it is crazy what happened."

She asked, "Are we going to the football game tonight?"

"No," I said. "We're going to a Bible study."

At this point, the Bible study was being held at the Catawba Association building. This would be the second time I'd ever seen Jaime, and it would be the first time he'd ever met my girlfriend. As we walked in, we didn't look sad or mad. We just looked like our normal selves – straight-faced – and we put on that little Christian front that can be read, "We're here. We're perfect. Blah blah blah." That's when Jaime approached us and asked, "Can I talk with you guys for a second?"

Dumbfounded, I answered. "Sure."

Jaime pulled us off to the side where others couldn't hear and said, "The Spirit of God just told me something about you guys. You guys are falling into sexual sin."

All of a sudden, I felt my body lock up and freeze. Cold chills ran through my body. My girlfriend, Brittany, was mad at this point and was staring at me with that silent "Why did you tell him?" look.

I stuttered a reply. "I didn't say anything. He doesn't even know me. The only little bit he knows about me is from a conversation we had about spiritual warfare the last time I saw him."

Jaime directed his attention to me. "Do you not know you're a man of God?" Keep in mind I was nineteen years-old at the time. I'm twenty-four now. He continued, "Do you not know how much of a man of God you are? Do you not know she is a daughter of God, and she is precious to Him? Every time you can't contain yourself and keep your pecker in your pants, you are taking away from her and not giving anything to her. When you lust after her, you are taking away from her. That's not love. That's greedy, and you need to stop now."

Then he looked at Brittany and asked, "Do you not know what a precious gift you have? This is a man of God, and he is a pastor. He is going to preach. You're taking him away from his ministry when you engage with him in sex."

I turned and hurried to the car where I cried like a little baby. When I returned, she was still mad and was convinced I'd told him something. Once again, I didn't believe this was happening because I'd been raised in a church where they didn't talk about the gifts of the Spirit or word of knowledge. This was just mind-blowing and mind-opening to me. And I wasn't thinking, *Look at this Jaime Torres guy. He's such a great guy*.

***

Brittany and I were saved early on in life and had been walking with the Lord. But we'd been dating a long time prior to our decision to follow Jesus. As a result, we had sex all the time. When we started to follow Christ, we knew we had to stop, but it was extremely hard to let go. We'd been trying, but it had become hard to handle. We'd fall under temptation and repent. This was a repetitive process. We'd mess up, feel horribly, repent, and try again. We'd made it a whole week once before falling again. That night before we came to Bible study and received that word, we'd messed up. It was about the fifth time that week, and we literally had a conversation before we walked in.

I confessed to her. "This is too hard. There is no way it is possible to live this life. I know plenty of friends who say they are walking with God, and they have sex all the time. They just do it and play the grace card, 'God loves us. It's cool.' I never wanted to be one of those people, but I don't know what else to do. I'm tired of feeling like crap and tired of messing up. I guess we'll just have to roll with it and know God loves us, and it's all right. This is why I went to the car to cry."

I told God, "Wow! You care so much about me God that you gave another man a word. I don't even know this guy, but You gave this crazy Puerto Rican man some word to speak to me because You heard me ready to give up. You love me so much You put it into someone else to speak to me."

As I mentioned earlier, I had been raised in a Christian home my whole life and had been raised in church my whole life. But about the time I turned sixteen years-old, I wanted to see what drinking was like and what sex was like. My youth pastor had advised us not to mess around by explaining how awful everything was.

"Don't ever drink alcohol because hangovers just suck. You throw up all the time when you go party. Don't have sex because there are STDs (sexually transmitted diseases). But when I heard my friends talk about drinking and sex at school, it sounded awesome. So I thought, *One of you is lying. I'm going to try it for myself.*

Of course, I loved it because the Bible said I would love it: "Sin is good for a season." Obviously, convinced my youth pastor didn't know what he was talking about, I began drinking, partying, and having sex. By the time I got to my senior year, my goal was to sleep with as many girls as possible. Every day I came to school high on marijuana. I wouldn't say I was an addict, but I enjoyed being high all the time. Eventually, my parents caught wind of what I was doing, so they lectured me a lot. By the time I graduated high school, I told myself, *I'm not going to put up with them lecturing me. I'm going to do what I want to do.*

After graduation, I moved out of my parents' house, got my own place, and finally had a job. Now I could earn my own money, buy my own drugs and alcohol, and invite girls over whenever I wanted to. I lived this life for a few months, up until my freshmen year in community college. I remember hosting a party at my house. I'd invited a bunch of buddies and girls, and we were all drinking. I remember sitting on the front porch alone while I smoked a cigarette and thinking, *I have everything I ever wanted. I wanted to get away from home. Check. I wanted to sleep with girls. Check. Buy my own weed. Check. I have lots of people in the house. Check. I have all this stuff, but why am I so miserable. I feel so empty, and I don't understand. I have everything I wanted.*

At about this same time, Graham, this guy I worked with at Food Lion, started coming up to me at work. Graham knew me from my parents and knew I attended church, but he didn't know anything about me other than that. He must have assumed that because I attended church, I would want to hear his sermon. Graham was teaching the youth at the time, so when he asked if I would listen, I said, "Yes." Graham enjoyed talking and giving his full sermon of what he'd teach that night. As I sat and listened, everything he spoke made me wonder, *Did he just see everything I did? Has he been watching my life play out? Is he speaking to me? This is weird.*

It wasn't long before another guy, Brad, from church called and asked, "Would you like to sit down and do a Bible study with me? It's just going to be you and me. We're going to read scripture."

Here I was, attending church and flying under the radar. Actually, I was attending church because my parents wanted me in church. Not wanting to be mean to Brad, I said, "Okay."

When we met, he explained, "I just want to go through the 'Book of Mark' and find what stands out to us and talk about it."

We began reading, and I can't tell you how ridiculous it was that everything we read spoke directly to me. What in the world was happening? After our second Thursday night, I began thinking, *This is freaky. I don't want to keep going. This is almost scary. I don't like going there. Every time I go, I get a huge sense of ....* I didn't know the word at the time, but it was conviction. It was ridiculous how convicting this was and how it was speaking directly to me. *I'm going to stop coming.* But for whatever reason, I kept going and listening to Graham give his sermons and Brad read scripture with me.

Eventually, I began reading the Bible for myself. I came across the scripture in 1 John 2:17 (paraphrased), "The world along with its desires will pass away, but the man who does the will of God will live forever." That's when I began thinking, *This makes sense. I've been chasing after the world for so long. Now it is all passed away. It may have been good for a minute, but it's all gone. Everything sucks. I'm still empty. Everything and anything I've chased after besides God will pass away, but the man who*

189

does the will of God will live forever.

Maybe all this weird stuff that was happening was God sending people into my life. Maybe God was trying to talk to me. Maybe God was saying, "I want to give you life, and I want to give you life abundantly, not this synthetic stuff you've been getting by on. I want to give you true life."

This led me to have a conversation with God. "Hey," I said. "Obviously, I think You are trying to talk to me – get a hold of me. You're sending Graham to me at work and Brad to me from church. The timing isn't a coincidence. As soon as I'm getting tired of this partying life, You begin sending these people into my life."

So I traveled alone to a place in Valdese, North Carolina, called McGalliard Falls, where I usually went to smoke weed. Instead, I hit my knees. I wasn't emotional. I just said to God, "If I'm going to do this, I'm going to do this for real. I give You my life."

That's it and where my life started. I followed it by making a profession of faith and being baptized by Brad in my church.

I don't want my testimony to be the end of this chapter because it is a beginning. Everyone thinks that once he/she answers the altar call and gives his/her life to God, "I've finally made it. I finally made the right decision." But as soon as you make the decision to follow Jesus, this is where the story begins, and you start walking with the Lord. The God I know says I will bring you from glory to glory. When I give my testimony, that's just a small portion of my life – a single event. I've seen so many more miracles happen and experienced so many more manifestations of God changing me throughout my life than just my little testimony. It's just the beginning of my story. A lot of people miss that.

Jaime is part of my story of how God brought me from glory to glory and how God used him as a divine instrument to bring me to the next place where I needed to go when I was trapped in sin. God knew Jaime would speak some stuff and not worry about his reputation. I think God puts a lot of conviction on people's hearts, but they don't speak it or say anything because they are worried about marring their reputations or losing their jobs. Some ministers fear if they preach the messages God has placed on their hearts, their congregations will stop tithing or giving offerings. But God knows Jaime is going to speak what's true no matter what people think. For me, I can't imagine when God put me on Jaime's heart.

I can hear God saying, "Here's a guy. You see that guy walking through that door? I need you to rebuke him. That's my child, my son, and he's about to give up on me."

I think that says a lot about salvation's definition. Not to get all into theology, there is a big debate among Baptist churches and the Church of God regarding "once saved, always saved" and "can you lose your salvation?" I don't take sides for either category, but I do ask, "What do you call salvation?" Salvation isn't a one-time decision to follow Jesus. Where in scripture do you find where someone comes up to Jesus, and asks, "What do I have to do to be saved? And Jesus' response is, "Just accept me in your heart or pray this prayer with me." No, Jesus says, "Repent and follow me." It's that simple. Follow me.

In Romans, it says to renew your mind daily. Jesus told the parable about the master coming home and finding the slave sleeping. The master beat him and tossed him away. But if he came home and found the slave working and doing what he was supposed to do, he would say, "Well done, my good and faithful servant."

I think so many people are living the lie they are saved because they made the decision when they were seven years-old at Vacation Bible School to repeat a prayer with the preacher. Oh, I think they are saved even though they are living life in sin right now. They think they will come up to God whenever they die and say, "Hey this is the decision I made when I was seven."

That's when God is going to say, "I could care less what you did when you were seven. What did you decide today right before you came here? Were you striving after me? It looks like you gave up a long time ago. So I don't care what you did when you were seven. A lot of people can make decisions."

Does God not compare salvation to marriage in the Bible? If we look at it in that regard, so many people who decide to get married end up getting divorced. I'm not saying that you can lose your salvation – I'm saying salvation is not a one-time decision. Salvation is making a daily decision to follow Jesus throughout your life. At any time, you can give up and go.

At many times in my life, I have said, "I'm done with this. I can't do it anymore. It's too hard to fulfill this calling you have for me. The things you want me to give up, I don't want to give up. That's when God sent people like Jaime to remind me, "No, I love you and still have life for you. So put your pecker back in your pants."

Life has just begun. God took me from that nineteen year-old kid, who was struggling in sin with his girlfriend, who is now my beautiful wife. Brittany and I have a wonderful marriage that began with Jaime conducting our marriage ceremony. I'll never forget that day. Brittany is more godly than I am, and He's given us two beautiful daughters (Love and Peace) who already pray for us. It is amazing. It is what God does. He doesn't stop there. He brings us from glory to glory. Sadly, sometimes people want to be brought from glory to glory, but they don't want to be rebuked. They don't want to be disciples. They want to be Christians and not disciples. But Jesus didn't want Christians. He wanted disciples. The word "disciple" comes from the root word discipline. He wants people who can accept rebuke and instruction. If you don't want to be rebuked or uncomfortable, then you absolutely would have hated Jesus.

Within the next month, I am hopeful to become a full-time youth pastor at a church. We've been going through an interview process for a couple of months now. They will be making a decision soon if they want us to come on board with them. I keep Jaime updated on this. I called him before I even got serious with this church. Anytime I make a decision like this, I figure I need to give him a call, especially the man who has prophesized over my life and told me I am going to be a pastor. Jaime is my spiritual father. He calls me son, and I call him papa.

There are guides we have in our lives. I can name you probably ten guides who have helped me in my life to get to the next level in my walk with God. They have given me spiritual wisdom when I needed it. But if I can only think of one spiritual father in my life, that is Jaime. I run to him when I'm making decisions, when I'm struggling with sin, and when I'm just wanting to tell him what God has done in my life and want to rejoice with somebody. He is a father and a safe haven for me. He has rebuked me when I've needed it. Like any dad, he's not afraid to tell me when I am being stupid. He's not afraid to use those words in a loving way, which is what I want – not someone who is going to sugar coat stuff and watch me walk into trouble. I want someone in my life who is going to be 100% honest with me, even if it hurts a little bit at first. He has always been that person.

Sometimes, his response is, "Son, what are you thinking? You already know. Examine your own heart. You know you are doing that because you are being selfish right now."

That's what I need to be told out of love. He has inspired me to do that for other people. In my ministry, I want to be that same guide to young people. I don't want to be a guide like a therapist who sits and listens to all your sinning and expects you to work it out yourself. I want to speak the truth in their lives even if offends them.

As Jaime says, "Not everyone hangs around me because they don't like my being honest with them."

I can say from my standpoint, I need this guy, and I love it when he rebukes me because I know I'm getting truth. Yes – he is absolutely my spiritual father.

Chapter Thirty-One

Pam Hyman
He gives himself to everyone.

The first time Jaime and I met was about a year ago at Popeyes Louisiana Kitchen in Hickory. With all my heart, I believe it was a divinely-ordained encounter. I had ordered my usual lunch choice, a two-piece white, spicy, with mashed potatoes and gravy and was waiting at the counter when this handsome man entered the restaurant and stood beside me. You can't ignore Jaime when he enters a room because the minute you see him, his face lights up. He has a certain presence that foretells of his friendliness.

Jaime was wearing a shirt that read "Chaplain, Morganton Public Safety." Because I'm a born-again believer, I noticed the word "Chaplain" and knew if I spoke to him, he'd probably respond. With a big smile, he did, so we exchanged additional pleasantries. Before I knew it, we were talking about Jesus and God's goodness. We discussed how He brings people across our paths and how we never know what the outcome will be. We didn't sit down; we never moved from the counter except to get out of other people's way. When my food came, I didn't want the conversation to end.

As I paid for his lunch, I said, "I'll see you again."

Jaime thanked me, blessed me, and handed me his business card. "It has been so refreshing to meet another kindred spirit," he said.

When he reached his arms out to me, I couldn't help but to

reciprocate. We embraced like we'd known each other forever. Even though I'm a warm and friendly person, the fact that we embraced is something I normally don't do, especially to a man.

The cashier was so engrossed by the exchange we'd had in that few minutes, he said, "I wish there would be more kindness in this world like what I just saw between the two of you. I've never seen anything quite like the encounter y'all just had."

Well, I hadn't experienced anything like it either because some people – even some Christians -- are just not friendly.

I was born in Washington, D.C., and spent most of my adult life in Maryland. My parents were North Carolinians; Daddy was from Rocky Mount, and Mama was from Morganton, which is where my brother, sister, and I spent our summers while growing up. As I was getting older and had retired after thirty-three years from the Postal Service as secretary to the Chief Privacy Officer at headquarters in Washington and in other departments of the Postal Service, I found myself praying to God whom I affectionately call "Daddy."

"Daddy, this is really what I want to do – move to North Carolina. You know me because You made me. I think it is time for me to make a change. I don't want to spend the rest of my life in this crazy rat-race area, so I am going to pack it up, and it is just going to be You and me for the rest of my life. Whatever comes is because You want it to."

I didn't hear God say no; I didn't wait for an answer. I know that isn't how you're supposed to do it, but that's how I did it, knowing it would be a big adjustment. So I did some preliminary homework and found that the cost of living would be cheaper for me if I moved from Maryland to North Carolina, which I'd always called "home" because of my childhood summers. I learned that I wouldn't have to pay state taxes on my federal retirement income, which would be helpful in terms of finances.

The only relatives I have in North Carolina are two cousins

whom I am very close to. They live in Morganton. If it weren't for them, I probably wouldn't have moved here because I didn't want to come without having family to spend time with and whom I knew I could depend upon. Except for a few other cousins, all my relatives have died. My sister and I sold the house, leaving me with quite a bit of money. I wanted to start over, buying everything new, so I brought very little of what I already had with me. In pursuit of a more quiet and peaceful life, I moved to North Carolina three years ago on August 25, 2015. I was coming home.

At first, I couldn't find a place to rent in Morganton, so I telephoned my cousin to learn where the next biggest city was located. She said, "Hickory."

"Okay!" I said. "Let me go look there."

This is how I ended up living in Hickory, which was more in line with how I was living in Maryland and which was an eye opener for me. When I first moved to Hickory, it was a wonderful time in my life. Actually, it was almost unbelievable! I had money and could buy what I wanted.

One thing that had always interested me was learning ballroom dancing. You can imagine my disbelief when I learned that Hickory had the All American Dance Company downtown. I quickly joined. Then I saw that the city had a soup kitchen. All my life I had wanted to work in a soup kitchen. After signing up, I was able to volunteer at the soup kitchen beginning the second week after my move. So here I was ballroom dancing, furnishing my home with beautiful things, meeting lots of people, and working at the soup kitchen.

It wasn't long before a very friendly maintenance guy where I lived asked me if I were looking for a church. He invited me to his church, which is non-denominational. So I partnered with Freshfire Church in Hildebran, N.C., and I've been there ever since.

I was experiencing a lot of adjustments: moving to

a new place; attending a new church; getting adjusted to new surroundings; and, leaving my sister, one son, and two grandchildren in Maryland and one son in Colorado. But I was willing to start over again and accept the challenges I had placed upon myself.

A few months later, I found myself calling Jaime. I wanted to talk with him about life in general, what God expects of us, and what my calling might be now. We decided to meet at a chicken place in Morganton, where we enjoyed soft drinks and conversation. This was a time and place for me to share what was going on with me. Jaime is one of these wonderful people whom when you call him, he is going to find a way of coming to meet you, wherever, to learn what he can do to help you.

I shared my testimony with Jaime that day. I became a believer on February 6, 1976, when my oldest son was seven. I remember it like it was yesterday. Isn't that amazing? I was living life the way I wanted to. My son and I were living with my father, after having lived in Chicago for a few years. My father saw that I wasn't living the way I should as a mother. After all these years, I will never forget the note my father wrote to me:

You fiddled through breakfast.

You fiddled through lunch.

But don't fiddle through dinner because it just may be too late.

He was right! I was drinking a lot and smoking reefer with my friends at the law school. I began feeling unsettled like my life was crashing, spiraling out of control. I knew I wasn't living right or doing right, but I didn't know what to do about it. I had grown up in church, so it wasn't like I hadn't heard the truth and how to live.

I telephoned a girlfriend of mine who didn't come to work that particular day.

"I'm not feeling well," I said. "I think something is happening."

She said, "Oh well. Just take the rest of the day off, and come over here. We'll get drunk, and forget about the rest."

I left my job and went over to her house where we drank, but I wasn't feeling any better.

"I think I'm having a nervous breakdown." I was scared. "I'm going to call my sister and tell her to come and get me."

My sister taught school; I knew not to call on a whim or for any foolish reason, but I called her.

"Please come and get me. I think I'm having a nervous breakdown."

My sister came and took me to the hospital, where I thought they would keep me. I didn't think they'd send me back home, but they did.

"We don't keep people who think they are having a nervous breakdown," I was informed. Instead, they gave me the name of a psychiatrist, who happened to have an office down the street from the law school, so this made it easy for me to schedule appointments at lunchtime. But all the psychiatrist was doing was doping me up more. He gave me pills to sleep and tranquilizers to get through the day. I just got worse.

A few nights later, I told my girlfriend, "I want to come and spend the night with you. My father will keep my son."

She said, "Okay."

Still having uneasy, jittery feelings, I went home with her.

"Maybe you just need to take a hot bath, smoke another joint, and have a glass of wine while you're in the tub. That will probably make you feel better," she recommended.

"Okay." I stepped into the warm bath water, did all those things, but when I climbed out of the tub, my heart was racing.

"I'm scared."

"Do you want me to take you to the hospital?" my friend asked.

"No. I just want to lie down. Maybe what I'm experiencing will pass." By now my heart was really racing.

The last thing I said after lying down was, "Dear God, please don't let me die."

When I awoke the next morning, God told me, "Call and cancel your appointment with the doctor because you don't need him anymore."

That was the beginning of the rest of my life with Christ. This is my testimony of the goodness of God. I never thought I'd have a platform to share my testimony, but I do now thanks to this chapter of Jaime's book. I am not ashamed of the Gospel of Jesus Christ because it led me to salvation. Had it not been that walk of floundering through life as I was doing, I never would be able to give my testimony.

At the end of our conversation, Jaime invited me to attend his Bible study on Friday nights in Morganton. I was excited to drive the twenty-three miles from Hickory the next Friday night to hear him preach. Since then, I've attended more than half a dozen times, and I text or call him to learn where he is preaching around this area. Then I go hear him speak whenever I can.

When I think of Jaime, I am moved to tears. The thing about Jaime is I have never met anyone in the body of Christ who is so sincere and so earnest in reaching the lost. I've been saved for forty-two years, and I have met a lot of people and heard a lot of sermons. But Jaime is so genuine in his life's calling to save the least and the lost because sometimes that is how people are treated – as the least.

Jaime embraces everybody. I know he has ministries I don't even know about. I know there are times where he travels a lot sharing the Gospel of Jesus Christ. I know that one of his passions is for men and women who were and are incarcerated. I don't know the degree to that either, but I know his heart for them is because he was incarcerated himself.

My experience when I go to Jaime's Bible study, is everybody wants a piece of him, and he gives himself to everybody. Just to sit there and observe him in action while I'm listening and learning is amazing – how his heart is so full of the Word of God and how important it is to him for us to get it. Other people may share, and you may listen for an hour, but Jaime wants to ensure you get the message.

Even though Jaime and I don't see each other often, every time is like the first. Once when we were talking, I said, "I know life is happening to both of us. I wish we could see each other more often." Every encounter with him is such a blessing.

Jaime replied, "But our connection isn't how often we see each other. Our connection is spiritual. As much as I would like to see you more often on Fridays, it's okay because I know we are connected spiritually, and we always will be."

I am so grateful for Jaime. I'm not going to apologize for being so emotional even though I'm surprised that I am. It's because I've never met a soul that God is using so strongly – someone who has given his life for his ministries. It is easy for people to say "I do," "I will," and "I have," but Jaime has done it all.

At seventy-one, I figured, "What else would I want to do with my life except to give it away?"

Because of the peace in my soul, I believe I'm well-rounded and where I'm supposed to be. I have a wonderful relationship with my pastor, whom I love like a son. I am active in my church by giving devotions regularly before praise and worship and facilitating a women's prayer group every Tuesday.

I enjoy being hospitable and opening my home to people because the only way to get to know people is to spend time with them. Just like our relationships with Jesus: If you don't spend any time with Him, you won't have a relationship with Him. The ladies from the prayer group come to my house regularly afterward, and we talk about issues that are important to them and me. Everyone brings pot luck, and we'll stay until the last person wants to leave. If I can touch a handful of people, even if it's just five, I believe that my living has not been in vain.

I'm at a point where I'm content with my life. This is the life I've chosen, and "Daddy" has put me here for a reason. He doesn't make mistakes. Even though the dance studio closed, which absolutely broke my heart, I'm active in my community by volunteering at the soup kitchen (which I love above all my other volunteerism). I'm also a Hospice volunteer at Catawba Regional Hospice; Safe Harbor, a non-profit ministry for women; and I tutor two little ones in elementary school. I have a strong spiritual base of people – my prayer warriors – who pray for me continually. With them I know the prayers will reach heaven.

I'm grateful for the day I met Jaime at Popeye's. My life will never be the same. Our relationship is very special, and I know God will always use him to further the kingdom. He is a rare human being, and I am grateful that God brought him into my life for such a time as this. Jaime and I are not connected by blood, but we are connected by love – Christ's love.

Hopefully, one day soon, Jaime, Grace, and their two beautiful children and I can break bread together and enjoy fellowship with one another. I said for the rest of my life, I wanted to give my life away. I have a wonderful, Christ-centered life, and I'm determined to do just that.

Chapter Thirty-Two

Meredith Cline ("Mama")

I believe the Lord put me in his life to help him.

In December 2012, I had an appointment, so my husband Larry, dropped me off and headed to the tire store. Later when he came to get me, he told me, "I ran into this guy who had the most unusual testimony." Then he told me about it. Larry said he'd taken the man to the Baptist Center to meet the Director of Missions. Around the end of December, Larry was preparing for Baptist Men's Day in January and was worried. He asked me, "Who am I going to invite to come and speak at Baptist Men's Day? We've done this for many years, and I've run out of leads for speakers. I need to find someone to speak."

It was a "God thing" for me to think of Jaime. I replied, "What about the guy you talked to at the tire store? You said he had a good testimony that was so unusual. Why don't you contact him?"

Larry remembered Jaime was leaving for Georgia after they met, but he happened to have Jaime's cell phone number because Jaime had called Larry to thank him for the money. So he called him. Jaime agreed to come and mentioned the Baptist Men's Day was on his birthday, but he would be back in Morganton soon.

A few days later, I actually was able to meet Jaime when he drove to the church. He wanted to get a feel for the community and know the church's location. Then he came to our home and visited with us for about an hour. I think I fed him a sandwich that night.

On Baptist Men's Day Sunday, Jaime was accompanied by Victor Salvat. When he began speaking, I immediately knew there was something different about Jaime. I've sensed that difference with other preachers, and my impression was he was quite different. I thought, *The hands of the Lord are on this guy.*

I usually cook Sunday lunch, so after the service, I invited Victor and Jaime to our home to eat lunch. Before they left, Jaime said, "Let's hang out one day this week. What have you got going?"

"We have to go to the hospital in Asheville on Tuesday. We have a lady in our congregation who is having surgery," I replied.

Then he asked, "Can I go with you and pray for her?"

"Sure," I said. "I don't see any problem in it."

Well, Tuesday came and Jaime wanted to drive us in our car. Larry got in the front seat with Jaime, and I got in the back seat. I wasn't used to his driving, so here we were going up the mountain on a curvy road. Now, Jaime was one of those people who kept turning and looking in the backseat while he was talking to me. I began silently praying, *Lord, please take care of us. I hope this guy doesn't have a wreck. He's not looking ahead. He's looking at and talking to me in the backseat.* Jaime made me feel uneasy about his driving that day. I've learned since then he is a good driver, but on that particular day, I didn't think so.

We arrived at the hospital and visited with the lady. She was encouraged by his coming to pray for her. Jaime likes to sing, so I think he sang a song for her, too.

Afterward, we extended an open invitation for him to come by anytime, so he began dropping in to see us more often. He was used to different kinds of foods, but I would invite him to eat. Sometimes, he liked it, and sometimes he probably didn't like it, but it was a meal.

In March 2013, Jaime had moved here but didn't have a job. The Christian Outreach Center went to Virginia to pick up food and bring it back for distribution. When they needed someone to drive a truck to get the food, Javier, Jaime's cousin asked if this was something Jaime could do to earn a little money. I think they paid him $100 to drive the truck to Virginia, get the food, and return to the Outreach Center. Jaime wanted Papa to go with him, so they began getting up really early and going every Thursday.

On one particular Thursday, Papa couldn't go with him, so he'd invited his cousin, Victor Salvat, to go, but Victor couldn't go either. If either of them had gone with him, it would have been disastrous. Jaime was driving down Highway 181 when the brakes on the truck failed. I don't remember how many pounds of food he was hauling, but I think they had overloaded the trailer. Jaime wasn't wearing a seatbelt when he wrecked the truck. The guard rail actually went through the truck. Upon impact, Jaime was thrown clear from the driver's side. If he'd been wearing a seat belt, the guard rail would have killed him. Some lady, who was a nurse, helped him, as well as another onlooker. They were worried the truck was going to catch on fire.

I was in the middle of cooking when Larry and I received a call from the hospital. Jaime had asked the nurse to telephone us. "He's been in an accident and is asking for you," she said.

I asked Larry to go check and see what was going on. "If you need me to come, call me, and I'll come over."

By the time Larry arrived at the hospital, Jaime's cousin, Javier, was there, and they would allow only two people in the emergency room at a time, so I didn't go. But this is when I realized how much I cared for Jaime. It was kind of like knowing somebody that you're around, but you don't know your feelings about the person until something like this happens.

I didn't know what condition Jaime was going to be in. When Larry called from the hospital, he said it was a miracle -- they were releasing Jaime. "In fact," Larry continued saying, "the patrol officer said in the condition that truck was in, the Lord made a mouse out of Jaime, or he wouldn't have gotten out of that truck alive." His description of the truck made it unbelievable that he could have survived.

"Larry, if he needs someone to stay with him, bring him home with you, and I will take care of him," I said. We had an extra bed, but Jaime decided to return to his cousin's house. He was able to get up and wait on himself.

Jaime told us, "The devil is trying to kill me. I've moved to this town, I'm trying to work for the Lord, I'm holding Bible studies, and then I have a wreck. The devil is trying to kill me!"

After he felt better, he began coming to our house, and we'd sit around the table and listen while he shared his desire to have a ministry, but he didn't have the funds.

I remember asking him, "Jaime, have you ever considered having a Jaime Torres ministry like Billy Graham has a ministry and different evangelists have ministries? If you feel that is your call, then why don't you set up a ministry?"

I could tell from his reaction he didn't know how to go about setting up a ministry. Then another God thing happened. It just so happened a lady in our church handled the business for A Caring Alternative in Morganton. So we contacted her, and she volunteered to handle the preliminary paperwork and contacts to get the ministry started. She contacted her lawyer and her accountant to ask questions and research information. As a result, we got the ministry started in the fall of 2013.

Larry and I already had begun attending his Bible studies on Friday nights during the summer months of 2013. We were meeting at Victor's apartment, but when it began growing, and we'd run out of space, a woman, who was bringing youth to the study, allowed us to meet in her church's fellowship hall.

But after a while, her church decided to build a new building, and they needed to use the fellowship hall, so we moved to the Baptist Center.

I kept thinking and meditating on how we could get financial support for Jaime. I thought of how the churches had supported Paul and his ministry and the different churches he went to. I thought, *Well, if our church – Pleasant Hill Baptist Church – has people, who are willing to give a little money each month to support Jaime and his ministry, it would be great!* I realized that sometimes when you mention money, you may receive flack. *What can we do? What can we call this?* Really, the Lord answered me with two words: Invest Five. Hopefully, people would be willing to sacrifice a hamburger and drink each week to donate $5 (or $20 - $25 monthly) to the ministry.

My husband preached a message about Paul and provided examples. We invited the congregation to Invest Five by setting aside a weekly amount and giving it once a month designated to Jaime's ministry. Because we were approved as a ministry, all contributions were tax deductible. Quite a few people accepted our invitation, and the first month, we collected $1000. Over time, some of our contributors have passed away, but many of our widows and others still faithfully give the ministry $25 each month. I feel the Lord answered my prayers by giving me Invest Five as a way to support Jaime Torres Ministries.

The Bible study has proven to be extremely successful and rewarding. We have people attending on Friday nights who wouldn't come to a church on a regular basis. Then, of course, sometimes the Bible study helps people to get involved in their churches. It's a starting place for some people who are unchurched and facing issues. They learn people will accept them for who they are and as they are. They receive encouragement, so it is a good ministry.

We knew we had to get out and get involved in the community. Jaime's heart is in prison ministry and that is where he loves to minister. Scottie Barnes with Forgiven Ministry had spoken about her prison ministry at our church, so I had her contact information. I telephoned Scottie and told her about Jaime's ministry. I explained we were interested in getting involved in other ministries, and perhaps she could give us pointers. Jaime, Larry, and I met with Scottie and her husband at Abele's Family Restaurant in Morganton. That's how we began working with Forgiven Ministry.

***

If I were to try and describe my relationship with Jaime, I'd say it is like Abraham's wife, Sara, in the Bible. I didn't know the Lord was going to give me another son after I was seventy years old. I tell Jaime, "You are the most expensive son I have ever had." He just grins when I say that because he knows it is true. He's always saying, "Mama, I need this," or "Mama, I need that," or "Mama, I need you to do this."

This isn't meant to be bragging, but looking back, if we hadn't been able to help Jaime, I don't know how he would have made it. There are more people helping him now than for a while, but he really had to depend on us. The ministry is trying to pay him a monthly salary; we are doing this by faith. His family needs a housing allowance because rent is very expensive this day and time. Jaime wants to live in Burke County because this is where his ministry is. He's also the chaplain at the police department, and he was recently named the head chaplain for the Burke-Catawba District Confinement Center. These are voluntary positions, not paid positions.

And I'm not just talking about finances. Larry and I have known people who could help Jaime, like the lady who helped with the paperwork for the ministry or the lady who helped us meet in the fellowship hall at her church. It seems ironic that Larry took Jaime to meet the Director of Missions at the Baptist Center where we are now holding the Bible studies on Friday nights. The director recognized the ministry work we are doing; he doesn't charge us anything even though we are non-denominational and not Baptist.

Jaime's wife, Grace, immigrated to the U.S. in December 2013. Their son, JonathanDavid was born on September 22, 2014. He has been a grandchild for Larry and me. And now with Isabella Grace being born February 2, 2018, we have another grandchild. We do our best to make their young lives happy.

I've also felt like God gave me another responsibility. Jaime says he didn't have a mother and father, really. Because his mother spoke Spanish, and they spoke English at school, he got discouraged and dropped out of school at an early age. Then his mother sent him to live with his father where he got into the drug business. He didn't have a two-parent family to guide him and instruct him is what I'm trying to say. I'm sure his mother loved him with a mother's love, but she had four other children by Jaime's step-father. She stayed busy with them, while his step-father shunned Jaime. He was left out.

I've actually tried to fulfill the mother role in his life by helping him, instructing him, and supporting and promoting his ministry. He doesn't always want to accept my advice. It's just like when you have children, and you tell them what you think is best for them. They don't always agree with you. I've never wanted Jaime to think I was trying to control him. I've even said that to him. "Jaime, I'm not trying to control you. I'm just trying to help you. I just want to give you instruction. As we get older, we gain a little bit of wisdom we can share." If I think he is doing something bad in the long run, I will bring it to his attention by saying, "Jaime, you shouldn't do that," or "Jaime, you should do this." I believe the Lord put me in his life to help him.

Since knowing Jaime, I've repeatedly said, "If you had told me two years prior to Jaime coming into our lives that I was going to reach out to a Hispanic person and accept him into our lives, I would have said, 'You've lost your mind.'" But we never know what plans God has for our lives. It seems really strange in some ways because Larry says Jaime and I are a lot alike. Even Jaime says, "Mama, you could have birthed me."

If we go out to eat pizza, I'll say, "I don't like mushrooms, and I don't like olives." Jaime will agree. "That's right, Mama. I don't like mushrooms or olives either."

And if we get into an argument, Larry will say, "You're both hard-headed. You've got the same DNA." He knows that each of us wants to win, and neither of us wants to give in.

I believe our lives can be compared to a puzzle. We don't always know how to connect the pieces, but we need to try to fit the pieces together as they are supposed to go. Let me give you an example of what I'm saying.

Our home is located close to the house where I grew up. It was my parents' home and we rent the house out. About eight years ago, we had spent a lot of money and done a lot of work on the house. We didn't want to rent it to just anybody. Larry's sister, Shirley, was paying rent in Lenoir, so we encouraged her to move into the house and gave her a better rate than what she was paying because we knew she would take care of it.

Jaime came to our home with us sometimes when we'd come to check on our own house while it was empty during the time we lived in the parsonage. We introduced Jaime to Shirley, who had been diagnosed with cancer. Jaime began going and praying with Shirley. This is how Jaime met Sara, her granddaughter. After Shirley died, Sara got on drugs. One day when we had come to mow the grass because we were moving back in, Sara's mother stopped and asked me, "Do you think Jaime would talk to Sara? I'm really worried about her."

"Yes, I'm sure he would be glad to talk to Sara."

So the next time Jaime came to visit us, we called and asked Sara to come to our house. We told her Jaime was here and wanted to see her. Sara liked Jaime and was impressed when he would come and talk with her grandmother and pray with her and sing to her. Actually, Sara had asked him to say something at her grandmother's funeral because she and her grandmother were very close.

When Sara arrived, Jaime took her into our living room. He said, "Girl! You're going to have to get it together, or you're going to die." He encouraged her to come to the next Bible study. From there, he knew she needed professional help and got her admitted into Grace Home in Santee, S.C. Now Sara is serving the Lord and is clear of drugs.

This is why I say life is like a puzzle. If we hadn't met Jaime, and if Jaime hadn't met Shirley, and if Sara hadn't met Jaime and had confidence in him and accepted his help, I don't know where she'd be today. I don't know if she'd even be alive today. You just have to fit the pieces together.

***

I was born and raised in a Christian family in Granite Falls, N.C. To this day, I tell people I am so glad I had a godly influence in my life and had parents who taught me right from wrong. They made sure I was always in church and involved. I am thankful for that.

I was attending Bible school when I was around eleven years-old. I was fond of our preacher and stayed at his house a lot. I could walk to the church because it was close enough to where I lived. I remember him talking to me, and I got under conviction and could hardly wait for the invitation. I had always been in church, but that day when they presented the plan of salvation, it clicked with me. I think I was the first one at the altar.

Later, as I emerged from the church doors and began walking down the road, it was as if the sun was shining brighter. Because my parents wanted to be certain I knew what I was doing, they had me wait to be baptized, but I knew there was a change in myself.

Soon after I was saved, my parents began attending a

Methodist church when there was a division in our Baptist church. Nothing was much different from our church, but we didn't join that church – we only visited it. Later, I was actually baptized at the church where Larry got saved -- Community Baptist Church. Both of us were baptized in the river because the small church didn't have a baptismal. Being baptized in a river is a cool thing, and I can attest it was cool. I was about to freeze to death. Being close to the mountains, the water was cold enough to take your breath away.

I met Larry when I was a junior in high school. We went to rival schools. Larry was at Hudson High School, and I attended Granite Falls High School. Now, the two schools have consolidated and is known as South Caldwell. After we graduated from high school, we got married and began our family. We've been married fifty nine years.

As I look back, I can see there is purpose in our relationship with Jaime just from the things, which have happened in our family and the things I've seen happen in other families. I've witnessed people giving testimonies of how their lives have been changed. We had two other girls who came to our ministry and went through drug programs. They are doing well now. One of the girls recently stated, "A year ago, I was out on the street. Now I'm working for the state." Her life has turned around. Another girl went to Grace Home and then to Wilmington to receive more help. She came to the Bible study and seems to be doing well. I've witnessed things that have occurred because of Jaime's ministry.

As for me, I've never had an opportunity to worship with people of another race. I've always been in a white environment, so I've learned to appreciate the Hispanic and African-American people. I've never been a prejudiced person, but I have learned to love these people more and to accept these people more. In the Friday night Bible study, they refer to us as Mama and Papa, just like Jaime. In turn, God has given us an opportunity to be a witness for them.

I'm so glad this book is being written. Jaime has talked about having a book written for a long time. Just the other day, Jaime said to me, "Mama, if you hadn't known Scottie Barnes, and if Scottie Barnes hadn't known Sandi Edwards and the Westmorelands, and if Sandi hadn't had a Christian publisher, then this book might not have happened."

It's just another piece of the puzzle.

Chapter Thirty-Three

Raquel Henderson
We can count on him.

The Republic of Costa Rica in Central America is my home country. That's where I grew up in an extremely religious Pentecostal church. Girls wore long skirts and couldn't wear makeup. In addition, members didn't go to the movies, didn't go skating, and girls couldn't cut their hair. But as a child, these strict tenets didn't bother me. I loved the church because it gave me a firm foundation and great teachings. But at the age of eleven, I began drinking alcohol behind my parents' backs. My country is very different from here, so it was a lot easier for me to begin drinking there. By the time I was fourteen, I was drinking heavily, and by the time I was sixteen, I was struggling with alcoholism. My school friends and I drank to an excess and became intoxicated three days a week.

On Mother's Day (always on August 15 in my country), I left school, hung out with my friends, and became intoxicated. On the way home, I felt weird because people stared at me. I wondered if they could smell the alcohol oozing from my pores. When I got home, I found a note Mom had left along with money to take a taxi to church that night. There was some type of church activity happening, but I had forgotten about it. I stepped into the shower and allowed the hot water to pour over my body. I tried to decide whether or not I was going to church. That's when and where God began ministering to me, and it was then and there He changed me. My decision was to attend church that night. I didn't drink again, and from that night on, all I wanted was to be baptized and serve God. And I did well for about a year and a half.

When I turned seventeen, I wanted to date a guy from high school, but because he wasn't from my church, it wasn't to be allowed. I was teaching a Sunday school class at the time, as well as being involved in other church activities, so when the pastor and his wife confronted me and explained I was going to be disciplined because I was breaking the bylaws of the church, I got mad and walked out of the church, never to return. My teenage rebellion followed me into my young adult years. I stayed away from church and religion for fourteen years.

My parents moved to Philadelphia in 1998, but my mom didn't like it. She was used to the lovely countryside in Costa Rica. One of our cousins had married a missionary and had moved to Morganton, so they invited my parents to come and visit them. Once Mom and Dad saw the mountains, they fell in love and moved to Morganton. When I finished high school, I came to visit my parents in America. I quickly learned Mom was pregnant at the age of forty-six. Knowing she would need my assistance, I decided to stay longer than I'd anticipated. Then I decided to stay a little longer and a little longer. I never left and have been here for twenty years.

As long as I can remember, my mom has always invited people to her house to eat. She loves to cook for people – especially pastors and brothers and sisters from church. On the day I met Jaime for the first time, there was a missionary from Costa Rica and a pastor from Panama, who were visiting the U.S. and staying with my parents. Mom had invited them, Jaime, and me to eat lunch with her. I had not attended church for a long time, not because I was angry with God, but because I just didn't have an interest in forming a deeper relationship with Him.

I was uncomfortable being here with these ministers. For

eight years, I had been living with a man who was abusive to me, plus when you aren't attending church, you're used to people approaching you and reminding you, "You need to get your life right with God" especially if your parents are believers and are vested in the kingdom of God. It had become an expectation for people to reproach me about not going to church, and of course, I wasn't disappointed this time.

The two men asked me if I had been attending church. So the meal began with me feeling defensive. But Jaime just sat quietly beside me as we shared our meal. Then he began talking about God in a different way. He shared how he had been in prison and "out in the world" and all that God had done to change him. For the first time in my life, I felt like he was a different kind of person – not the usual religious Christian who just wants to look down on everybody else.

Jaime had caught my attention, and his conversation stayed with me over the next few months. When his wife, Grace, immigrated to America from Ecuador around Christmastime, I saw Jaime again when Mom had invited them to her house. That's when God began transforming my life. God was dealing with me – calling me back to Him.

The first thing God put on my heart was the question, "Why don't you find out about Jaime's Bible study?" It was true I didn't know where he was holding it or when. I sent Jaime a text message, which he quickly answered, giving me the requested information. So I began attending Jaime's Bible studies on Friday nights.

The Bible speaks of how the Word of God is like a river of living waters. I remember feeling differently than when I'd attended churches before. Even though I'd grown up in the church and had been surrounded by the knowledge of God, sitting in Jaime's Bible study was so refreshing. I felt like I'd been wandering around for many years but now had found a place of nourishment. I had found a place of living waters.

I recall sitting there staring at Jaime and imagining I was one of the twelve disciples with Jesus. I heard the Gospel delivered in a different way – non-traditionally, non-religiously, and non-judgmentally. As I left the Bible study that first night, I couldn't wait until the next Friday evening when I could come again and receive more.

From the first time I met Jaime until now, I have considered him not only a great man of God and a spiritual leader for many, but a friend. He is a person who always makes himself available at a friend level. It never mattered if I called him at two in the morning or at midnight or at one in the morning, he always took my calls and was available to talk to me about whatever was on my mind or in my heart. It was always amazing to hear the wisdom and love that God gave him to share with me. I can remember talking about any circumstance I was facing and never feeling judged. On the contrary, he would tell me to take my time and not to allow anyone to pressure me into progressing or achieving anything according to his/her time or advice. "Just allow God to do things in His own time in your life." Having Jaime tell me this took the pressure off my shoulders and gave me freedom from the judgement of other people.

On the subsequent Friday nights at the Bible studies, every word Jaime spoke was as if the Holy Spirit had given him the words to speak exactly to the circumstances or difficulties I was facing or had gone through that week. To me, this was mind-blowing to know a person whom the Holy Spirit would give so much revelation and speak to my life in such a powerful way at a time, which truly was difficult for me. No one knew – not even my family – I was living with an abusive man. I couldn't trust anybody; I just wanted to get out of the relationship. God talked to me and confirmed so many things that strengthened me, so I left that relationship and met my husband, Jonathan Henderson, at Jaime Torres Ministries. Jaime officiated our marriage.

217

Having Jaime's support through everything I've been through has been amazing. You usually don't experience this feeling in many churches. Honestly, it is very difficult to find. I believe pastors have very hard jobs, and it is difficult to minister to many people the way Jaime does because they have so many people for whom they are responsible. Personally, I can attest that the way Jaime has always approached me and cared for me has been more than just as a spiritual leader or spiritual father. He has been a brother in Christ.

Never once have I felt that I couldn't come to him and be 100% honest as I shared whatever I was going through without feeling like he would dodge me. I've only felt free to communicate and discuss my issues with him. I've never felt he would judge me or pass condemnation. When you are struggling with challenges in your life and trying to overcome them or feeling ashamed about situations that are not under your control, it is good to know a person can receive God's love. The last thing I ever felt was judgement.

The wisdom and love God gave Jaime when he first met and ministered to me was necessary and wise. At the time, I wasn't willing to go to church on a permanent basis. Sure, I had visited churches for a few weeks before getting discouraged and quitting. But the entire setting of Jaime Torres Ministries was comfortable and not the same as what I left so many years ago. It was different, so it was easy to allow him to minister to my life and help me.

God came to perform a 180-degree transformation in my life. He changed me and got me out of the abusive relationship, which I didn't have the strength to leave on my own. He brought a man of God into my life who loves me and respects me. He restored everything I had lost over the years – the respect of my family and finances. God used all the years to fulfill and transform my life.

I believe Jaime understands many of the things that have

happened in my life. The love and support I've received during the four years since I first heard his ministry are true blessings in my life. If I were to call him or leave a message, saying, "Hey brother, I need prayer," or "I need to talk," he would never turn me away. I'm grateful a person can have the level of love for people the way Jaime does. He dedicates his life to honoring God. He is all about honoring God. People are imperfect; we fail one another sometimes. But when we love God and do things to honor God, we can love imperfect people without allowing our own emotions to get in the way. I'm grateful Jaime can be that person.

When it came to making a decision about getting married, I was afraid. From the time I met my husband until we were to be married was only a period of three months. I was afraid of commitment. The night before we were to marry, I went to Jaime's house at 10:00 p.m. and sat on his couch and cried. He patiently listened, advised me, and gave me many scriptures that were powerful. I still hold onto them. With honor and glory for God, I have been blessed with a good marriage. I never thought a love like ours existed, but I feel when you honor God and obey Him, He can bring those things into your life. And I believe if Jaime had been a different type of person, more judgmental or religious, I would have completely shut him off that first day in my mom's house. I was defensive, hurt, and couldn't allow anyone to mind my business or tell me anything about how I was living my life. But when Jaime approached me, he didn't approach me with that mindset. Instead, he approached me with love, understanding, and wisdom. There was no reason to feel defensive with him.

I've always allowed Jaime in, and he's always known what to say because the Holy Spirit gives him the words I need at the right time. Jaime means a lot to Jonathan and me. We love his wife and children; we always can count on him.

Chapter Thirty-Four

Reverend Glenn Usry

Meeting someone like Jaime was a breath of fresh air.

A friend of mine, Pastor Steven Dietz, of Resurrection Church in Hickory, North Carolina, told me he knew a gentleman whom he thought I really would like to meet. He said, "He has your kind of flavor – your kind of vibe. I would like to send him, so you two can meet." So he did. Pastor Dietz sent Jaime Torres to me on a Wednesday, while I was conducting a Bible study at the Christian Outreach of the Piedmont, where I am the Pastor in Statesville, North Carolina.

Jaime and I met, we fellowshipped, and he shared his testimony with me. I was excited to make his acquaintance. By having come from New York and the type of background I had experienced, I was immediately blessed by Jaime's testimony because of several things, which had happened in my home. My brother had been incarcerated after getting involved with drugs -- selling and using. My father was an alcoholic. There were so many different things, which were encouraging to hear in his testimony of how God had brought him out of prison and out of his old lifestyle. These are the things that drew us together. Now, there isn't a month that goes by when we're not communicating a couple of times, if not just praying for each other.

After spending more time with Jaime, I asked him to share his testimony. There were some people in our church who needed to hear the message that there is hope after the lifestyle in which they had been involved. They needed to know they weren't alone in having a criminal record and things in their past, which had gotten them involved in drugs. So to have Jaime come and share his testimony has been a blessing for our congregation. He frequents here from time to time to share his testimony or just to be a part of the service. We are glad to have him here and glad we made the connection. In addition, the Lord has shared certain things with me to share with Jaime, so he is aware God has tremendous things planned for his life from an international standpoint.

I grew up in Hempstead, New York, and spent a lot of time in Jamaica, Queens. I began following my brother's lead and getting involved in drugs to a certain degree, but the grace of God was on my life in a heavy way.

I got saved when I was fourteen years-old, but I didn't realize it. I had been frustrated most of my life by my father, who was an alcoholic and was abusive to my mom and the whole family. Even so, he was a good man and introduced me to the Bible. One of the first things he showed me in the Bible was the Ten Commandments. The commandment we promised was to "honor our father and mother." Of course, I had a problem promising that. How could I honor this man who chases us out of the house at 3:00 in the morning? There we'd be, out in the street, looking for a place to stay. This had happened on several occasions.

Sometimes, my father would hit my mom and be unfaithful to her or do other things of that nature. I often encouraged my mom not to stay with him. At the same time, my brother saw our father's lifestyle, and that's what pushed him into the street where he became a drug user, as well as a drug pusher. By living in that volatile environment, I gravitated toward using drugs – mainly out of curiosity and the need to fit in with my friends. So I experimented until I was sixteen.

By the time I reached fourteen, there had been several

episodes of the police coming to the house whenever fights broke out in the house. I found myself lying on the floor one day and asking Jesus to come into my life. I hadn't been going to church or reading the Bible, so it had to be amazing grace. That's when God revealed this truth to me: My father was not a problem person; he was a person with a problem.

After my prayers on the floor that night, I didn't feel that much of a change or difference, but two years later, around 1977, I was walking home from middle school. That's when I fully understood that according to the Word, what I did by surrendering my life to Jesus and repenting, I had been saved. I heard the Holy Ghost reveal this to me. I hadn't realized it because I wasn't going to church and learning how to become a disciple.

It wasn't long after this experience when my mom received a phone call from my aunt who lives in Denver, Colorado. She asked if I could come and spend the summer with her to get away from all the abuse and drugs. I had other relatives who were getting involved in drugs, and she feared I was getting ready "to get out there, too."

My mom and I were walking around at the Kennedy Airport and were about to board the plane. When I looked back, I noticed Mom wasn't coming with me.

She called after me. "I'm not going with you. You're going to get away from all this madness."

I couldn't believe Mom was putting me on that plane, but she did. And I couldn't believe I was riding alone in a plane for the first time and flying three hours to Denver, Colorado. When I arrived and left the plane, my aunt met me. She showed me all the mountains and took me on tours. The view was shocking because I had never seen mountains or had gone up and touched a cloud. It was mind-blowing. That's when I began to say, "There is a God."

While I was there, I began training to get my body in shape, so I could play varsity basketball when I returned to New York. One day while I was out playing ball, shooting hoops in a broken-down, abandoned schoolyard, I saw my reflection in a window. I heard the Spirit of God speaking to me again, "That which I called you to do I need you to do now."

I thought, *I'm too young for this. I can't do that.* I knew He specifically meant pastoring. *I barely go to church, don't really want to go to church, and You're calling me to be a pastor. It's crazy!*

God had called me, and while I was riding on the plane heading homeward and staring at the Rockies, I accepted the call to ministry. I looked at those mountains and thought, *Man this is too beautiful. God is too great. There is no place I can run to.*

I returned to the church where I had attended every now and then. I asked the pastor if he could share with me because I had received a call into the ministry. The pastor said he could see God's grace on me. He didn't sit me down and go through a lot of stuff. He simply said, "You learn by doing." Later he became a bishop in the African Methodist Episcopal Zion Church.

Following his advice, I became a student of the Word. I went to Bible study and church and didn't miss for any reason. I just took off and grew and grew. I never missed a revival or any of that stuff. I just kept on growing.

The pastor and I had planned to begin a ministry in New York, but when I heard about Statesville and all the drug problems and other things, I felt another calling. The Lord was calling me to leave the Methodist church and to start a non-denominational church in Statesville where I could focus on this city and start several ministries which God placed on my heart. This included starting a school, a men's home, and a recreational center for kids. God did all this for us! He is amazing!

Meeting someone like Jaime was a breath of fresh air. Even

though I went to seminary and he didn't, the most important lessons I learned were outside of seminary. And by the time I got to seminary, I'd already read the Bible a couple of times. Seminary was something I did for my mom because no one in her life had ever finished college, much less graduate school. So I went to college and ended up getting an academic scholarship, which was something I was told I'd never get. I went to graduate school at the Theological Seminary and never paid a cent. My belief is this was because of the scripture, "Honor thy father and mother."

I had honored my mother by doing what she wanted me to do. I had honored my father by realizing he wasn't a problem person; he was a person with a problem. I remembered every good thing my father had told me even when he was drunk. I later discovered his father had been an alcoholic as well. He had been a real embarrassment to my father. Sometimes he'd get drunk, go outside, and direct traffic. These experiences really scared my father. It gave me compassion for alcoholic people.

By seeing what my brother had gone through, it gave me compassion for drug- addicted people. But there is no place for selling drugs. And now I am able to understand another angle, which I am crazy about and passionate about – people who are abusive to women, even though my father was. Now, I have a better understanding and empathy. Even though my father was physically hitting my mother, he was really striking out at his own life. He was constantly frustrated. There is a fine line, but

I hate the fact people sell drugs.

I hate the fact people abuse women.

I hate the fact people cheat on women.

I hate the fact people go to jail and are incarcerated.

My experiences have helped me to gain an understanding of why people get in these situations. Jaime's testimony is the assurance you can come out of whatever you are in.

***

Today, I am the caregiver for my mother who is eighty-seven years-old. She is battling with dementia, but she is an amazing woman. She isn't handicapped; she is handicapable. That's my word. Everything in the house to eat is cold because I do the cooking and don't allow her to have access to anything hot, like a stove. It's only turned on when I arrive. But even though she is forgetful and has some physical things going on like a bad case of diverticulitis, she goes into the kitchen to eat, locks her doors, and puts herself to bed. Mom is driven to do for herself because she wants to be alone. She's always been like that. Every now and then she'll slip up and think I'm her husband, but it's only for a short period of time until she bounces back because of the prayers of the Saints and her own prayers. I don't want to place her in a nursing home – she deserves to live at home. As long as Mom can remember who I am and who the kids are and is able to safely perform the tasks she currently does, we'll be fine. God is amazing!

My mother has lived a hard life. That's why I've rolled with her and am still rolling with her. My baby sister, who was my only sister, died of cancer when she was only thirteen. That put my mother on a downward spiral. She never had a relationship with her own mother when she grew up. It was toxic. My father's alcoholism took him out early because of cirrhosis of the liver. But he was proud of what I'd become. My father didn't have a relationship with his father. My brother passed away when he was thirty-six. He was an IV drug user and ended up contracting the AIDS virus. But the good news is I was able to lead both my father and brother to the Lord before they passed.

For the end of this chapter, I'd like to share a poem God gave me one day when I was in undergraduate school. I was sitting in class and bored. I began thinking, *I've got to get out of here.* Then I began reminiscing about my life and was given this poem. I think it describes Jaime's life and testimony.

225

Don't Give Up

The dark clouds of today can wholly dim your view.
The bright skies of tomorrow means that you pursue.
To stay within the race there is a winner's cup.
Never ever lose your hope.
Don't you dare give up.
 If you are discouraged, becoming faint in heart,
And trouble steals your courage before you even start
Just strive for your life's goals;
You know they're right for you.
Keep your determination.
Great will see you through.
Cast not away your confidence.
Hold to your faithful dream.
Your vision of success in life, you'll reach although it seems
The odds are all against you to bring you to an end.
Face your trials with bravery, I say to you my friends.
The dark clouds of today can wholly dim your view.
The bright skies of tomorrow means that you pursue.
Put your total trust in God, for He will fill your cup.
Never ever lose your hope.
Don't you dare give up.

Reverend Glenn Usry

Chapter Thirty-Five

Caron Cline

His is nothing short of a miracle.

I met Jamie Torres on January 27, 2013, which was his birthday. He came to our church to speak for Baptist's Men's Day. I had heard about Jaime from my mom and dad, Reverend Larry and Meredith Cline, but I had yet to meet him. And to be honest with you, when I met him that Sunday morning in the balcony of the church where I operate the sound system, he was nothing that I expected.

As Jaime approached to hand me a CD to play during his part of the program, I noticed how different he seemed. As we exchanged pleasantries and talked for a short while, I began thinking, *Boy, there is something really different about this guy*, aside from being friendly, of course. When it was time for Jaime to speak, he arose in the pulpit, and I began playing the song he'd instructed me to play. Then he did the first thing he does everywhere he goes to preach. He began singing and beckoned the congregation to join him. The minute I heard him begin speaking, I thought, *The power of God is on this guy.* I could feel it, and I could see it. Jaime was different.

I remember the service being remarkable even though I can't remember what he preached about. I just remember thinking, *This guy has the power of God on him.* He was a fresh wind in our church that day, which isn't to say our church was dead. He was somebody very different.

As time passed, Mom and Dad got to know Jaime better,

and I got to know him, as well. He began visiting my parents' home whenever I'd be there, so I began talking to him. One thing led to another, and Jaime became more involved in ministries in the area, and as a result, Mom, Dad, and I began to get involved in those ministries. I wasn't around him as much as my parents were, but he began attending their church and performing different tasks.

On Sunday nights, Dad would begin the service by reading a passage of scripture. Then he would teach about the passage before asking the congregation, "What's your take on this? What do you think? How does this scripture apply to your life?" At that point, he'd turn to Jaime and say, "Jaime, let's get your perspective on this scripture."

Jaime seemed pleased to do this. He'd reply, "Well, I believe God was saying ...." Then he'd search through his Bible to locate other scriptures to support his beliefs. This was an open forum where people could ask questions, make comments, or discuss issues they were facing or Biblical questions they had. Dad and Jaime took turns going back and forth, answering the people's questions and addressing their comments. People were excited to have this opportunity because it was an unusual thing.

Jaime is very unorthodox, and that can be a stressor for people who are really religious. He reminds you of somebody with a simple faith – a child-like faith. If God says something in His Word, Jaime doesn't try to explain it away or believe it won't happen again. Jaime believes that God does what He says He will do. Sadly, this is rather unique when you hear some people preach and minister today. It shouldn't be unique, but it is.

As time went on, I began to get to know Jaime better. Within a year, my mother had the vision to birth Jaime Torres Ministries. Jaime and friends already held a Bible study on Friday nights in an apartment, so my parents began attending the session. When the participants multiplied and outgrew the apartment, Dad used his connections to find another place,

Praise Assembly's Fellowship Hall, where I was able to attend twice. Soon, the group needed a larger place, so they began using the Baptist Associational Building in Morganton, and the Bible study took off and began to grow because of having more room. Fortunately, it worked out where I could begin attending the study more often. By knowing Jaime and attending the Bible study, I was introduced to different people, certainly different cultures. I've never been a prejudiced person, but like so many people, it's difficult to find opportunities to spend time with people of other cultures. As we go through our daily routines, you just don't think about it.

In our Bible study, we had Hispanic, Asian, African Americans, and white people. I got to learn about different cultures and a lot about people I'd never been able to spend time with. I'm sure they learned more about white people, too. The other aspect was, by coming from more of a mainline denomination, a Baptist church, I was exposed to some things but not as many pertaining to gifts of the Spirit or things of the Spirit. Definitely, not like I have been since meeting Jaime. He has opened up a different world for me -- culturally and spiritually. This new world has changed me in a lot of ways and, hopefully, made me a lot less orthodox. I would describe Jaime's and my relationship as more family-like. He always says he is my parents' son, and I'm his sister. So I consider him as a brother.

I work for Quality Oil and manage some gasoline stations. Jaime hasn't done this in a long time, but he used to go by some of the stations and ask, "Do you know Caron Cline?" Repeatedly, he'd receive the same answer: "Oh, yes! We know Caron." Then he'd smile and say, "She's my sister." When their faces would change to puzzlement, and they looked at him in a funny way, he'd hurriedly explain, "I'm the black sheep of the family."

Jaime has a spiritual gift that I can't explain. I guess you would call it a Word of God. He has a discerning spirit. Jaime can hit the nail on the head. I've invited several people to attend the Bible studies on Friday nights. When they agreed, I was careful never to tell Jaime anything about them; some of these folks were facing big problems in their lives. Almost every time I've done that, he'd end up speaking directly to them and telling them things that addressed the problems they were having when he didn't know anything beforehand. Usually, these people would become mad at me, asking "Why did you tell him everything about me?"

I'd quickly and honestly explain, "I didn't tell him anything about you."

Jaime's gift -- whatever you want to call it – is a gift of discernment. I don't mean he does this to every single person, but you can tell before he does. He'll get quiet for a second, and then he'll go directly to that person and address them. It's easy to tell by the puzzled look on their faces – even people I don't know – that he has pegged it, and they can't figure out how he would know. Then he'll share a word with them that the Lord has given him to give to him / her.

One night there was a married couple attending the Bible study. They hadn't been married long. I'd seen them once or twice, but they hadn't come very often. Jaime knew who they were, but I don't believe he knew them. Jaime was speaking when all of a sudden, he turned to stare at the man. Jaime said, "You're just now getting over a depression. You were depressed all of your life until you married her."

The man didn't say a word. The wife looked shocked. Finally, she spoke aloud, "That's the truth. That's the truth." Jaime turned around and continued preaching where he'd left off. I've seen this great gift put in operation many times.

Now, Jaime can be as stubborn as a mule. Sometimes that's good, and sometimes it can be bad. As a Board member of Jaime Torres Ministries, the Board will discuss and decide on an issue that needs to be handled. But if Jaime strongly believes God has told him something different, he will emphatically say, "No. God is telling me to …. So this is what we're going to do."

The Board respects him and his beliefs, so we'll reply, "Well, if God has told you that, and you're sure, then that is what we need to do." We don't want to make a wrong decision.

Then there are times when he will bend if he hasn't received a direct word from the Lord, and he'll say, "Well, y'all know better about that than I do." He submits to the Board to handle more business-related decisions. But when there is a spiritual aspect, he won't back down if he believes God is instructing him. We want to follow the vision God wants.

Jaime told my mother for a year, "God is going to give me a car."

After a while, my mother said, "I don't know about that."

His response was, "Mama, God is going to give me a car."

Sure enough, a dealership gave him a second-hand car with some mileage– the first car he received for his ministry. Then a year afterward, another dealership gave him a second-hand van, which had some mileage but more room for his growing family. It is amazing how God has moved in Jaime's life. I don't think I've ever known anyone in my life who has the faith Jaime has. If I had a quarter of his faith, then, of course, the Bible says I could move a mountain. Jaime constantly says, "I'm a faith man. I'm a faith man." And he really is. He believes that nothing is too hard for God. Jaime will do anything and everything that will glorify God's name.

I have seen Jaime pray over people who have asked him to pray for them when they want to have children. He has a special, unique gift. I've seen him pray over several couples who didn't seem to be fertile and failed to get pregnant. Then the women have gotten pregnant! I believe there is nothing too hard for God, too, but I don't step out in faith as much as I should.

Throughout the Bible, we read about God doing wondrous things. He allows us to partner with Him in many ways. When

God shows us something, we believe Him because we have seen it. But there are just some things He directs us to do that we can't see. We get in trouble when we decide that we want something now, and we don't check with Him before we go about our way and make it happen. We need to remember God can do anything and will in His own time.

***

I was raised in church and made a profession of faith when I was nine years-old. Some people say, "Well, you probably were saved then." But I think I just didn't understand what the significance was and just repeated the words because I wanted to be baptized. Everyone else was doing it.

When I became a teen, I wasn't in a lot of trouble, but I was a typical rebellious teenager. When I turned sixteen, I didn't want to go to church because I no longer had a real interest in church. I had a lot of friends who partied – the typical partying you did back in the '70s in high school – nothing compared to what partying is today. By the time I was eighteen, I had moved farther and farther away from the church and the Lord, so I didn't go to church. I'm sure there probably were a lot of people praying for me, but I wasn't conscious of that.

In 1990 when I was twenty-eight-years-old and the Gulf War happened because Iraq invaded Kuwait, interestingly enough, I began to watch the events on the news. These events made me think, especially when I'd hear people talking about the "end times." Well, that began to click with me. I thought, *Wait a minute. I was taught all of this in church. Maybe this is the end times. Maybe this is typical.* Obviously, the Lord was dealing with me, but I didn't realize it at the time.

The amazing thing was I lived in Hickory – about twenty-three miles from Morganton, where my parents lived. I was never at Mama and Dad's on a Saturday night, and I can't remember why I was there on a Saturday night in August 1990, right after the invasion. There I was sitting and watching television when the phone rang. Dad answered the phone; I didn't pay a lot of attention to what he was saying and had no idea who he was talking to. But when I heard him say, "Yeah, this is lining up with prophesy. The second coming could be around the corner," I didn't act like I was listening, but I was hearing every word he said.

These words began to shape me. *Man, this is real*, I thought. That's when God began to work on my heart. I didn't say anything to anybody even though I couldn't get it off of my mind. When I went to bed that Saturday night, I couldn't sleep. I kept thinking about the words. The Lord began to tell me, "You're not ready. You're not ready. You're not ready."

I began to sweat it, and it bothered me for a couple of days. But remember, a lot of the time, the enemy will help you, which he did. So I didn't think about it; it left my mind. But oddly enough, the following Saturday night, I was back at Mama and Daddy's house. I repeat. Never ever was I at my parents' house on Saturday nights, but now, I had been there two weeks in a row. I didn't know why I was there. The exact same things began happening. I was sitting there watching television when the telephone rang. Dad answered it and had almost an identical conversation with the unknown person as he'd had the previous week with the other unknown person. I was listening, and I was shaken, but I didn't say anything to them.

When I left that night, my parents had no idea I was a basket case inside. The following day was Sunday; I actually worked in my office, but the entire day, I felt what people might refer to as the *Holy Ghost conviction*. I didn't know what it was, but I felt like I had a fever; I felt sick. I remember arriving at my home in Hickory around 3:00 p.m. That's when I began to walk the floor. I thought I was going to die if I didn't do something, but I didn't know what that something was. The Lord was pressing me, and I kept hearing a voice, "You need the Lord. You need the Lord."

233

When I finally said, "Yes," and received the Lord and asked Him to forgive my sins, it felt like a fever broke in my body. I felt something completely change in the speed of a heartbeat, and I remember thinking, *I'm going to church tonight.*

I hadn't been to church in ten years, but I went. I'm sure everyone wondered what in the world I was doing there on a Sunday night. I shared that I'd gotten right with the Lord and had gotten saved.

When I look back on that night, August 26, 1990, it was amazing. God really dealt with me even though I was hard-headed and stubborn. We all have a choice to say "Yes," or "No," but looking back then, I felt like I had no choice. I was going to die if I didn't change my life; God changed my life. It was wild. But the very next day, the enemy attacked me. I've struggled just like everyone does. I've even asked, "Is this real? Is this not real?"

That's when God gave me a great desire to read the Bible. I wanted to know what the Bible said. I began to read every chance I got – all the time. I read all the way to Revelation in eight or nine months. God really has taken me on a great journey in these twenty-eight years. There is no doubt that God was calling me and drawing me to Him. We know God knows from the beginning who is going to receive Him.

As for my relationship with Jaime, I hope I mean something to Jaime and his family. Since we've been together for five years, I've seen a lot of things happen, especially JonathanDavid's birth and Isabella's birth. We've been tied up together, and I've adopted his kids as my nephew and niece. Our families celebrate Christmas together and have a family gathering at Thanksgiving. We are Jaime's family; he is part of our family.

Jaime has a lot of faith and power in prayer. When you think of his story, from the events and experiences he has endured to now, Jaime is nothing short of a miracle. He is a miracle.

Chapter Thirty-Six

Curt Johnson

To say Jaime has made an impact on my life is to put it mildly.

My younger sister, brother, and I grew up in a Church of God parsonage with our parents, who were wonderful, loving, and godly people. Our father was a Pentecostal preacher. My dad was saved and called to preach in his early thirties when I was about five. He was never reared in church; that influence came from my mom after they were married. We were taught and our mother and father modeled what it meant to live for the Lord. I was taught the scriptures and witnessed first-hand the evidences of God working in people's lives.

As I recall, I don't believe there was ever a time when I didn't believe in God / Christ. By growing up in a minister's home, I had witnessed firsthand the sacrifices and commitments that went into serving the Lord. I never saw myself going into ministry. My daddy was a good business man, but I saw him turn down many business opportunities because he told me he was called to be a pastor, not a business man or shop owner. He wanted to pastor, and he was really good at it. I knew he could have done a lot better in the secular world. I guess I may have had a little resentment about that. So pride, arrogance, selfishness, and a lust for worldly things began to dominate my young life.

It broke my parents' hearts to watch me making some of the choices I made in life. From age seventeen to thirty-four, you could say I was the quintessential *prodigal*. I can remember many times when I was in my twenties, I would awaken and find my dad standing at the foot of my bed, praying after I had been out all night and partying and doing things. He would be praying and asking the Lord to save me. But despite my unfaithfulness, God was always faithful.

In June 1990, my daughter was born. Unfortunately, her mother and I were not married, but as I reflect on it, I'm certain the moment I first gazed upon my baby's face was the beginning of a process and a plan God had to return this *prodigal* home. Tragically, my father passed away suddenly from a massive heart attack in February 1991. His death was devastating for my family and me.

My father was the greatest man I have ever known. He was strong in character and his faith in the Lord. He was my hero, as well as my best friend. Truly, I regret he never knew me as a saved man in this life, but my heart leaps with joy to imagine the moment I will see him again in the life hereafter. Because of my father's faithfulness in God, I realize my relationship with the Lord today is in big part because of him and the call on his life. It is with certainty I know my father had prayed, "Whatever it takes, Lord, please save my family." Regrettably, it may have taken his death to break through the hardness of my heart.

In 1995-1996, I endured a bitter custody battle, which I won. Then my daughter and I moved from Vicksburg, Mississippi, to Patterson, Georgia, so we could be close to my mother and sister, who had also moved to Georgia after the passing of our father. In January 1997, I remarried, thinking I had finally reached a place of complete satisfaction. I had a beautiful wife whom I loved, a wonderful daughter, a good job, and I was living close to family. Life was great for a little while, but I have found when God has a call on your life, you will never find lasting peace and satisfaction until you submit yourself to His perfect will for your life.

Despite all the good things that were occurring in my life,

there was still the desire for something more. Even though I'd been clean in order to gain custody of my daughter a few years earlier, drugs became an everyday need. This time was worse than before; I needed more to achieve the same high. I spent money as fast as I could make it. I had everything, yet I had nothing.

The first event God used to place me in a position where He could deal with me was two weeks before September 17, 1999, when I narrowly escaped being busted by the law. I was in possession of a fairly large number of narcotics. How I got through was really a miracle, but this narrow escape began a process, which had me looking at my life and where I was headed and where I was leading my family. For the sake of my family, I decided to clean up. This brings us to the night of September 17, 1999.

For a couple of days, I had not done any drugs; I didn't want to. But on this night, I was restless and uncomfortable in my bed; I tossed and turned and tried to resist the ferocious cravings in my body and the pounding thoughts in my mind to get high again. The only thing I wanted was sleep, but my body and mind wouldn't allow me to sleep. A series of events had gotten me to this place, this night, and this time. Little did I know God was about to change my life.

The night was cold with a misting rain, but I still just had to get out. I got out of bed, dressed, and headed for the front door, while whispering to my wife, "Everything is okay. I just need a walk."

Engrossed in my thoughts, I started walking down the old dirt road in front of my house. I barely noticed the cold dampness of the night. I just walked and talked; the farther I walked, the more I talked. Suddenly, I stopped and noticed I was quite a distance down the road and standing in the middle of the woods in the dark and rain, talking. That's when something amazing happened. I believe I was arguing when it dawned on me God was talking back. I was experiencing something so real and clear. God was reasoning with me. He didn't have to, but He did.

God began to reveal my life and how lost I was. He showed me the times in my past how He had kept me until this day -- not just because of me, but because of His faithfulness to my parents and because of His desire to work great things in my daughter's life. God charged me with reality, holding me personally responsible for the spiritual condition of my wife and daughter. God challenged me to become the example I had been given.

Futilely, I even attempted to argue, reminding Him I had tried to live a "Christian" lifestyle several times but had only succeeded in making myself and Him look like a fool every time. That is when I heard Him say something very clearly and distinctly in my heart.

God said, "Curt, this is what I have been waiting for you to see. You can't do it, but I can." Then He spoke something that ran right through me. "It is not by might nor power, but it is by My Spirit, says the Lord." Since then, I have discovered this verse is in Zachariah 4:6, but at the time, I had no idea if I had heard this before or if it was in the Bible.

I broke, knowing this was my time. It was now or never. With certainty, I knew there wouldn't be another opportunity. Now, I had to choose. I remained in the woods for about two and a half hours -- just talking and listening. Truly, September 17, 1999, was the beginning of my life. I had tried to *commit* to being a better person, a better Christian, but the one word that summarizes that night was submit. I had to submit. Submitting is a lot different than committing. The difference for me was I submitted. I submitted to do whatever the future held or brought. I had to lay down my aspirations. The best I could do hadn't turned out that well. I had expectations when I surrendered to the Lord, I would have peace and a resolve to it. I knew what the right decision was. I just had to submit and accept whatever life had, which in my estimation was going to be a great deal of sacrifice and self- denial and loss of friends and activities I enjoyed doing.

It sounds foolish, but as I was walking home that night, I was thinking, *I might be kind of miserable and not have fun and do without, but at least when I die I can go to heaven.* That was such a weird and false expectation because the Lord has more than exceeded my imagination or anything I could have thought of He would have for my life – nowhere near. By submitting, all the things I really wanted in my life, I've been able to do. There are many things to share about that night, but I can attest that when I returned home, I was not only wet, but a changed man. I've never been the same. Since that night, I've never done drugs. My family and I found a church we began attending, but my life didn't get any easier. It did, however, get clearer.

When I first met Jaime, I was working for the Felton Burke Automotive Group as a finance/sales manager of a pre-owned automobile lot in Jesup, Georgia, in the fall of 2000. I was a very young Christian at the time, having served the Lord for only about a year. I remember getting a call from Mr. Burke, asking me if I would take on a new guy, who had been released from the federal prison in Jesup. I remember being opposed to bringing in an ex-convict, especially one fresh out of federal prison into an already stressful job situation.

Mr. Burke said, "This fellow became a Christian while in prison and was some kind of preacher in prison."

My response was negative. "Great! That's what we need, an ex-convict with jail house religion."

Nevertheless, Mr. Burke moved from asking me to telling me Jaime Torres was going to be arriving at my store. I am so glad Mr. Burke didn't listen to me!

The first time I saw Jaime, I noticed a few things right off the bat. 1) He liked to look sharp. 2) I wondered if he were

African-American or Hispanic. It could go either way. 3) He had a presence about him. 4) He had the biggest and most genuine smile you could imagine.

Over the next couple of years, God began growing me spiritually. He created a hunger and desire to grow closer to Him. Jaime played a vital role in this. He was so outwardly open with his faith, it was quite shocking. I'd never met anyone like him, coming out of prison and never having been in church or knowing anything about church, church politics, or what goes on in church. What he knew was what the Bible had said about church and about groups of believers and how they did it in prison. When he came out, his excitement and boldness and desire to do things for the Lord were quite motivating and contagious. As I grew, I began to realize the call God had on my life, and for the first time, I felt a passion for ministry.

Sadly, my wife did not share this vision. Ultimately, she decided our paths were going in two different directions. Other than the death of my father, I don't believe any event in my life was more devastating than not being able to save my marriage. My brother was tragically killed on May 5, 2002. My wife left me on May 25, 2002. In less than a month, the company for which I worked went out of business. The year 2002 was a time of testing me, and Jaime stood beside me through all of it, encouraging me to read Biblical scriptures and pray. I never doubted the Lord was going to heal my marriage. I had purchased a new book, *The Power of a Praying Husband*.

Jaime came into my office. "Look, Jaime, I'm going to start this book tonight."

Jaime just stared at me. I could tell something was wrong.

"Jaime, what's up? What's wrong?"

Jaime began crying. He said, "Curt, the Lord wants me to tell you something, but I don't want to tell you."

I said, "Well, if the Lord told you to tell me, you have to tell me."

He said, "The Lord wants to know even if she never comes home, will you still trust Me?"

That's the first time it really sunk in that the Lord may not heal my marriage. It was a powerful moment. But it was then when all the worst Satan had to throw at me, God honed me, shaped me, and made me who I am today. I began to release my marriage vows and stayed single for eleven years. I focused on raising my daughter and asking the Lord to select my next wife.

I became active in my church, too, serving as youth pastor, teaching an adult Sunday school class, leading the choir, serving as back-up clerk, and being a member of the pastor's counsel and finance committee.

Later, it was Jaime's impact on me, which led me to found and lead a successful men's ministry in 2005, Men of the Way Ministries, a 501c3 organization with between thirty and forty young men meeting every Thursday night for a meal and Bible study. It began in my home and was focused on marriages. My divorce had caused a lot of pain. I realized how much the families in church in America were under assault. I recognized the devil was attacking men, and we were losing masculinity in the church. In addition, Jaime's influence gave me a passion to learn and teach God's Word and to seek God's purpose for my life. As the Bible study group grew, the Lord made it possible for me to purchase seventeen acres of land and build a nice building with fireplace, kitchen, and bathrooms. This is where we've been meeting ever since.

At Jaime's insistence, I preached my first sermon along with him in a tent, no less. He stretched my faith in ways I don't think I would ever have except for his compelling words of affirmation and faith. His knowledge and strong defense of the Bible inspired me to read more, learn more, and believe deeper. I began to have a real desire to do whatever I could for the Lord. I had wasted seventeen years of my life as a prodigal, and at least ten years of those I was high every day. I had lost so much ground. I wanted to make up.

There was a night that has always been etched in my mind because it was a turning point for me. It was a cold and rainy night when I came home from church hungry for the Lord. I went into my bedroom and prayed fervently beside my bed.

"Lord, will you please use me in ministry? I don't care what it is, or what I have to do. If you want me to go to Africa and be a missionary, I will. If you want me to go to a small church in the country, I will. I don't care about the money. I just want to be used by you."

The Lord really spoke to my heart that night – deeply. It was a shocking thing. "Curt, I can't use you."

It hurt me really bad. My spirit was crushed. "Lord, why can't you use me?" I cried.

That's when the Lord shared that over the years, I had allowed my finances to get in bad shape. My credit score wasn't good. I made good money, but I lived week to week. "You are so far in debt, you couldn't go on a mission trip for two weeks, or you'd have to file bankruptcy. How can I use you?"

I began to say, "Lord, if you'll help me, I'll change. I'll fix it."

I studied the Word about finances and stewardship and all the things the Bible taught about it. From that time, I began to change my finances. Now, I have been able to care for my mother and travel with my wife. The Lord changed it, so He could use me.

You know, the night I was saved, my perspective on the Christian life was warped and screwed up. In my mind, to become a Christian was to give up having fun, lose all your friends, become poor and miserable, and be locked down and maybe even prosecuted. Then you would die and maybe go to heaven. Boy was I wrong! Never have I been happier, more fulfilled, and more blessed in my life than when I accepted His call. It is true what Jesus said, "The devil came to steal, kill, and destroy. But I have come to give life and to give it more abundantly."

It is clear in retrospect now that God, Himself, placed Jaime in my life because He knew what I needed and whom I needed to knock off my rough edges and challenge me to dive deeper into whom God was calling me to be. Other than my father, no other man in my life has had more of an impact on me spiritually and as a man of God than Jaime. He has been so influential to me

Maybe the greatest thing I learned from Jaime, though, is I truly think he taught me to love people again. Jaime's heart for people knows no bounds. Jaime is uncompromising when it comes to Biblical truth and doctrine, but his ability to love people despite their failures, their mistakes, and their sins is truly a gift. Jaime never meets a stranger, and he never meets anybody without mentioning Jesus to them. Jaime taught me to be bold in my faith and public about it.

He was with me one day when we pulled into a gas station, and we were standing there talking while we were pumping gas. A guy from the Northeast was pumping his gas beside us. Jaime leaned against the car, looked at him, and said, "I just love Jesus. Do you love Jesus?" The guy didn't know what to say. I thought *I wish I could do that.*

One day, we went into a body shop to pick up a car. Some people were waiting in the waiting room. A little girl was in there with her mother and didn't feel well. She hadn't been able to go to school that day. Jaime didn't break his stride. He walked to where she was lying with her head in her mother's lap and knelt by her. He put his hand on her and asked, "Do you mind if I pray for her?" He prayed for her in the middle of the business and told her how much Jesus loved her and how He wanted her to feel better. I think it was his boldness and childlike enthusiasm and expectation that he had that was so exciting and fresh and encouraging. In that respect, he began to push me beyond what my expectations of what the Lord had for me in my life.

Today I am credentialed and an ordained minister through the Church of God, president of Men of the Way Ministries, and my wife and I travel weekly, ministering across the country and sometimes overseas. My wife is Beth Stephens-Johnson, an evangelist. Her ministry is Beth Stephens Ministry. Even though we're both from Georgia, we didn't meet each other until we were in Beijing, China, ministering to the Underground Church. I didn't know she preached for a living, but she was a pretty well-known evangelist. We were long-distant friends for seven years. Then things changed, and we got married.

My wonderful daughter is twenty-eight now. She has two small boys, runs our business, and faithfully serves the Lord.

Jaime has made a huge impact on my life. To this day, I'm a hugger because of Jaime, although, I'm not so much the kisser he is. Jaime actually takes the verse literally to "greet the brethren with a holy kiss." We used to laugh like crazy at the look that came over some of the men's faces in the places we went to preach. You can imagine when the big Puerto Rican from New York would walk up to them with a huge smile and give them a big hug and kiss on the cheek how they reacted. They didn't know what to do. As time went on, people just learned to expect Jaime to hug and kiss them. But at first, it was quite a cultural shock for us in Southern Georgia, to say the least.

I don't think I could ever stop writing about all the great things God has done and is doing in and around my life. I just know that I love and need Him more today than I ever have in my life. My passion and heart's desire are to simply fulfill His purpose and destiny in my life in whatever capacity He desires for me. I am forever grateful He would use someone like me. It is truly an honor to serve Him. My journey continues to grow and mature to this day.

Chapter Thirty-Seven

Felton Burke, Jr.

God used Jaime to save my family.

I'm a proud resident of Jesup, Georgia. It was around the year 2000 when a couple of ministers from the Church of God came to my Chevrolet dealership, which was located in Alma, Georgia. They informed me of a guy who was getting out of prison soon. The guy had served roughly ten years in the federal prison in Jesup and had started ministering while he was in prison. They mentioned he needed a job and asked if I'd consider interviewing him for a job. I told them I would consider it and for them to bring him over for an interview whenever he was released.

A short period of time later, maybe a couple of weeks, they brought this guy to my dealership and introduced him to me. His name was Jaime Torres. After exchanging pleasantries, I invited Jaime into my office to talk. That's when I asked him why he had been in prison. He was straight-forward and didn't hesitate or dodge my questions.

After Jaime finished talking, I said, "You know what? I probably don't need to hire a guy who may have been sitting in prison for ten years, trying to figure out how he is going to con me, but I feel like God sent you here, and God is telling me to give you an opportunity."

So I hired him even though I really didn't have a job opening. I hired Jaime as a "go to" guy. He did whatever was needed. He rode back and forth with me from Jesup to my Alma store, which is forty miles away. Later, I got him a little car, so he could drive back and forth. Jaime cleaned toilets and cleaned up the dealership. He did whatever I asked him to do.

As our relationship matured, he began to feel comfortable talking to me about faith and religion and started witnessing to me constantly. I am the son of a Church of God minister. My father preached from the time he was sixteen years-old until his death at the age of seventy-six. Because we were raised in the strict Pentecostal faith and could not have televisions or other stuff, I ran away from the church because I didn't want to follow that type of life. I actually ran away from God.

When Jaime witnessed to me, he did so in a very easy way – never being pushy at all. We built a relationship where he became more of a son than an employee because I grew to totally trust him. I feel confident in saying Jaime would do anything in the world for me. If he ever told me something, I had zero doubt. I knew he was telling me the truth because I watched the way he lived his life. I saw him at times and places when other people didn't see him. I also saw what he could do. I knew then as I know now that Jaime is a true man of God.

Jaime became interested in the car dealership business, so I helped him get started with that. There was a little Spanish church in Jesup where his ex-wife was pastoring while Jaime was in incarcerated. Once he had been released from prison, he took it over and began pastoring it. I was glad to attend some of their services and enjoyed meeting a lot of his Hispanic friends.

I became a daily drinker after I sold my automobile dealerships. Convinced I needed to change my life and seek help, I went for rehabilitation at St. Simons by the Sea. While I was there, I went into the courtyard and looked up to heaven. That is when I asked God to either change me or let me die. As soon as my prayer was over, it felt like a fifty-five-gallon drum of warm oil was dumped on my head and was penetrated through my body. I began to cry because I knew God was communicating with me and telling me He would change me. After I was saved that day, God's purpose for me was realized. He wanted me to teach the Lord's Prayer, so this became my lifelong mission: I would preach and teach the Lord's Prayer.

During this difficult period in my lifetime when I was getting sober and after I left rehabilitation, Jaime was beside me. His support meant everything because he could empathize and sympathize with me. He, himself, had experienced what I was going through. He'd shared his own trials and tribulations with me and how he had attended Alcoholics Anonymous meetings while he was trying to stop drinking and drugging. I joined the same organization, so we had that in common. Never did Jaime say a word to me about my drinking. Jaime just prayed for me.

My new-found sobriety and salvation led me to get my ministerial license. My purpose was not to preach, but to go into the jails and prisons to counsel with alcoholics and drug addicts. As a new member of Alcoholics Anonymous, I wanted to share my experiences and work in the program to help others. I began sponsoring people, so they could learn as I had there is a better way of life through Jesus Christ.

I built a little church in Jesup and purchased five acres of land for Jaime to build a church, but unfortunately, it didn't work out. Instead, they decided to open another church. But the great thing about the five acres of land, which I purchased, was they sold the land to another guy, and he now has a church on that property that serves about three hundred people for worship services on Sundays. God used it for His purposes anyway.

After a while, Jaime and I began traveling on mission trips with the Church of God. The first mission trip we went on together was to Panama. We went with the pastor from the Church of God and a nice group of people. In addition, I asked Brother Sammy to go with us.

Jaime had been on several other mission trips, but one had been to Ecuador where he had met a young woman in whom he was interested. He asked me to go with him and interview the young woman because he didn't know if he was making the right decision about getting involved. He didn't want anything to interfere with his work for the Lord, so he valued my opinion and ultimately, my advice. Without hesitation, I agreed to accompany him to Ecuador on another mission trip, of which there would be time for us to meet with this young lady.

Jaime and I spoke at several churches. Then we traveled to this young woman's town where I interviewed her. I was happy to be introduced to the pretty young woman known as *Grace*. I had prayed hard about the interview and had prayed for God's will regarding this relationship to be made known. I was a tough interviewer that day because I was seeking the truth. I knew Jaime needed someone to be there for him while he preached the Word of God. Jaime didn't need another Jaime. He didn't need anyone trying to replace him in the pulpit. He needed someone to support him and serve him while he served God. At the end of our time together, I felt like Grace was exactly who Jaime needed.

After I got on the plane in Ecuador, we were sitting on the tarmac, waiting to take off. While there, I met a missionary from the Benny Hinn Ministry and told him all about my Lord's Prayer ministry. For whatever reason, I began to question myself and asked God, "Is this still what you want me to do?"

God didn't hesitate to answer. In my spirit, He asked, "What month did you leave the U.S. to go on this mission trip?"

"January."

God asked, "What day did you leave?"

"The seventh."

Again, God asked a question. "What day are you coming back home?"

"The thirteenth."

Then God instructed me to retrieve my carry-on bag from the compartment above my seat and take out my Bible, which I did. Confused and not understanding what God was trying to tell me, He said, "Turn in your Bible to the Lord's Prayer."

As I flipped through the tissue-like pages, I finally found it and began reading the red letters in its entirety before I was able to put the pieces together. When I finished and scanned the entire page, I was turned to the first book of the Gospels (Matthew), the seventh chapter, and the thirteenth verse: Matthew 7:13. I never questioned God again.

Jaime has spent many a night with us over the years. Just recently, we were delighted to host him, Grace, and their two babies at our home, while they were traveling through Jesup to do ministry work. I believe God blessed Jaime by giving him Grace as his wife. He is a great man of God and has been a wonderful inspiration to my wife, my son and daughter, and me. My son, who is now forty-eight years-old, was witnessed to by Jaime. Now he attends church regularly and is serving God. My wife and children love him.

I'm proud to be a recovering alcoholic. Actually, I will celebrate twelve years of sobriety on December 10, 2018. I took my last drink on December 10, 2006. In addition, I'll celebrate eleven years the same month of not smoking. I smoked my last cigarette the following year in December 2007. It may seem as though I did Jaime all these favors, but in reality, God used Jaime to save my family.

I continue to carry on my work at Alcoholics Anonymous and teaching the Lord's Prayer. Jaime and I stay in contact with each other, normally talking a couple of times every month. There isn't anything in the world that I wouldn't do for him. He helped me turn my life around. If it had not been for Jaime loving me and living the life of Christ on a daily basis in front of me, I don't know what might have happened to my soul.

Chapter Thirty-Eight

Keith Morgan

Jaime lays it down where you can pick it up.

I owned a car dealership in Jesup, Georgia, where I was born and raised. In the year 2001 or 2002, a friend introduced me to Jaime Torres. After I met Jaime and saw him several times, I'd overhear people saying things about him.

"Yeah, that's Jaime Torres." Then they'd make comments about his past. "He just got released from prison early."

I don't say a lot, so I just watched and listened to them. As Jaime's path and my path began to cross, slowly we struck up a conversation. I actually was talking to him and getting to know him for myself, rather than hearing what others had to say. During the process of building a relationship, it got to where Jaime would drop by the dealership every once in a while and come to my office. He'd say, "Hello! How are you doing, sir?" Then we'd continue making small talk, so I could "check him out." As time passed and our friendship progressed, instead of saying, "Hey," and sharing a few comments, we began to sit in my office and talk. Our conversations lasted longer while we discussed deeper subjects. Then he'd throw out some Word of the Lord to me.

As a Southern Georgia white man, and as a Puerto Rican with a darker complexion, it's obvious we're from different places, with different backgrounds, and have different cultures. We also speak English but with different dialects and accents. Jaime and I used to laugh, cut up, and make jokes about the way we spoke.

I'd say, "Jaime, you have to speak where I can understand you. You have to give me some slack here."

Our many conversations shifted to discussing the Word of the Lord. I'd always been a believer in the story of Christ and in God, but Jaime kept talking to me. One day, I reached across my desk, pulled open a drawer, and withdrew a Bible. That's when our conversations became even more focused. Jaime would flip through the Bible, read a verse or two, and then we'd talk about the meaning of the words. We began doing this on a regular basis for about two years, all the time growing into close friends as we learned more about each other.

Jaime enjoyed cars and being around car lots. Sometimes when he came by the dealership to pick up a used car one of his friends had purchased, or to perform another task, or just to say hello, my wife would be in the office. She would hear his soft-spoken voice and watch his humble actions. When he arrived or before he left, he would say, "I love you, sir." Then he'd hug my neck and kiss me on the cheek. With me being born and raised in Southern Georgia, this was awkward, and I kept thinking, *Okay. Slow down a little, buddy.*

Afterwards she'd say, "There ain't no way that guy can be that genuine."

Eventually, Jaime came to work for us on a full-time basis. His role was to do anything we needed, like transporting vehicles from one town to another. He'd do anything in the world to help and be a part of. When Jaime went to different locations, he'd talk to employees, pray with employees, and pray over the car lot.

My wife, Clarissa, has always been a believer in God and a sweetheart. After she got to see Jaime more often, she began to say, "I've never met anyone so humble. When I first met him, I didn't think there was any way he could be so genuine." As time rocked on and he was the same each time we met, she realized that's who Jaime is.

By this time, Jaime and I had become closer friends. I really enjoyed his company when he'd come by the dealership. He'd always walk the car lot and pray for our business. Then he'd pray for Clarissa and me before he left. I began going with him on Sunday nights to a few church services where he had been invited to preach. These were usually out of town -- in Waycross or other surrounding towns or cities. I always tried to go and support him.

We shared a lot of good stuff in our deep conversations. I had lots of questions. Jaime was honest and told me anything I asked about his past, years of dealing drugs, troubles he'd gotten into, or the times he was shot and stabbed. It was amazing! Even today, I tell people, "Jaime is one of those guys you love to sit and listen to his life's story, but it's a story you don't want to live yourself. He has a testimony you love and pulls you in; you love to hear it, but you sure wouldn't want to be the one with that testimony."

I discovered Jaime could open the Bible and talk to me in a way that most preachers couldn't. Now, I'm not bad-mouthing any preachers that I've sat under at any denominational church. But I could listen to a preacher's sermon for twenty or thirty minutes and not understand the meaning, whereas Jaime could read the Word and break down the meaning in a dialogue that I could understand and grasp what the Word was saying. One of my favorite sayings today is "Jaime lays it down where you can pick it up."

At the time Jaime came into my life, the Lord really was working on my heart and my walk with Him. There were lots of things happening and changes being made in my life. Even though I'd always been a believer, the Lord was pursuing me, and He was using Jaime in a really big way to be a part of His pursuit. Rather than just believing in the story, I began knowing Him and knowing the story. I began to know how real God is.

I had never experienced any type of life-changing encounter during the time I had been a believer because nobody ever talked about getting saved; they just preached about what the Bible said.

My paternal grandfather and the rest of the Morgan family had been very religious. My own father was a Vietnam Veteran; he wasn't a bad man, but he was a workaholic. My father believed that according to his family's religion, he couldn't live the life they told him he had to in order to be a Christian. He equated it to being like a person is standing on this oily, slippery log, and if the person falls off, he / she is going to hell. So in his mind, he'd never be able to stay on the log without falling. That is why he refused to try very hard.

On Sundays, my mother took my younger brother and me to a church in Jesup. We attended periodically, sometimes regularly, but my father never went with us when I was a boy. When Clarissa and I began dating, I accompanied her to a Methodist church. This is where we got married and continued attending afterwards.

Based on our conversations, I believed Jaime had always desired to be part of a family. He longed to be loved. As a young boy and a young man, he never felt loved. In his world were friends and compadres but never the love of a family. Whenever he became a part of something or was welcomed into a family, I could sense he felt special. He became a big part of my family's life, as well as mine.

I recall the time when my mother-in-law was scheduled to have surgery for a benign brain tumor in Jacksonville, Florida. We needed to arrive at the hospital early the next morning, so my wife, her brother and sister, and I drove to Jacksonville, where we were going to stay the night at my wife's sister's home, who also lived in Jacksonville.

Jaime drove from Jesup, which is about a two hour drive to Jacksonville, to my sister-in-law's house. He spent time at the house with us, prayed with my mother-in-law, and then drove back home. That was Jaime. It didn't matter that it was a three hour drive. He wanted to bless us. That's the kind of person he was.

Eventually, Jaime opened a car wash and ran a little painting business. I'd drop by his car wash on a regular basis, and he'd come by the car dealership on a regular basis. Gradually, as our friendship grew, I shared deep personal life experiences with him, things that had happened to me when I was young, which explained why I might think the way I did about different subjects based on my upbringing and experiences. I told Jaime things about me that no other person knows. Coming from where he did, he never knew anything but a life of drug dealing, which had shaped his experiences and explained why he felt the way he did about different subjects.

Those of us who were born in Southern Georgia or in the Bible belt, grew up where it was common to ask a blessing before a meal. It was common to attend church on Sundays. We grew up hearing about Jesus and God. It was in our minds. We knew the story. But to meet someone who had never seen a Bible or who had never heard a family member ask a blessing for a meal was inconceivable to me. It was hard to fathom how someone, anyone who had been raised in America didn't know of the Bible or church or blessings before meals. But under Jaime's past circumstances, he hadn't known the things I had taken for granted.

I remember when my wife and two young daughters, Sailor and Mercer, went on a vacation cruise to Nassau, Bahamas. As soon as we disembarked the ship in Nassau, a bunch of locals were waiting to sell us a tour of the island. After telling several of them, "No," we ran up on this guy, another local Bahamian. The minute I laid eyes on him, I thought, *Oh my goodness!* Something told me I was going to have to go on a tour with him.

The four of us went on the tour with him, and we ended

up spending the entire day together. Rather than going on a traditional island tour like was given on a daily basis, he took us to his church across the island. We visited inside his little church where he pastored and prayed with him. Over the years, we became good friends with his family and him. We invited them to America one summer. They came and spent two weeks at our home. While they were here, we invited Jaime and several other friends to come and meet our Bahamian friend, Pastor Anthony Johnson.

Pastor Anthony and Jaime clicked instantly and began talking. During their lengthy conversation, Jaime discovered before the Pastor had begun preaching, he had been a military policeman in the Bahamas. After that stint, he had been a police officer in the Bahamas.

Jaime shared how he had lived through a few instances when he was caught on an island in the Bahamas with a shipment of drugs. He had hid on an outer island with the shipment. By having been a member of the military police, Pastor Anthony had dealt with and tracked those people. After Jaime and Anthony shared their stories, Pastor Anthony pulled me aside.

"Brother Keith, it is a miracle – a miracle -- this man is alive. In the Bahamas, when a drug dealer is caught on an outer island, they are not taken to one of the interior islands like Nassau. They are killed. I'm telling you, it is a miracle this man is alive. He should have been killed in the Bahamas."

As they continued sharing stories back and forth, I reflected on how close their paths may have crossed during those years. It was amazing. The world is really small. You never know who you are going to meet or how close you were to meeting someone twenty or thirty years ago in totally different circumstances. I just found it ironic both of these men were here, sitting in my living room and sharing the Word of the Lord. And they both were pastors now.

There was a prophet I met through Jaime. After Jaime introduced us, we talked for a while and prayed before we left. As we were leaving, the man told me, "God is going to give you a son, and He will show you something with this son." I was surprised. Clarissa and I were blessed with our two beautiful daughters and weren't talking about having a third child. Anyway, a year later in 2006, our son, Noah, was born. The first time Jaime held him at his birth, he prayed for a blessing for Noah. This is a special memory. Whenever Jaime is around Noah now, he always prayers the same prayer over him as a reminder of the prophetic word of him being prophesized.

Jaime was married to his first wife during these years. Clarissa and his wife never bonded or developed a friendship like Jaime's and mine, but the four of us would always speak, hug, talk, and laugh when we were together. In 2008 when the economy tanked and things were going bad in the banking industry, the car business took a tremendous downturn, a hit. At that point, we lost our business and had to close.

Jaime was there every day with me while I closed the business. He would just sit in my office, never saying a word at times unless he felt the need to speak, but if there was anything I needed, he would stand up and go do it. No matter what was going on in his life, he was there every day, checking on me.

In 2009 or 2010, his business wasn't doing well; finances became difficult for his family with bills stacking up, which can cause a lot of stress in a marriage. They were struggling with the burdens of stress, so the marriage was destroyed. When his divorce was happening, I did my best to support him. Jaime really struggled because he had gotten out of prison and really was trying to fit in. He had been trying to make amends and live a better life by doing things the right way.

In the community, he was known for being a good Christian man. Jaime had made a lot of friends. Many people respected and loved him. Jaime felt as if he had let a lot of people down.

He felt he had disappointed the public, the friends he had preached to, and the Hispanic people in his church, who he had preached to for years. I tried to do the best I could for Jaime. Whether he was wrong or right, he was my friend and brother, and he'd always been my friend whether I was wrong or right. He'd never judged me, and I never judged Jaime.

I believe what bothered Jaime the most about the divorce was feeling like a failure. Here he was preaching and performing good works, but his life was falling apart. Most of all, Jaime thought he had failed God. The divorce tore him pretty good. I also believe one of the things Jaime had to learn after coming out of prison was living in the real world again. In prison, the inmates had a ton of down time and could attend church seven days a week, all day long. There really wasn't a lot to do other than play basketball and things like that because they had no responsibilities of holding down a job or the daily grind of running a business or supporting a family. This isn't to say that while a person is incarcerated, all of this isn't on his/her mind. I'm sure there are worries of how he/she had disappointed family members. Over the years, I've met a bunch of the guys who were in prison with Jaime but were still incarcerated. They were constantly reading and praying and praising the Lord.

When a person is released from prison and is acclimating to the real world, it's necessary to realize that just because some of us call ourselves Christians, we are still human. We make mistakes. We're trying to run a business or make a living for our families. Jaime had a big sense of gullibility, which meant if John Doe attended church every Sunday and claimed to be a Christian, Jaime couldn't understand how John Doe might function differently on a daily basis in the real world.

Unfortunately, some Christians stab each other in the back. It may not be intentional, but they are trying to survive and are human. Jaime took everyone at his / her word. If things didn't work out the way that had been intended, he had a hard time

257

comprehending why it didn't. Sadly, life doesn't always produce peaches and cream; there are those rough patches we have to battle and fight to get through.

Jaime and I stay in contact even though he lives in North Carolina. If we go a week or two weeks without talking, one of us is calling to check on the other. "How are you doing?" "How is your family?"

Today, thank God, my mother and father are different people. They are saved and have different perspectives about the Lord and what they did during those years. They attend church regularly. And in 2004, I remember getting fire insurance. Anyway, I am glad I did because of my life-changing encounter that set me on fire. I accepted Christ, and He saved me from my sins. For the past ten plus years, my family and I have attended non-denomination churches because they are spirit-filled. We all need our spirits filled.

A few weeks ago, Jaime was preaching in Orlando. He traveled to Tampa where his father lives and got him. They were on their way traveling I-95, so they stopped here in Brunswick where I have my business and spent some time with us. I was happy to see my friend again.

If you look around our world today, there is much division between races, political parties, and other things. Jaime and I come from two different places, two different backgrounds, and two different cultures but I love him. Recently, a really close friend passed away two weeks ago. This made me reflect on my life and the people in it. This man, Jaime Torres, and one other person were the top three names on my list of friends.

Yes, I love Jaime. I just love him. And I know he loves me, too.

Conclusion
From Jaime's Heart

Our God is a Great God

Fight the good fight for the faith. Keep holding on to eternal life, to which you were called and about which you gave a good testimony in front of many witnesses. – 1 Timothy 6:12 (ISV)

Even after becoming a Christian, there were a lot of things that bothered me. We serve a merciful God and certainly a forgiving God, but consequences linger. I found it hard to forgive myself. I have to be reminded daily that we fight a real enemy, and he is an accuser of the brethren. His job is to undermine what God has done. For me, it is an ongoing battle. The scripture says "to fight the good fight for the faith." It is a battle I fight every day; some days are better than other days. If it weren't for the fact that I believe He really forgave me, I don't think I would be here now. It's important for me to remember the work was finished on Calvary. This gets me through the day because there are a lot of things, especially our vulnerabilities, the enemy brings up. And it will be a constant battle to fight until we are raptured. But the key and the armor are knowing there is a God.

Because I am a scripture man, I enjoy referencing the Word of God, whom I love to call "Big Papa." Big Papa inspired it, so that settles it for me. I can't even talk, much less preach, if I don't reference Big Papa's Word.

There are scriptures that are so dear to me. Here are a few. Psalm 27:13-14 says, *I had fainted, unless I had believed to see the goodness of the LORD in the land of the living. Wait on the LORD: be of good courage, and he shall strengthen thine heart: wait, I say, on the LORD* (KJV).

I love that David said if it wasn't for the fact he served a faithful and good God, he would have given up. If it weren't for the fact that I know deep in my heart that God is full of goodness, and mercy, and compassion, I would have given up, too. This is what keeps me going.

I have received many honors and certificates during my ministry. One that I'm really proud of is a certificate from Billy Graham. While I am grateful for them, all I want is God. I'm incomplete without God. I appreciate the Lord; I long for Him.

I've been out of prison for eighteen years. If I've given my personal testimony five times, then that is too much. I'm careful not to give my testimony. I hardly ever give my personal testimony because I don't want to give the impression, especially to children and young people, you have to go down a similar path as I did to have something to talk about. I don't want people to think you have to go to prison or eat crap or go to a hog pen to have a testimony because they don't. I don't want it to be about me. It's not about me. I give it when the Spirit of God prompts me to. I'm writing this book for those people who have fallen on their faces and made some horrible, stupid choices like I did, so they can understand we serve a God of second and third chances.

Mark 3:14 is a very important scripture. *And he ordained twelve, that they should be with him, and that he might send them forth to preach* (KJV). He didn't choose the disciples to give them a calling. A lot of times we run after the ministry and say, "I want to be a preacher." "I want to be a deacon." "I want to be an elder." He ordained the twelve that they should be with Him. I want to be with Him, too.

Why did Jesus die? He died to reconcile you and me to Him. The calling comes afterwards. It's a byproduct of your relationship with Him, but sometimes we miss that point. Sometimes we chase the calling by believing it is important to have our names on the board, attend the biggest church, or be listed in the church directory. I'm chasing Jesus because He ordained the twelve that they should be with Him. He wants us so desperately to be with Him. But seek ye first the *kingdom of God, and his righteousness; and all these things shall be added unto you* (Matthew 6:33, KJV). When we miss the important fact that Jesus is about relationships – God is a relational God – we miss everything. This is what means the whole world to me. I appreciate the Lord.

Can I be honest with you? Sometimes I feel so inadequate. But I realize (I'm not stupid) it is Jesus, and only He, who equips me to preach to thousands even when I feel inadequate or unprepared. And at the end of the day, I walk with my head down, and I say, "Lord, thank You. I shouldn't be here. I should be in hell." I don't ever want to get too big for my britches because at the end of the day, I know from where He reached down and pulled me.

I'm a preacher of the Gospel; that is what I love to do. I love to talk about God's goodness. I love people, and I love to encourage people. I love His word. I love His presence. I love presenting at Forgiven Ministry's One Day with God camps. I love my ministry: Jaime Torres Ministries. I enjoy visiting prisons and doing a lot of out-reach work in the streets and in the hood. I love teaching Bible studies. These are among the many things I love to do for the Lord. And I want to do more. I believe this is what God called me to do: to speak life into the people.

God took a man in prison who didn't know how to read. But because of His grace and mercy, He has given me a revelation of His Word. When I die and leave this earth, the only thing I want people to say is, "Ol' Jaime believed God."

And I'll tell you what will happen when you believe God.

People will call you stupid, ignorant, unlearned, and foolish. They've called me those names, but I don't care. Do you want to know why? Because when I walked with the devil, I did some stupid stuff. The things I did were stupid, and the devil made a spectacle of me. So if you want to call me stupid for Jesus, go right ahead and do it because I'd rather be stupid for Him.

This is my story. I'm a miracle created and saved by the blood of Jesus Christ. I didn't know Him, but He knew me.

Epilogue

Who hath believed our report and to whom is the arm of the LORD *revealed?*—Isaiah 53: 1 (KJV)

In Isaiah 53:1, we are asked a question: *Who hath believed our report* (KJV).The problem is sometimes we believe what the devil is saying quicker than we believe God. In 1 Corinthians 15:33, the Bible says, *Be not deceived: evil communications corrupt good manners* (KJV). In Proverbs 18:21a, we are warned *The tongue has the power of life and death...* (NIV). And in Romans 10: 9-10, we are reminded, *For one believes with the heart and so is justified, and one confesses with the mouth and so is saved* (NRSV). What report are you going to believe? Let me warn you. Following Jesus is not for the faint of heart. It's difficult. But following Jesus is greater than anything you will ever do.

He is despised and rejected of men; a man of sorrows, and acquainted with grief: and we hid as it were our faces from him; he was despised, and we esteemed him not. Surely he hath borne our griefs, and carried our sorrows: yet we did esteem him stricken, smitten of God, and afflicted. But he was wounded for our transgressions, he was bruised for our iniquities: the chastisement of our peace was upon him; and with his stripes we are healed (Isaiah 53:3-5, KJV).

Remember, the devil is a masterful liar; he is excellent in what he tries to do. But you can't let your guard down and entertain his thoughts. Whenever he is wrestling with you and

263

whispering bad thoughts, just say, "Get behind me, liar. God didn't bring me this far to fail. Thank you Jesus."

I have learned to live by faith alone; I don't charge anyone anything when I preach. I never see the money that is donated to our ministry; I have a Board of Directors who handles the money and other decisions regarding my ministry. God has never let me down. Sometimes, when I have been low on gas, I have found gas cards on my door. When I was sick and my liver shut down, I was healed. I've never been late on my bills. When you believe and trust in God, He honors His Word. God didn't bring me to the cross to "who-do" people or to make money. My goal is to die with dignity and by honoring His name.

If God can save Lazarus, clean me up, wipe me down, package me up, and send me forth, He can do it for somebody else. I'm grateful I have the opportunity to talk and write about Jesus and to spread His Word.

Finally, if this book is the vehicle God has used for you to get to know Him, then Hallelujah! This book has served its purpose. But remember, He already knows you.

Jaime Torres

Jaime Torres has a special place in his heart for young people. Their salvation is his priority, so he continues to speak at youth rallies in several states. Jaime has a burden for the unity among all people, especially the people of God, regardless of their culture or denomination. In addition to preaching in many states, Jaime has had the privilege of ministering in Ecuador, Peru, Belize, Panama, Mexico, Venezuela, and the Dominican Republic.

Jaime was born in Puerto Rico to an unwed mother of fifteen. She took her baby of nine months and left the island for New York City. Unfortunately, this was a place of hardships and rejections for Jaime, so he was returned to Puerto Rico to live with his biological father. This proved to be a downfall for Jaime, as his father was one of the larger drug leaders on the island. Sadly, Jaime followed in his father's path. He returned to New York, where he became a drug dealer. After many trials and tribulations and stints in jails and prisons, God's patience with Jaime won out when he accepted God's grace and mercy in a federal prison.

Jaime has five grown children: Richard, Michael, Ashley, Kira, and Vanessa. He and his lovely wife, Grace, have two younger children: JonathanDavid and Isabella Grace. Jaime and Grace enjoy traveling wherever God sends them to spread the Good News to all people that there is a God who loves them enough to send His Son to die for their sins in order that those sins may not be counted against them. The family resides in Morganton, North Carolina.

Sandi Huddleston-Edwards

For you, O Lord, are good and forgiving, abounding in steadfast love to all who call upon you. -- Psalm 86:5 (ESV)

Sandi Huddleston-Edwards loves being a Carolina girl. She has passions for God, her family, and writing novels and memoirs. She holds a B.A. and M.A. in English from the University of North Carolina at Charlotte. She is a former adjunct professor of English and has taught at Central Piedmont Community College, Montreat College, Johnson & Wales University, and the University of North Carolina at Charlotte.

Sandi has written articles for *Lake Norman Publications, Tarheel Wheels,* and *Reader's Digest.* She is the author of two novels, a historical novel, two memoirs, a children's book, two devotionals and this book.

She and her husband Barry are the proud parents of three grown sons (Jeremy, Jeff, and Todd), six grandchildren, and six great-nieces and nephews. One of Sandi's greatest supporters of her writing is her sister, Teresa George, for whom she is thankful.

Sandi and Barry enjoy traveling and spending time with their two Yorkshire Terriers at their home in Myrtle Beach, South Carolina.

I have been blessed and honored to write this beautiful and inspirational memoir for God and with Jaime. Without a doubt, Jaime is the model for "how to be God's faithful servant." God clearly took a broken life of chaos and sadness and miraculously molded it into one that is ordered, beautiful, spiritual, and devoted to His Lord.

While interviewing many people, family and a wealth of friends, it has been amazing to hear how his life as a bornagain Christian has impacted, intersected, and transformed the lives of so many through God's amazing love and mercy. Jaime has been blessed with a welcoming and contagious smile that is genuine, penetrating, and wins you over immediately. He's been blessed with platforms and wide-spread audiences (nationally and internationally) where he's willingly traveled to serve the Lord in places some people shun or frown upon. But we know our Lord Jesus Christ loved everyone and instructed us to love one another the way He loves us. If you want to know how that's done, just watch Jaime in his daily life and when he's focused on his work.

This book can only touch on all that he is or does for God's kingdom. But by reading it, you'll read about miracles. It's a wonderful witness of God's will, given with mercy and grace, and how He has the power to take the impossible and make it possible. God can do all things.

I'm forever grateful to God for bringing Jaime and his lovely and supportive family into my life. It's impossible to describe the blessings I've reaped by traveling this year-long journey, which began by hearing Jaime's profound, miraculous, and intriguing testimony, as well as hearing the different testimonies of all the special people who have generously given their time and willingness to share in the writing of this book for their beloved Jaime and most of all God. God brings us to Him in many different ways, as you have read.

Remember, **You Can't Kill the Miracle: I Didn't Know Him, but He Knew Me.** Aren't we glad this is true? *To God be the glory – now and forever.*

---Sandi Huddleston-Edwards

Works Cited

Fisher, George P. 1900. *Manual of Christian Evidences.* New York, NY: Charles Scribner's Sons.

"Puerto Rico." History. 2019. W&E Television Networks, LLC. Accessed 25 March 2019. https:www.history.com

CPSIA information can be obtained
at www.ICGtesting.com
Printed in the USA
LVHW080242230719
624964LV00023B/2110/P